Lecture Notes in Computer Science   14096

Founding Editors

Gerhard Goos
Juris Hartmanis

The series Lecture Notes in Computer Science (LNCS), including its subseries Lecture Notes in Artificial Intelligence (LNAI) and Lecture Notes in Bioinformatics (LNBI), has established itself as a medium for the publication of new developments in computer science and information technology research, teaching, and education.

LNCS enjoys close cooperation with the computer science R & D community, the series counts many renowned academics among its volume editors and paper authors, and collaborates with prestigious societies. Its mission is to serve this international community by providing an invaluable service, mainly focused on the publication of conference and workshop proceedings and postproceedings. LNCS commenced publication in 1973.

Bhavna Antony · Hao Chen · Huihui Fang ·
Huazhu Fu · Cecilia S. Lee · Yalin Zheng
Editors

Ophthalmic Medical Image Analysis

10th International Workshop, OMIA 2023
Held in Conjunction with MICCAI 2023
Vancouver, BC, Canada, October 12, 2023
Proceedings

 Springer

Editors
Bhavna Antony (iD)
Alfred Health
Melbourne, VIC, Australia

Huihui Fang (iD)
Pazhou Lab
Guangzhou, China

Cecilia S. Lee (iD)
University of Washington
Seattle, WA, USA

Hao Chen (iD)
Hong Kong University of Science
and Technology
Hong Kong, China

Huazhu Fu (iD)
A*STAR
Institute of High Performance Computing
Singapore, Singapore

Yalin Zheng (iD)
University of Liverpool
Liverpool, UK

ISSN 0302-9743 ISSN 1611-3349 (electronic)
Lecture Notes in Computer Science
ISBN 978-3-031-44012-0 ISBN 978-3-031-44013-7 (eBook)
https://doi.org/10.1007/978-3-031-44013-7

This Springer imprint is published by the registered company Springer Nature Switzerland AG
The registered company address is: Gewerbestrasse 11, 6330 Cham, Switzerland

Paper in this product is recyclable.

Preface

The 10th International Workshop on Ophthalmic Medical Image Analysis (OMIA-X) was held on October 12th, 2023, in conjunction with the 26th International Conference on Medical Image Computing and Computer-Assisted Intervention (MICCAI). It was hosted in Vancouver, Canada. To encourage more scholars to participate, this year was a hybrid (virtual + in-person) conference.

Age-related macular degeneration, diabetic retinopathy, and glaucoma are the main causes of blindness in both developed and developing countries. The cost of blindness to society and individuals is huge, and many cases can be avoided by early intervention. Early and reliable diagnosis strategies and effective treatments are therefore a world priority. At the same time, there is mounting research on the retinal vasculature and neuro-retinal architecture as a source of biomarkers for several high-prevalence conditions like dementia, cardiovascular disease, and of course complications of diabetes. Automatic and semi-automatic software tools for retinal image analysis are being used widely in retinal biomarkers research, and increasingly percolating into clinical practice. Significant challenges remain in terms of reliability and validation, number and type of conditions considered, multi-modal analysis (e.g., fundus, optical coherence tomography, scanning laser ophthalmoscopy), novel imaging technologies, and the effective transfer of advanced computer vision and machine learning technologies, to mention a few. The workshop addressed all these aspects and more, in the ideal interdisciplinary context of MICCAI.

This workshop aimed to bring together scientists, clinicians, and students from multiple disciplines in the growing ophthalmic image analysis community, such as electronic engineering, computer science, mathematics, and medicine, to discuss the latest advancements in the field. A total of 27 full-length papers were submitted to the workshop in response to the call for papers. All submissions were double-blind peer-reviewed by at least three members of the program committee. The paper selection was based on methodological innovation, technical merit, results, validation, and application potential. Finally, 16 papers were accepted at the workshop and chosen to be included in this Springer LNCS volume.

We are grateful to the Program Committee for reviewing the submitted papers and giving constructive comments and critiques, to the authors for submitting high-quality papers, to the presenters for excellent presentations, and to all the OMIA-X attendees from all around the world.

August 2023

Bhavna Antony
Cecilia S. Lee
Hao Chen
Huazhu Fu
Huihui Fang
Yalin Zheng

Organization

Steering Committee

Emanuel Trucco	University of Dundee, UK
Jiang Liu	Southern University of Science and Technology, China
Tom MacGillivray	University of Edinburgh, UK
Yanwu Xu	South China University of Technology, China

Workshop Organizers

Bhavna Antony	University of Edinburgh, UK
Cecilia S. Lee	University of Washington, USA
Hao Chen	Hong Kong University of Science and Technology, China
Huazhu Fu	IHPC, A*STAR, Singapore
Huihui Fang	Pazhou Lab., China
Yalin Zheng	University of Liverpool, UK

Program Committee

Dewei Hu	Vanderbilt University, USA
Guanghui Yue	Shenzhen University, China
Hai Xie	Shenzhen University, China
Hanyi Yu	South China University of Technology, China
Hao Zhang	Shandong University, China
Haofeng Liu	Southern University of Science and Technology, China
Heng Li	Southern University of Science and Technology, China
Huaying Hao	Chinese Academy of Sciences, China
Huihong Zhang	Southern University of Science and Technology, China
Huihui Fang	Pazhou Lab, China
Jingliang Zhao	Guangdong University of Technology, China
Jiong Zhang	Chinese Academy of Sciences, China

Jui-Kai Wang	University of Iowa, USA
Junde Wu	Institute for Infocomm Research, A*STAR, Singapore
Justin Engelmann	University of Edinburgh, UK
Lei Mou	Chinese Academy of Sciences, China
Likun Xia	Capital Normal University, China
Mohammad Shafkat Islam	University of Iowa, USA
Peng Liu	University of Electronic Science and Technology of China, China
Peng Yang	Shenzhen University, China
Pengshuai Yin	South China University of Technology, China
Samuel Gibbon	University of Edinburgh, UK
Shaodong Ma	Chinese Academy of Sciences, China
Shihao Zhang	National University of Singapore, Singapore
Shuang Song	University of Science and Technology Beijing, China
Xianqi Meng	Beijing Institute of Technology, China
Xingyue Wang	Southern University of Science and Technology, China
Yan Hu	Southern University of Science and Technology, China
Yifan Yang	South China University of Technology, China
Ying Chen	Beijing Institute of Technology, China
Yingpeng Xie	Shenzhen University, China

Contents

Associations Between Retinal Microvasculature Changes and Gray Matter Volume in a Mid-Life Cohort at Risk of Developing Alzheimer's Disease

Darwon Rashid[1(✉)], Ylenia Giarratano[1], Charlene Hamid[2],
Tom MacGillivray[2,3], Graciela Muniz Terrera[2,8], Craig Ritchie[3,4],
Baljean Dhillon[3], Megan Reid-Schachter[2], Audrey Low[6],
Maria-Eleni Dounavi[7], John T. O'Brien[7], and Miguel O. Bernabeu[1,5]

[1] Centre for Medical Informatics, Usher Institute,
The University of Edinburgh, Edinburgh, UK
d.rashid@sms.ed.ac.uk, miguel.bernabeu@ed.ac.uk
[2] Edinburgh Clinical Research Facility and Edinburgh Imaging,
University of Edinburgh, Edinburgh, UK
[3] Centre for Clinical Brain Sciences, University of Edinburgh, Edinburgh, UK
[4] Edinburgh Dementia Prevention, University of Edinburgh, Edinburgh, UK
[5] Bayes Centre, University of Edinburgh, Edinburgh, UK
[6] Department of Clinical Neurosciences, University of Cambridge, Cambridge, UK
[7] Department of Psychiatry, University of Cambridge, Cambridge, UK
[8] Department of Social Medicine, Ohio University, Athens, OH, USA

Abstract. Alzheimer's Disease (AD) presents a formidable global health challenge, with a predicted rise in affected individuals in the coming years. Consequently, the development of methods for early detection and monitoring methods are crucially important. Recent studies have highlighted the potential of retinal microvasculature changes captured through optical coherence tomography angiography (OCTA) as a promising tool to be further investigated for the early detection of asymptomatic AD. However, the relationship between retinal microvasculature changes and gray matter volume (GMV), a neuroimaging biomarker for symptomatic AD, is still vague when the disease is asymptomatic. This study investigates the potential associations between retinal microvasculature changes and gray matter volume (GMV) in a midlife cohort at risk of developing AD. The study investigated the potential association between OCTA metrics and GMV measures in participants ($n = 108$, mean age = 51 years old) with and without the known Apolioprotein E4 (APOE4) gene. We observed that foveal avascular zone (FAZ) area and acircularity, foveal vessel skeleton density (FVSD), vessel graph density (VGD), vessel curvature and tortuosity showed significant correlations with various GMV regions. Our findings strengthen the potential for investigating retinal microvasculature changes for the early detection of AD.

Supplementary Information The online version contains supplementary material available at https://doi.org/10.1007/978-3-031-44013-7_1.

Keywords: Gray matter volume · OCTA · Alzheimer's Disease

1   Introduction

Alzheimer's Disease (AD) is a neurodegenerative disorder characterized by cognitive decline and functional impairment. This poses a global health challenge, with the number of affected individuals expected to rise exponentially in the coming years [16]. There is a need to explore novel early disease detection and monitoring methods. Gray matter volume (GMV) is crucial in various cognitive functions, such as memory and attention. Neuroimaging studies utilizing magnetic resonance imaging (MRI) techniques have demonstrated consistent GMV loss patterns in individuals with AD [19]. However, such MRI-based methods are often costly, time-consuming, and less accessible in routine clinical settings.

The retina and the brain not only share embryological and anatomical origins, but growing studies suggest cerebral microvascular changes mirrored through retinal microvascular changes [14]. This positions the retina as a potential window into the brain's vascular and neurodegenerative processes. Optical coherence tomography angiography (OCTA) has emerged as a promising imaging modality that allows non-invasive visualization of retinal microvasculature changes in high resolution. OCTA offers several advantages, including its rapid acquisition, relatively low-cost, and non-invasive nature. Previous studies reported that retinal microvasculature changes that OCTA tracks may mirror cerebrovascular changes under the context of symptomatic AD [8,11,18]. These results piloted further studies that have begun investigating retinal microvascular changes tracked by OCTA in preclinical AD. Furthermore, studies have also reported a potential link between retinal microvasculature changes and increased white matter hyperintensity (WMH) burden measured obtained through MRI [23,27]. These ongoing studies make a strong case to investigate OCTA in relation to the early detection and monitoring of AD before symptoms manifest. Given GMV's importance in symptomatic AD [17], it is crucial to investigate potential associations between retinal microvasculature changes and GMV.

Recent studies have begun investigating whether associations exist between OCTA and GMV measures obtained through MRI. Positioned as a pilot study, Yoon *et al.* recruited 16 participants with known AD and mild cognitive impairment (MCI) statuses and explored any potential link that retinal vessel density (VD) and perfusion density (PD) could have with cortical gray matter, inferolateral ventricle (ILV), lateral ventricle (LV), and hippocampus (HP) MRI volumes. The authors reported that VD and PD were only correlated to ILV [25]. A study by Ruilin *et al.* recruited 135 participants (median age = 50 years) who were healthy and classified as dementia-free. The authors still reported a correlation between the superficial vascular complex density and hippocampal GMV [21]. A recent study by Hu *et al.* recruited 25 cognitively impaired (AD, MCI) and 21 cognitively normal participants (mean age = 64.2 years)and extracted OCTA VD and MRI white and gray matter volumes. The authors reported significant associations between VD and GMV in the hippocampal region in cognitively impaired participants [10]. Lastly, a study by Zhao *et al.* recruited 28 participants that were classified as mild AD and 28 participants that were classified as healthy controls (mean age = 64.9 years). The authors reported a correlation between OCTA VD (inside-disc radial peripapillary capillary) and total GMV. However, the statistical significance vanishes after adjusting analyses for multiple comparisons [26].

The results of the aforementioned studies provide valuable insights into the potential associations between OCTA and GMV obtained through MRI. These studies have mainly investigated these associations in individuals with AD and MCI or healthy elderly participants (dementia-free). However, it is important to note that none of the studies have specifically explored the relationship between OCTA and GMV in a mid-life asymptomatic cohort with known risk factors (40–60 years old). This age group represents a critical stage in which early detection and intervention for AD could have a significant impact [20]. In addition, it is important to acknowledge the relatively small number of participants recruited in the aforementioned studies under the context of AD (<60). We can strengthen any potential findings' statistical power and generalizability with a larger cohort.

This study will investigate potential associations between OCTA and GMV measures in a mid-life cohort consisting of a risk group of participants with and without known Apoliproprotein E4 (APOE4) gene. Previous studies have detailed APOE4's involvement as a risk factor for developing AD [13]. We will investigate whether OCTA tracks total GMV, subcortical GMV, and left and right hippocampal GMV.

2   Methodology

2.1   Dataset

Participants were from the PREVENT-dementia cohort. Previous studies have described the cohort in detail [20,22]. The participants are individuals aged between 40 and 59, averaging 51 years. Participants analyzed for this study were those with and without APOE4 gene. Positive APOE4 status is an individual carrying one or more copies of the APOE4 allele. OCTA and MRI scans were obtained from 108 participants with and without APOE4. Participants with prior eye surgery or any ocular disease were excluded. Important participant covariates, including blood pressure (BP), and Cardiovascular Risk Factors, Ageing and Dementia (CAIDE) score, were collected for this study. Previous studies have detailed the CAIDE score's role as a risk factor [15].

2.2   Image Processing

We obtained $3 \times 3 \, mm^2$ scans of both eyes' superficial and deep capillary plexuses from participants using the RTVue XR Avanti OCTA machine [18]. Not every scan was of acceptable quality for this study. Scans classified as poor quality by the OCTA device were excluded from this analysis [1]. Acceptable scans were

Table 1. Top: A summary of the available cross-sectional dataset for this study, including the total number of OCTA retinal images per left and right eye, the number of male and female participants per left and right eye, and the total number of participants. For each participant, there is one MRI scan, and for each OCTA retinal image, there is a corresponding superficial and deep capillary plexus scan. Both left and right eye OCTA retinal images correspond to only one MRI scan per participant. (OD): right eye, (OS): left eye.

Groups	n-retinal images	n-female	n-male	n-participants
At baseline				
APOE4 +	OS:31/OD:36	OS:18/OD:20	OS:13/OD:16	38
APOE4 −	OS:54/OD:63	OS:32/OD:38	OS:22/OD:25	70

binarized and processed into graph objects to quantify metrics that characterize the retinal microvasculature across each region of interest (ROI) on the ETDRS grid [7]. The ROIs include temporal (T), inferior (I), superior (S), nasal (N), foveal (F), and whole retina (W). The U-net architecture was used to process the retinal scans [5,12]. Metrics that describe the Foveal avascular zone (FAZ) in terms of area and acircularity were included in this study. Vascular density across the microvasculature was characterized by vessel graph density (VGD), parafoveal vessel skeleton density (PVSD), and foveal vessel skeleton density (FVSD). Concerning vessel morphology, metrics that describe vessel tortuosity and curvature were included. To explore the functional characteristics of the vascular network, vessel resistance was computed and extracted on every ROI except the whole image (W). Metrics related to the FAZ were quantified by using both the superficial and deep capillary plexuses, while all other metrics in this study were derived only from the superficial capillary plexus. Table 1 summarizes the dataset for this study. Further information about the framework used in this study for processing and extracting metrics from OCTA images has been previously detailed [5,6]. GMV was divided into total GMV, subcortical GMV, and left and right hippocampal GMV. The GMV volumes were normalized using the total intracranial volume (TIV) to account for different individual head sizes. Further information about the acquirement and quantification of GMV are previously detailed [3,4].

2.3 Statistical Analysis

To investigate whether OCTA metrics are correlated with GMV, we fitted a Generalized estimating equation model (GEE) [9]. The GMV was the dependent variable, and the independent variables were the OCTA metric and covariates: BP and CAIDE score. The CAIDE score accounts for both age and sex, eliminating the need for including them as separate covariates in the analysis. Available scans of both eyes were accounted for and used within the GEE model when fitting. The correlation structure within the GEE model was picked to be exchangeable, assuming a correlation between the left and right eyes [24].

We fitted the model with each OCTA metric included in this study against each GMV included and acquired the p-values and standardized beta coefficients from each run. Since we ran multiple experiments between various OCTA metrics and GMVs, it is necessary to adjust for multiple comparisons. We used false discovery rate to adjust for multiple comparisons in this study [2]. The p-values from OCTA metrics that passed the false discovery rate were reported as statistically significant findings in this study.

3   Results

108 participants (mean age = 51 years) with known APOE4 statuses were analyzed in this study. Our results revealed significant correlations between OCTA metrics and GMV measures in a mid-life cohort across the total GMV, subcortical GMV, and the left and right hippocampal GMV. We observed that as GMV decreases, there is an increase in OCTA metrics that were correlated. Table 2 summarizes the OCTA metrics that are statistically correlated to GMV. FAZ area and acircualrity, FVSD, and vessel curvature and tortuosity exhibited consistent associations with each region of interest (ROI) in the retina. Vessel resistance showed no significant correlations with any of the GMV regions. Furthermore, PVSD was correlated to only the right hippocampal and total GMV. VGD (Whole image and foveal region) was significantly correlated to each GMV region. Table 3 presents the p-values of each OCTA metric in relation to every GMV region. A Table containing the standardized beta coefficients of each OCTA metric in relation to every GMV region can be found in the supplementary material of this study.

Table 2. A baseline summary of the OCTA metrics that are significantly correlated (p-value < 0.05) to GMV after adjusting for blood pressure and the CAIDE score. (VC): vessel curvature, (VT): vessel tortuosity, (VR): vessel resistance, (FAZ): foveal avascular zone, (PVSD): parafoveal vessel skeleton density, (FVSD): foveal vessel skeleton density, (VGD): vessel graph density, (F): foveal, (N): nasal, (I): inferior, (T): temporal, (S): superior, (W): whole image, (ALL): association across all retinal ROIs (F, N, I, T, S, W). (↑) means an increase in the OCTA metric as GMV decreases.

OCTA metric	Total GMV	Subcortical GMV	LH-GMV	RH-GMV
FAZ area	↑	↑	↑	↑
FAZ acircularity	↑	↑	↑	↑
VGD	(W)↑, (F)↑, (S)↑	(W)↑, (F)↑, (N)↑, (T)↑, (I)↑	(W)↑, (T)↑, (F)↑, (N)↑, (I)↑	(W)↑, (F)↑, (N)↑, (I)↑
PVSD		↑	↑	
FVSD	↑	↑	↑	↑
VC	(ALL)↑	(ALL)↑	(ALL)↑	(ALL)↑
VT	(ALL)↑	(ALL)↑	(ALL)↑	(ALL)↑
VR				

Table 3. A baseline summary containing the p-values of the OCTA metrics in relation to every GMV region after adjusting for blood pressure and the CAIDE score. (VC): vessel curvature, (VT): vessel tortuosity, (VR): vessel resistance, (FAZ): foveal avascular zone, (PVSD): parafoveal vessel skeleton density, (FVSD): foveal vessel skeleton density, (VGD): vessel graph density, (F): foveal, (N): nasal, (I): inferior, (T): temporal, (S): superior, (W): whole image.

OCTA metric	Total GMV	Subcortical GMV	LH-GMV	RH-GMV
	p	p	p	p
FAZ area	0.013	0.010	0.042	0.021
FAZ acircularity	0.001	0.001	0.001	0.002
PVSD	0.301	0.231	0.001	0.738
FVSD	0.003	0.001	0.004	0.004
VGD (W)	0.003	0.005	0.007	0.002
VGD (T)	0.184	0.231	0.001	0.222
VGD (F)	0.003	0.002	0.004	0.004
VGD (N)	0.480	0.371	0.003	0.002
VGD (I)	0.406	0.014	0.001	0.004
VGD (S)	0.001	0.003	0.372	0.376
VC (W)	0.002	0.002	0.004	0.004
VC (T)	0.001	0.002	0.002	0.001
VC (F)	<0.001	0.001	0.001	0.015
VC (N)	<0.001	<0.001	0.001	<0.001
VC (I)	0.001	0.002	0.002	0.003
VC (S)	<0.001	<0.001	<0.001	<0.001
VT (W)	0.007	0.008	0.004	0.011
VT (T)	0.001	0.001	0.001	0.001
VT (F)	0.018	0.022	0.022	0.026
VT (N)	0.001	<0.001	0.001	<0.001
VT (I)	0.011	0.014	0.010	0.016
VT (S)	<0.001	<0.001	<0.001	<0.001
VR (T)	0.907	0.940	0.941	0.946
VR (F)	0.127	0.071	0.063	0.055
VR (N)	0.166	0.198	0.167	0.164
VR (I)	0.106	0.071	0.146	0.162
VR (S)	0.110	0.071	0.185	0.162

4   Discussion

The present study investigated potential correlations between changes in the retinal microvasculature and GMV in a mid-life cohort of participants with and without APOE4 status at baseline. We observed significant correlations between OCTA metrics and various GMV measures, including total GMV, subcortical GMV, and left and right hippocampal GMV. Furthermore, there were consistent associations between OCTA metrics and GMV measures across different ROIs in the retina. These findings suggest that retinal microvasculature changes could reflect global and region-specific gray matter alterations in the brain. To our best knowledge, this is the first study to investigate the associations between OCTA metrics and GMV measures in a mid-life cohort at risk of developing AD based on APOE4 status.

Comparing our results to related studies in the literature, a pilot study by Yoon *et al.* that consisted of 16 participants with known AD and MCI statuses reported that VD and PD were only correlated to ILV. Other GMV measures, such as LV, HP, and cortical gray matter were not reported to be correlated to either VD or PD. However, the limited sample size of their study may have impacted the potential broader associations between OCTA metricss and GMV measures. The authors still concluded that the relationship between the retinal microvasculature and volumetric brain measures should be studied further [25]. Next is a study by Ruilin *et al.* that investigated whether the retinal microvasculature was linked to any brain volumes such as WMH and GMV in a cognitively healthy and dementia-free elderly cohort ($n = 135$, median age = 58 years). Even though the cohort was cognitively healthy, there was still an observed significant association between vascular density in the superficial plexus layer and hippocampal GMV. AD is related prominently to hippocampal atrophy, and the authors have suggested that microvascular impairment could potentially be followed by hippocampal atrophy [21]. Another study by Hu *et al.* recruited 25 cognitively impaired participants based on AD and MCI statuses and 21 cognitively healthy participants (mean age = 64.2 years). The authors investigated whether retinal VD extracted from OCTA images was associated with any hippocampal subfields. The authors reported that GMV of the whole hippocampus and hippocampal subfields were correlated to VD. The authors concluded that the hippocampus contributes to the association between VD and cognitive function [10].

Our results align with the findings of Hu and Ruilin et al. as we also identified a significant correlation between OCTA metrics and GMV measures, including left and right hippocampal GMV. A recent study by Zhao *et al.* recruited 28 participants defined as mild AD and 28 as healthy control (mean age = 64.9 years). The authors reported a positive correlation between VD in the inside-disc radial peripapillary capillary and total GMV. However, all statistical significance would disappear once the results were adjusted for multiple comparisons [26]. It is worth noting that the low sample size in their study may have influenced the statistical power. In comparison, VGD (W, F) in our study with a larger sample size has been statistically significant to each GMV measure after adjusting for multiple comparisons. Moreover, we observed distinct correlations between specific VGD ROIs and GMV regions. Specifically, VGD (T) exhibited a correlation exclusively with the left hippocampal GMV, VGD (N) showed correlations with both the left and right hippocampal GMV regions, VGD (S) demonstrated associations solely with total and subcortical GMV regions, and VGD (I) displayed correlations exclusively with subcortical as well as left and right hippocampal GMV regions. Furthermore, our investigation has uncovered associations between OCTA metrics related to vessel morphology, specifically vessel curvature and tortuosity (across all ROI), and each region of GMV included in this study.

One possible explanation for the observed correlations between OCTA metrics and GMV measures is the presence of common underlying vascular processes in both the retina and the brain. The retina provides a unique window into the microvasculature, allowing for non-invasive assessment of vascular changes that may reflect systemic vascular dysfunction and cerebrovascular pathology [14]. Additionally, the hippocampus, a crucial region for memory and cognition, is known to be among the earliest affected by AD [17]. The associations between OCTA metrics and hippocampal GMV may suggest that retinal microvasculature changes could track early hippocampal atrophy. Our study's age cohort (mean age = 51 years old), consisting of individuals between 40 and 59 years old, is younger than previous studies focusing on elderly participants. By examining individuals at this critical stage, we have the opportunity to understand the underlying pathological processes that occur before the onset of clinical symptoms.

In conclusion, our study highlights the promising potential of retinal microvasculature changes as a non-invasive method to investigate neurodegenerative processes in the brain. Ultimately, there should be further investigation into the identification of reliable biomarkers from OCTA metricss for early monitoring of AD.

References

1. Ali, N., et al.: Clinical validation of the rtvue optical coherence tomography angiography image quality indicators. Clin. Exp. Ophthalmol. **48**(2), 192–203 (2020)
2. Benjamini, Y., Hochberg, Y.: Controlling the false discovery rate: a practical and powerful approach to multiple testing. J. Roy. Stat. Soc.: Ser. B (Methodol.) **57**(1), 289–300 (1995)
3. Dounavi, M.E., et al.: Volumetric alterations in the hippocampal subfields of subjects at increased risk of dementia. Neurobiol. Aging **91**, 36–44 (2020)
4. Dounavi, M.E., et al.: Macrostructural brain alterations at midlife are connected to cardiovascular and not inherited risk of future dementia: the prevent-dementia study. J. Neurol. **269**(8), 4299–4309 (2022)
5. Giarratano, Y., et al.: Automated segmentation of optical coherence tomography angiography images: benchmark data and clinically relevant metrics. Transl. Vision Sci. Technol. **9**(13), 5–5 (2020)
6. Giarratano, Y., et al.: A framework for the discovery of retinal biomarkers in optical coherence tomography angiography (OCTA). In: Fu, H., Garvin, M.K., MacGillivray, T., Xu, Y., Zheng, Y. (eds.) OMIA 2020. LNCS, vol. 12069, pp. 155–164. Springer, Cham (2020). https://doi.org/10.1007/978-3-030-63419-3_16

7. Early Treatment Diabetic Retinopathy Study Research Group, et al.: Grading diabetic retinopathy from stereoscopic color fundus photographs–an extension of the modified Airlie house classification: ETDRS report number 10. Ophthalmology **98**(5), 786–806 (1991)
8. Gunes, S., Aizawa, Y., Sugashi, T., Sugimoto, M., Rodrigues, P.P.: Biomarkers for Alzheimer's disease in the current state: a narrative review. Int. J. Mol. Sci. **23**(9), 4962 (2022)
9. Hardin, J.W., Hilbe, J.M.: Generalized Estimating Equations. CRC Press, London (2012)
10. Hu, Z., et al.: Retinal alterations as potential biomarkers of structural brain changes in Alzheimer's disease spectrum patients. Brain Sci. **13**(3), 460 (2023)
11. Hui, J., Zhao, Y., Yu, S., Liu, J., Chiu, K., Wang, Y.: Detection of retinal changes with optical coherence tomography angiography in mild cognitive impairment and Alzheimer's disease patients: a meta-analysis. PLoS ONE **16**(8), e0255362 (2021)
12. Liang, Z., Zhang, J., An, C.: Foveal avascular zone segmentation of octa images using deep learning approach with unsupervised vessel segmentation. In: ICASSP 2021–2021 IEEE International Conference on Acoustics, Speech and Signal Processing (ICASSP), pp. 1200–1204. IEEE (2021)
13. Liu, C.C., Kanekiyo, T., Xu, H., Bu, G.: Apolipoprotein e and Alzheimer disease: risk, mechanisms and therapy. Nat. Rev. Neurol. **9**(2), 106–118 (2013)
14. London, A., Benhar, I., Schwartz, M.: The retina as a window to the brain–from eye research to CNS disorders. Nat. Rev. Neurol. **9**(1), 44–53 (2013)
15. Low, A., et al.: Caide dementia risk score relates to severity and progression of cerebral small vessel disease in healthy midlife adults: the prevent-dementia study. J. Neurol. Neurosurgery Psychiatry **93**(5), 481–490 (2022)
16. Nichols, E., et al.: Estimation of the global prevalence of dementia in 2019 and forecasted prevalence in 2050: an analysis for the global burden of disease study 2019. Lancet Public Health **7**(2), e105–e125 (2022)
17. Rao, Y.L., Ganaraja, B., Murlimanju, B., Joy, T., Krishnamurthy, A., Agrawal, A.: Hippocampus and its involvement in Alzheimer's disease: a review. 3 Biotech **12**(2), 55 (2022)
18. Rifai, O.M., et al.: The application of optical coherence tomography angiography in Alzheimer's disease: a systematic review. Alzheimer's Dementia: Diagnosis Assessment Disease Monit. **13**(1), e12149 (2021)
19. Risacher, S.L., Saykin, A.J.: Neuroimaging biomarkers of neurodegenerative diseases and dementia. In: Seminars in Neurology, vol. 33, pp. 386–416. Thieme Medical Publishers (2013)
20. Ritchie, C.W., Ritchie, K.: The prevent study: a prospective cohort study to identify mid-life biomarkers of late-onset Alzheimer's disease. BMJ Open **2**(6), e001893 (2012)
21. Wang, R., et al.: Association of retinal thickness and microvasculature with cognitive performance and brain volumes in elderly adults. Front. Aging Neurosci. **12**, 1010548 (2022)
22. Wiseman, S.J., et al.: Measuring axial length of the eye from magnetic resonance brain imaging. BMC Ophthalmol. **22**(1), 1–9 (2022)
23. Xu, Z., et al.: Associations of macular microvascular parameters with cerebral small vessel disease in rural older adults: a population-based oct angiography study. Front. Neurol. **14**, 1133819 (2023)
24. Ying, G.S., Maguire, M.G., Glynn, R.J., Rosner, B.: Tutorial on biostatistics: longitudinal analysis of correlated continuous eye data. Ophthalmic Epidemiol. **28**(1), 3–20 (2021)

25. Yoon, S.P., et al.: Correlation of octa and volumetric MRI in mild cognitive impairment and Alzheimer's disease. Ophthalmic Surg. Lasers Imaging Retina **50**(11), 709–718 (2019)
26. Zhao, B., et al.: The correlation of retinal neurodegeneration and brain degeneration in patients with Alzheimer's disease using optical coherence tomography angiography and MRI. Front. Aging Neurosci. **15**, 1089188 (2023)
27. Zhou, X., et al.: Abnormalities of retinal structure and microvasculature are associated with cerebral white matter hyperintensities. Eur. J. Neurol. **29**(8), 2289–2298 (2022)

Improved Automatic Diabetic Retinopathy Severity Classification Using Deep Multimodal Fusion of UWF-CFP and OCTA Images

Mostafa El Habib Daho[1,2]($\boxtimes$), Yihao Li[1,2]($\boxtimes$), Rachid Zeghlache[1,2],
Yapo Cedric Atse[1,2], Hugo Le Boité[3,4], Sophie Bonnin[5], Deborah Cosette[6],
Pierre Deman[7,8], Laurent Borderie[8], Capucine Lepicard[9], Ramin Tadayoni[3,5],
Béatrice Cochener[1,2,10], Pierre-Henri Conze[2,11], Mathieu Lamard[1,2],
and Gwenolé Quellec[2]

[1] Univ Bretagne Occidentale, Brest, France
[2] LaTIM UMR 1101, Inserm, Brest, France
mostafa.elhabibdaho@univ-brest.fr, yihao.li@etudiant.univ-brest.fr
[3] Ophthalmology Department, Lariboisiere Hospital, APHP, Paris, France
[4] Paris Cité University, Paris, France
[5] Ophthalmology Department, Rothschild Foundation Hospital, Paris, France
[6] Carl Zeiss Meditec Inc, Dublin, CA, USA
[7] ADCIS, Saint-Contest 14280, France
[8] Evolucare Technologies, Le Pecq 78230, France
[9] AP-HP, Paris, France
[10] Ophthalmology Department, CHRU Brest, Brest, France
[11] IMT Atlantique, Brest, France

Abstract. Diabetic Retinopathy (DR), a prevalent and severe complication of diabetes, affects millions of individuals globally, underscoring the need for accurate and timely diagnosis. Recent advancements in imaging technologies, such as Ultra-WideField Color Fundus Photography (UWF-CFP) imaging and Optical Coherence Tomography Angiography (OCTA), provide opportunities for the early detection of DR but also pose significant challenges given the disparate nature of the data they produce. This study introduces a novel multimodal approach that leverages these imaging modalities to notably enhance DR classification. Our approach integrates 2D UWF-CFP images and 3D high-resolution $6 \times 6\,\mathrm{mm}^3$ OCTA (both structure and flow) images using a fusion of ResNet50 and 3D-ResNet50 models, with Squeeze-and-Excitation (SE) blocks to amplify relevant features. Additionally, to increase the model's generalization capabilities, a multimodal extension of Manifold Mixup, applied to concatenated multimodal features, is implemented. Experimental results demonstrate a remarkable enhancement in DR classification performance with the proposed multimodal approach compared to methods relying on a single modality only. The methodology laid out in this work holds substantial promise for facilitating more accurate, early detection of DR, potentially improving clinical outcomes for patients.

B. Antony et al. (Eds.): OMIA 2023, LNCS 14096, pp. 11–20, 2023.
https://doi.org/10.1007/978-3-031-44013-7_2

Keywords: Diabetic Retinopathy Classification · Multimodal
Information Fusion · Deep learning · UWF-CFP · OCTA

1   Introduction

Diabetic Retinopathy (DR), a common ocular complication of diabetes, is a leading cause of blindness globally [19]. The disease is characterized by progressive damage to the retina due to prolonged hyperglycemia and is estimated to affect approximately one-third of all people with diabetes. As such, timely and accurate diagnosis of DR is crucial for effective management and treatment. However, the subtle and complex nature of the disease's early stages presents a challenge for such a diagnosis.

Recent advances in imaging techniques have significantly enhanced the ability to detect and classify DR. Ultra-WideField Color Fundus Photography (UWF-CFP) imaging and Optical Coherence Tomography Angiography (OCTA) are two such techniques that have shown great promise. UWF-CFP imaging offers a panoramic view of the retina, allowing for a more comprehensive assessment [16], while OCTA provides depth-resolved images of retinal blood flow, revealing detailed microvascular changes indicative of DR [18].

Despite the individual merits of these imaging modalities, each offers a unique perspective on retinal pathology. Leveraging the information from both could potentially enhance the diagnosis and classification of DR [8,24]. However, the integration of these modalities poses a significant challenge due to the disparate nature of the data they produce, especially in terms of dimensionality (2D versus 3D) and field of view.

In recent years, deep learning (DL) has emerged as a powerful tool for medical image analysis, demonstrating great performance in a wide range of tasks [7,9, 14,15]. These models, particularly Convolutional Neural Networks (CNNs), have shown their ability to learn complex, hierarchical representations from raw image data, making them a natural choice for multimodal image fusion.

In the quest to enhance DL models, the field has benefitted significantly from incorporating innovative techniques like the Manifold Mixup [20]. Through its unique method of generating virtual training examples via the convex combinations of hidden state representations, this technique has made a profound impact by significantly reducing a model's sensitivity to the data distribution and encouraging smoother decision boundaries.

Building upon these advanced techniques, several proposed methods in the state of the art have employed multimodal imaging [10,17]. These methods aim to utilize the complementary information available in different types of images. Recent works have effectively used mixing strategies to enhance multimodal DL models. For example, the M^{3}ixup approach [11] leverages a mixup strategy to enhance multimodal representation learning and increase robustness against missing modalities by mixing different modalities and aligning mixed views with original multimodal representations. The LeMDA (Learning Multimodal Data Augmentation) [12] method automatically learns to jointly augment multimodal data in feature space, enhancing the performance of multimodal deep learning architectures and achieving good results across various applications. MixGen [5] introduces a joint data augmentation for vision-language representation learning to boost data efficiency, generating new image-text pairs while preserving semantic relationships. This method has shown remarkable performance improvements across various vision-language tasks. Furthermore, TMMDA (Token Mixup Multimodal Data Augmentation) [27] for Multimodal Sentiment Analysis (MSA) generates virtual modalities from the mixed token-level representation of raw modalities, enhancing representation learning on limited labeled datasets.

Despite the significant results obtained, these methods are proposed for vision-language and vision-audio fusion but are not suitable for 2D image/3D volume fusion. This study proposes a new multimodal DL approach for DR classification, integrating 2D UWF-CFP images and 3D OCTA images and incorporating a custom mixing strategy. Regarding the used modalities in this work, recent research has used UWF-CFP and OCTA imaging for the diagnosis of diseases such as Alzheimer [21]. However, to the best of our knowledge, our study is the first to develop a DL model for the classification of DR using both UWF-CFP and OCTA imaging modalities, which contributes significantly to the existing body of knowledge.

2   Methods

2.1   Model Architecture

We utilize two separate CNN architectures, ResNet50 and 3D-ResNet50, designed to process 2D UWF-CFP and 3D OCTA images, to extract features from each imaging modality. ResNet50 was chosen as a backbone for feature extraction due to its remarkable performance in computer vision tasks. Its structure provides a balance between depth and complexity, allowing the network to learn complex patterns without suffering from overfitting. To further improve such models' performance, Squeeze-and-Excitation (SE) blocks have gained attention in the DL community [6]. As shown in Fig. 1(d), the SE blocks dynamically recalibrate channel-wise feature responses by explicitly modeling the interdependencies between channels, thus helping the model focus on more informative features. They have been demonstrated to significantly improve the representational power of deep networks without a significant additional computational cost.

The 3D-ResNet50, a 3D extension of the ResNet50 architecture, integrated with SE blocks, is applied to process OCTA images (Fig. 1(a)). This model expands traditional 2D convolution operations into the 3D space, making it particularly appropriate for volumetric image data. This enables the network to decipher spatial hierarchies inherent in volumetric data, thus facilitating a comprehensive feature extraction from OCTA volumes. SE blocks in the 3D-ResNet50 model perform a similar role as in the 2D ResNet50 model, thus enhancing the performance of the 3D backbone. For the rest of the paper, we will refer to these models as SE-ResNet50 and SE-3D-ResNet50.

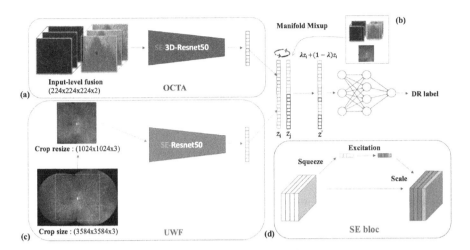

Fig. 1. Proposed pipeline.

2.2 Fusion Strategy

The fusion of multiple modalities has been an area of active research due to the enhanced performances it offers [2,13,28]. Such fusion can be executed at input, feature, and decision levels, each offering distinct advantages and disadvantages.

In this work, we employ an input-level fusion for merging the structure and flow information embedded in OCTA images. Numerous studies affirm that merging these distinct types of information can significantly enhance the accuracy of DR diagnosis [10,25]. Input-level fusion involves integrating multiple modalities into a single data tensor subsequently processed by a DL model Fig. 1(a). This method is effective without the need for registration, as the structure and flow data align with each other by design.

On the other hand, the fusion of UWF-CFP and OCTA images is performed through a different approach, primarily due to the absence of inherent alignment between these imaging modalities. Here, a feature-level fusion strategy is adopted, which allows us to use different backbones for each modality (SE-ResNet50 and 3D-SE-ResNet50), thus effectively addressing the alignment challenge. We have chosen feature-level fusion over decision-level fusion to capitalize on the rich interplay between the modalities at the feature level. This strategy facilitates the extraction of features and the fusion of high-dimensional feature-level information, making it especially suited for unregistered or dimensionally diverse data [3,4,22,23].

2.3 Manifold Mixup

To enhance the model's robustness and generalization capabilities, we implemented a multimodal extension of Manifold Mixup into our training process. The original Manifold Mixup method [20] is a recently introduced regularization technique. It generates virtual training examples by forming convex combinations of the hidden state representations of two randomly chosen training examples and their associated labels.

Extending the concept of Input Mixup [26] to the hidden layers, Manifold Mixup serves as a robust regularization method that provokes neural networks to predict interpolated hidden representations with lesser confidence. It leverages semantic interpolations as an auxiliary training signal, leading to the cultivation of neural networks with smoother decision boundaries across multiple representation levels. Consequently, neural networks trained with Manifold Mixup can learn class representations with reduced directions of variance, thus yielding a model that exhibits enhanced performance on unseen data [20]. The operational process of the Manifold Mixup approach is as follows:

1. The original Manifold Mixup performs the mixing of the hidden representation randomly on a set of predefined eligible layers. Instead, in our proposed implementation, we have purposefully selected the layer containing the concatenated feature maps from UWF-CFP and OCTA images to process the Manifold Mixup. This strategic choice is not only the simplest way to introduce Manifold Mixup but also ensures we are capitalizing on a layer that encapsulates a high-dimensional, multimodal feature space. Creating numerous virtual training samples from the fusion layer significantly improves the model's ability to generalize to new data.
2. Feed two images into the neural network until the selected layer is reached.
3. Extract the feature representations (z_i for multimodal data x_i and z_j for multimodal data x_j).
4. Mix the extracted feature representations according to Eq. 1 in order to derive the new representation (new features z' associated with new label y').

$$(z', y') = (\lambda z_i + (1 - \lambda)z_j, \lambda y_i + (1 - \lambda)y_j) \qquad (1)$$

where z_i and z_j are the features of two random training examples, and y_i and y_j are their corresponding labels. $\lambda \in [0, 1]$ is a Mixup coefficient sampled from a Beta distribution $Beta(\alpha, \alpha)$, where α is a hyperparameter that determines the shape of the Beta distribution.

5. Carry out the forward pass in the network for the remaining layers with the mixed data.
6. Use the output of the mixed data to compute the loss and gradients. Given $\mathcal{L}$ the original loss function, the new loss $\mathcal{L}'$ is computed as:

$$\mathcal{L}' = \lambda \mathcal{L}(y_i, y') + (1 - \lambda)\mathcal{L}(y_j, y') \qquad (2)$$

Through this process, Manifold Mixup enhances our fusion strategy by operating on the joint feature representation (Fig. 1(b)), thereby ensuring that the model can generalize from the learned features of UWF-CFP and OCTA images.

3 Experiments and Results

3.1 Dataset

The data used in this study arise from the "Évaluation Intelligente de la Rétinopathie diabétique" (EviRed) project[1], a comprehensive initiative that collected data between 2020 and 2022 from 14 hospitals and recruitment centers across France. This database included UWF-CFP images and OCTA images from patients at various stages of DR. The dataset comprised images of 875 eyes belonging to a total of 444 patients, and was carefully divided into one (fixed) test set, and multiple train and validation sets (through 5-fold cross-validation) to ensure a broad representation and unbiased learning. Each patient's eye was labeled by an ophthalmologist into one of the 6 DR classes: Normal, mild non-proliferative diabetic retinopathy (NPDR), moderate NPDR, severe NPDR, proliferative DR (PDR), or Pan-Retinal Photocoagulation (PRP).

The UWF-CFP images in the dataset, captured using the Clarus 500 (Carl Zeiss Meditec Inc., Dublin, CA, USA), varied in size, ranging from 3900×3900 to 7900×4900 pixels. This size variation arises from the image stitching process for montage creation, not from changes in the device's resolution. Considering the clinicians' focus on the seven Early Treatment Diabetic Retinopathy Study (ETDRS) fields [1], we carried out center cropping on each image to 3584×3584. This process ensured that all seven fields were included in the image. Subsequently, we resized these cropped images to 1024×1024, a size that guarantees no loss of details.

The high-resolution $6 \times 6 \, \mathrm{mm}^3$ OCTA images, offering $500 \times 224 \times 500$ voxels and centered on the macula, were captured using the Zeiss PLEX Elite 9000. Each OCTA volume includes 2-D en-face localizer, structural, and flow 3D volumes. Due to the restrictions posed by the graphics processing unit (32Gb GPU) hardware, our 3D-SE-ResNet50 could only accommodate inputs up to $224 \times 224 \times 224 \times 2$ input tensors. This limitation guided our data pre-processing. In the training step of our deep learning network, we employed random crop processing. During the prediction process, we extracted multiple volumes from the OCTA image using $N = 10$ times random crop, which were simultaneously processed with the full UWF-CFP image to make predictions. The final prediction for an examination was determined based on the severest prediction among these N predictions (test-time augmentation).

3.2 Implementation Details

Our models were implemented using the PyTorch[2] deep learning library, and all experiments were conducted using an NVIDIA Tesla V100s GPU. For UWF-CFP images, we used the SE-ResNet50 architecture with weights pre-trained on ImageNet, while for OCTA images, we trained from scratch our implementation

---

[1] https://evired.org/.
[2] https://pytorch.org/.

of the 3D-SE-ResNet50 backbone with input-level fusion for structure and flow volumes. The key to our model enhancement process included incorporating SE blocks in both ResNet models and using Manifold Mixup on multimodal features for model regularization. In our implementation, we set the reduction ratio, a crucial SE hyperparameter, to 16, following the practice from the original SE network paper [6]. For Mixup, we carried out a grid search focusing on the α parameter, which is essential for deriving the adequate Beta distribution $Beta(\alpha, \alpha)$ for sampling the right λ interpolation parameter during Manifold Mixup training. This comprehensive exploration determined 0.2 as the optimal value for α, which yielded the best model performance. The two models were trained jointly on the UWF-CFP and OCTA datasets, using a cross-entropy loss function and an AdamW optimizer. During training, we used a learning rate of 0.001 with the OneCycle scheduler, a decay factor of 0.0001, and a batch size of 4 over 200 epochs.

3.3   Results and Discussion

To compare the performance of our proposed method with the individual modalities, we trained standalone models using either UWF-CFP or OCTA images with the same training settings as described above. This provided a baseline performance for each modality, against which the performance of the multimodal approach was compared. In addition, an ablation study was conducted to further understand each component's impact and contribution to our pipeline. We compared the performance of our model without the Manifold Mixup and the SE blocks.

The performance of the proposed models was evaluated in terms of the Area Under the Receiver Operating Characteristic (ROC) Curve (AUC). This metric was chosen due to its ability to provide an aggregate measure of performance across the four DR severity cutoffs ($\geq$ mild NPDR, $\geq$ moderate NPDR, $\geq$ severe NPDR, $\geq$ PDR).

Table 1 presents the performance of the different models: the ResNet50 model trained on UWF-CFP images, the 3D-ResNet50 model trained on OCTA images, the proposed multimodal pipeline, the multimodal models without SE, the pipeline without Manifold Mixup (MM in the table), and the pipeline without SE and Manifold Mixup.

Our approach that combines both UWF-CFP and OCTA images using a multimodal pipeline notably outperformed models based on individual modalities. Specifically, when evaluating DR severity cutoffs, the multimodal model achieved an AUC score of 0.8566 for $\geq$ mild NPDR, notably higher than 0.7983 for UWF-CFP alone and 0.8316 for OCTA alone. This trend continued with $\geq$ moderate NPDR and $\geq$ severe NPDR, where our multimodal model attained AUC scores of 0.8037 and 0.7922, respectively, compared to 0.7925 and 0.7906 for UWF-CFP and 0.7627 and 0.7338 for OCTA. These outcomes underscore the importance of capitalizing on diverse image modalities to provide a more comprehensive, holistic analysis, thereby enhancing the robustness and accuracy of

Table 1. Performance of Models in DR Classification

Data	SE	MM	≥ mild NPDR	≥ moderate NPDR	≥ severe NPDR	≥ PDR
UWF-CFP	✗	✗	0.7983	0.7925	0.7906	**0.9159**
OCTA	✗	✗	0.8316	0.7627	0.7338	0.7576
Multimodal	✓	✓	**0.8566**	**0.8037**	**0.7922**	0.8820
Multimodal	✗	✓	0.8241	0.7969	0.7682	0.8522
Multimodal	✓	✗	0.8431	0.7782	0.7566	0.8420
Multimodal	✗	✗	0.8140	0.7775	0.7525	0.8164

DR classification. Our study suggests that each imaging modality captures distinct aspects of DR, and the concurrent utilization of both modalities in our models appears to improve the diagnosis, which is aligned with clinical studies [8, 24].

The greater success of UWF-CFP in identifying the cutoff ≥ PDR can be attributed to its wide-field view of the retina, which allows for the detection of peripheral lesions and signs of PRP laser impacts. Conversely, OCTA images proved to be particularly useful for ≥ mild NPDR detection due to their central focus on the macula and the high-resolution imaging of the microvasculature.

Regarding the added components in our pipeline, the Manifold Mixup and the SE blocks were proven to enhance the model's performance. For example, omitting the SE blocks caused a decrease in AUC scores across all DR severities. This indicates the critical role of SE blocks in bolstering feature representations and overall model robustness. Similarly, when the Manifold Mixup was excluded, there was a noticeable drop in performance, corroborating the effectiveness of such a regularization technique in improving model generalization.

4   Conclusion

Our findings demonstrate the efficacy of the proposed multimodal model in improving DR classification. This model, which integrates UWF-CFP and OCTA images using a feature-level fusion strategy and employing both our proposed adaption of the Manifold Mixup technique and SE blocks, delivers a compelling performance. The ablation study further attests to the significance of each component within our pipeline. These findings reiterate the necessity and potency of multimodal approaches coupled with advanced regularization techniques, such as Manifold Mixup and SE blocks, for medical image classification tasks.

To the best of our knowledge, our study is the first to propose a pipeline for the classification of DR using both UWF-CFP and OCTA images. However, we believe several improvements and extensions could further enhance the classification performance. The application of cross-modal attention mechanisms may provide a more effective way of fusing features from different modalities by focusing on the most relevant information from each. Similarly, implementing Manifold Mixup at different levels of the model, rather than solely at the concatenation layer, could provide further regularization and performance improvements. Moreover, introducing novel components, such as Transformer blocks, might prove beneficial in capturing complex relationships within and across modalities.

Acknowledgements. The work takes place in the framework of Evired, an ANR RHU project. This work benefits from State aid managed by the French National Research Agency under "Investissement d'Avenir" program bearing the reference ANR-18-RHUS-0008.

References

1. Early treatment diabetic retinopathy study design and baseline patient characteristics: Etdrs report number 7. Ophthalmology **98**(5, Supplement), 741–756 (1991). https://doi.org/10.1016/S0161-6420(13)38009-9
2. Akhavan Aghdam, M., Sharifi, A., Pedram, M.M.: Combination of RS-fMRI and SMRI data to discriminate autism spectrum disorders in young children using deep belief network. J. Dig. Imaging **31**, 895–903 (2018)
3. Al-Absi, H.R., Islam, M.T., Refaee, M.A., Chowdhury, M.E., Alam, T.: Cardiovascular disease diagnosis from DXA scan and retinal images using deep learning. Sensors **22**(12), 4310 (2022)
4. El-Sappagh, S., Abuhmed, T., Islam, S.R., Kwak, K.S.: Multimodal multitask deep learning model for Alzheimer's disease progression detection based on time series data. Neurocomputing **412**, 197–215 (2020)
5. Hao, X., et al.: Mixgen: a new multi-modal data augmentation (2023)
6. Hu, J., Shen, L., Sun, G.: Squeeze-and-excitation networks. In: 2018 IEEE/CVF Conference on Computer Vision and Pattern Recognition. pp. 7132–7141 (2018). https://doi.org/10.1109/CVPR.2018.00745
7. Lahsaini, I., El Habib Daho, M., Chikh, M.A.: Deep transfer learning based classification model for COVID-19 using chest CT-scans. Pattern Recogn. Lett. **152**, 122–128 (2021). https://doi.org/10.1016/j.patrec.2021.08.035
8. Li, J., et al.: Ultra-widefield color fundus photography combined with high-speed ultra-widefield swept-source optical coherence tomography angiography for non-invasive detection of lesions in diabetic retinopathy. Front. Public Health **10** (2022). https://doi.org/10.3389/fpubh.2022.1047608
9. Li, T., et al.: Applications of deep learning in fundus images: a review (2021). https://arxiv.org/abs/2101.09864
10. Li, Y., et al.: Multimodal information fusion for glaucoma and diabetic retinopathy classification. In: Antony, B., Fu, H., Lee, C.S., MacGillivray, T., Xu, Y., Zheng, Y. (eds.) OMIA 2022. LNCS, vol. 13576, pp. 53–62. Springer, Cham (2022). https://doi.org/10.1007/978-3-031-16525-2_6
11. Lin, R., Hu, H.: Adapt and explore: multimodal mixup for representation learning. Available at SSRN (2023). https://doi.org/10.2139/ssrn.4461697
12. Liu, Z., et al.: Learning multimodal data augmentation in feature space (2023)
13. Qian, X., et al.: A combined ultrasonic b-mode and color doppler system for the classification of breast masses using neural network. Eur. Radiol. **30**, 3023–3033 (2020)
14. Quellec, G., Al Hajj, H., Lamard, M., Conze, P.H., Massin, P., Cochener, B.: Explain: explanatory artificial intelligence for diabetic retinopathy diagnosis. Med. Image Anal. **72**, 102118 (2021). https://doi.org/10.1016/j.media.2021.102118

15. Shamshad, F., et al.: Transformers in medical imaging: a survey. Med. Image Anal. **88**, 102802 (2023). https://doi.org/10.1016/j.media.2023.102802
16. Silva, P.S., et al.: Diabetic retinopathy severity and peripheral lesions are associated with nonperfusion on ultrawide field angiography. Ophthalmology **122**(12), 2465–2472 (2015). https://doi.org/10.1016/j.ophtha.2015.07.034
17. Sleeman, W.C., Kapoor, R., Ghosh, P.: Multimodal classification: current landscape, taxonomy and future directions. ACM Comput. Surv. **55**(7) (2022). https://doi.org/10.1145/3543848
18. Sun, Z., Yang, D., Tang, Z., et al.: Optical coherence tomography angiography in diabetic retinopathy: an updated review. Eye **35**(11), 149–161 (2021). https://doi.org/10.1038/s41433-020-01233-y
19. Teo, Z.L., et al.: Global prevalence of diabetic retinopathy and projection of burden through 2045: systematic review and meta-analysis. Ophthalmology **128**(11), 1580–1591 (2021)
20. Verma, V., et al.: Manifold mixup: better representations by interpolating hidden states (2019)
21. Wisely, C.E., et al.: Convolutional neural network to identify symptomatic Alzheimer's disease using multimodal retinal imaging. Br. J. Ophthalmol. **106**(3), 388–395 (2022). https://doi.org/10.1136/bjophthalmol-2020-317659
22. Wu, J., et al.: Gamma challenge: glaucoma grading from multi-modality images. arXiv preprint arXiv:2202.06511 (2022)
23. Xiong, J., et al.: Multimodal machine learning using visual fields and peripapillary circular oct scans in detection of glaucomatous optic neuropathy. Ophthalmology **129**(2), 171–180 (2022)
24. Yang, J., Zhang, B., Wang, E., et al.: Ultra-wide field swept-source optical coherence tomography angiography in patients with diabetes without clinically detectable retinopathy. BMC Ophthalmol. **21**(1), 192 (2021). https://doi.org/10.1186/s12886-021-01933-3
25. Zang, P., et al.: A diabetic retinopathy classification framework based on deep-learning analysis of oct angiography. Transl. Vision Sci. Technol. **11**(7), 10–10 (2022)
26. Zhang, H., Cissé, M., Dauphin, Y.N., Lopez-Paz, D.: mixup: beyond empirical risk minimization. CoRR abs/1710.09412 (2017). https://arxiv.org/abs/1710.09412
27. Zhao, X., Chen, Y., Liu, S., Zang, X., Xiang, Y., Tang, B.: TMMDA: a new token mixup multimodal data augmentation for multimodal sentiment analysis. In: Proceedings of the ACM Web Conference 2023. WWW 2023, pp. 1714–1722. Association for Computing Machinery (2023). https://doi.org/10.1145/3543507.3583406
28. Zong, W., Lee, J.K., Liu, C., Carver, E.N., Feldman, A.M., Janic, E.A.: A deep dive into understanding tumor foci classification using multiparametric MRI based on convolutional neural network. Med. Phys. **47**(9), 4077–4086 (2020)

Auxiliary-Domain Learning for a Functional Prediction of Glaucoma Progression

Sean Wu[1], Vahid Mohammadzadeh[2], Kiumars Edalati[2], Jack Martinyan[2], Arthur Martinyan[2], Joseph Caprioli[2], Kouros Nouri-Mahdavi[2], and Fabien Scalzo[1,3(✉)]

[1] Seaver College, Pepperdine University, Malibu, CA 90265, USA
fabien.scalzo@pepperdine.edu
[2] Glaucoma Division, Stein Eye Institute, David Geffen School of Medicine, University of California, Los Angeles (UCLA), CA 90095, USA
[3] Department of Computer Science, University of California, Los Angeles (UCLA), CA 90095, USA

Abstract. An accurate and early prediction of a patient's glaucoma progression can give ophthalmologists insight on how to mitigate the ramifications of the disease before they experience irreversible visual field loss or blindness. Our paper introduces an auxiliary-domain learning framework that trains a convolutional neural network to predict glaucoma progression (main task) and utilizes auxiliary tasks during training, including prediction of the patient age, mean deviation, and optical coherence tomography (OCT) data to improve its accuracy on the main task. The modalities of optic disc photographs and OCT data are often not utilized jointly due to costly machinery. However, we exploit informative features in the OCT, age, and mean deviation data as our learning objective to alleviate the need to acquire the data in clinical deployment. We compared baseline models with no auxiliary outputs to the ones built using auxiliary tasks, and observed a 6.5% increase in Area Under the Receiver Operating Characteristic Curve (AUC-ROC) in the final auxiliary-domain model ($91.3 \pm 2.6\%$) compared to the baseline ($84.8 \pm 4.9\%$). This study demonstrates the utility of auxiliary tasks when training ophthalmological models by leveraging important patient data that is difficult to acquire during training, even when it is not available as part of the model's deployment in routine clinical care.

Keywords: Glaucoma Progression · Auxiliary Domain Learning · Siamese Neural Networks

1 Introduction

Glaucoma is an optical disease responsible for the degeneration of the optic nerve and a gradual visual field loss. It is one of the leading causes of blindness

B. Antony et al. (Eds.): OMIA 2023, LNCS 14096, pp. 21–31, 2023.
https://doi.org/10.1007/978-3-031-44013-7_3

worldwide [1], affecting about 2.2% of the world's population [2]. While there is no cure of this disease, early diagnosis has demonstrated the ability to prevent further visual field loss through surgery and other treatments. Conventional computer vision techniques have been utilized in recent studies to diagnose progression of the disease by using optic retinal images [3]. While these methods show proficiency in classifying glaucoma progression, training a multi-task neural network has the potential to greatly enlarge the generalizability of a neural network. In this paper we discuss the benefits of hard parameter sharing between the convolutional and fully connected layers when training a deep learning model to classify glaucoma progression.

Machine learning has made a significant contribution to ophthalmic research, assisting ophthalmologists to treat various optic ailments such as diabetic retinopathy [4], glaucoma screening through optic disc photographs [5], and also volumetric deep learning algorithms to analyze optical coherence tomography scans [6]. In previous studies, visual field and clinical data such as mean deviation have been used to assess glaucoma progression [7]. Optic disc photographs have also shown promising prevalence in predicting symptoms of glaucoma [8]. In this paper, we constructed a deep learning model to utilize both optic disc photographs, clinical data, and OCT data as a multi-output neural network to enhance the predictability of glaucoma progression. A diagram of our methods is depicted in Fig. 1 where we use additional data as model outputs to facilitate the training process.

The addition of multi-modal features to a deep learning model has been shown to positively impact the network's performance depending on how predictive that feature is to the particular task [9]. For glaucoma progression, the mean deviation index, optical coherence tomography (OCT) clock-hour acquisitions, and global eye thickness (computed from OCT) hold crucial information to whether the patient's glaucoma will progress or not. However, acquiring these additional inputs can be costly due to requiring an OCT machine and additional visual field tests. To address this challenge, we trained a model to learn these external features through a multi-output convolutional neural network to be able to utilize the important characteristics of those features in relation to glaucoma progression prediction but without explicitly needing them as an input (Fig. 1). In this paper, we construct a model that captures multi-modal features in the training process and can be deployed on unseen data without the need of these additional, potentially costly and unavailable, modalities.

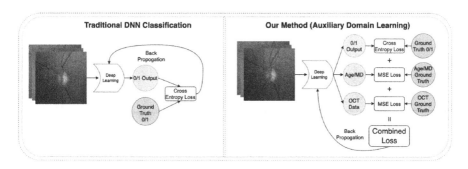

Fig. 1. Left: Conventional single task deep neural networks for glaucoma progression prediction with optic disc photographs. **Right:** Representation of our auxiliary-domain neural network to improve the prediction of glaucoma progression.

2   Methods

Our model consists of three parallel Siamese Neural Networks [10], where each encoding of the optic disc photographs "share" the exact copy of weights with one another. Additionally, we explore a composite loss function to weigh and propagate our multi-task losses through the model.

2.1   Data Acquisition

The dataset used in our experiments consists of 1,706 eyes acquired at the University of California, Los Angeles (UCLA) Jules Stein eye institute. Each sample has a minimum of one optic disc photograph and more than five visual field exams with at least 3 years of follow-up data. Each eye's mean deviation index was calculated with a linear regression model, and the visual field progression was determined as a statistically significant negative slope ($p < 0.05$) for at least two consecutive visits and at the final visit of the sequence. The three optic disc photographs that are inputted into our model were acquired at different visit dates, and the third visit photograph was taken at least one year before the diagnosed progression date. Due to the prolonged time between each visit, different devices were used to obtain the optic disc photographs. The Zeiss 450 camera (Carl Zeiss Meditec, Dublin, CA) and the FF 450 plus Fundus Camera with VISUPAC Digital Imaging System (Carl Zeiss Meditec, Dublin, CA) were the devices used to take the optic disc photographs. Each eye also has a corresponding retinal nerve fiber layer OCT data taken by the Cirrus SD-OCT machine that consists of thickness measurements for 12 clock-hour angles and an additional global thickness value that is the average of the clock-hour values. The use of this data was authorized by UCLA's Institutional Board Review.

2.2   Baseline Deep Learning Model

To train our model, we used the shallowest network in the residual neural network family ResNet18 [11], pre-trained on Imagenet [12] as the backbone for

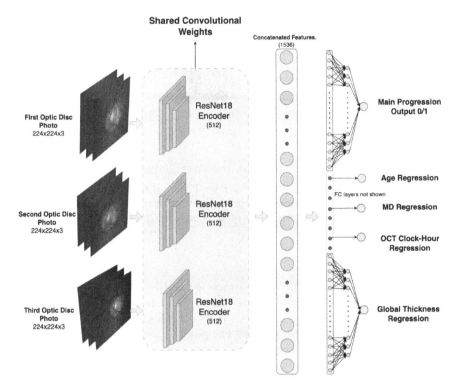

Fig. 2. Our multi-output pipeline, where three optic disc images are passed to a Siamese Neural Network with shared weights, then fed to their task-specific fully connected layers.

our Siamese Neural Network (SNN). Our SNN consists of three identical networks, where each encoding of the optic disc photographs "share" their weights with one another. The 512 features that are extracted from each instance of the ResNet18 encoder are then concatenated with one another, creating a vector of 1536 elements that can be fully connected to the binary glaucoma progression neuron.

The 1706 eyes were first randomly shuffled and partitioned into an approximate [80%/10%/10%] training/validation/testing split. To standardize the data, the left eye images (OS) were mirrored along the horizontal axis to represent a right eye (OD). This mirroring was done to reduce variance and variability in the data, helping guide the model for easier learning. Additionally, we applied data augmentation methods of shifting, scaling, and rotating geometric transformations with parameters of 0.0625, 0.2, and 90 degrees, respectively, to ensure that our model is invariant to any spatial changes and can generalize well on a broader population. In training, we set the batch size to 16 and the learning rate to 1×10^{-4}, and ran each network for approximately 100 epochs while saving the highest validation area under the receiver operating characteristic curve.

2.3   Hard Parameter Sharing and Combined Loss Function

To ensure that our model undergoes multi-domain learning, we utilized a common hard parameter sharing technique, where the initial network layers are seen as a common ground between tasks [13]. Figure 2 illustrates our method of hard parameter sharing, where the ResNet18 encoder weights are shared in a SNN amongst the three optic disc photographs. If a progressing sequence did not meet the criteria for three optic disc photographs, a padded image of numerical constants was used as a replacement. This is a common practice for temporal data such as glaucoma progression, where the number of visits for each patient is variant. To ensure consistent input shapes and prevent any input tensor mismatch errors during the forward pass to the model, we utilized blank tensors as placeholder inputs for these eyes. Sequence padding is a common approach for problems consisting of temporal data, such as glaucoma progression, where the number of visits for each patient is variant. We instantiate one fully connected layer for each auxiliary output task. For instance, the age and mean deviation predictions have their own fully connected layers consisting of a linear function mapping the 1536 features to one output feature. Each output task shares the convolutional layers from the SNN and ResNet18 backbone; however, they each have their own individual task-specific layers that predict a task-specific output.

To compute the loss for the binary glaucoma progression task, we used a binary cross entropy loss (BCE) [14] with a built-in non-linear sigmoid activation function. To address the slightly class imbalanced progressing/non-progressing class proportions, we set the positive class with 3.18 more weight when computing the loss. This value was derived by the ratio between the number of negative samples vs. the number of positive samples in our training dataset. This artificially "augments" the positive class in a way to ensure our model is learning both classes equally. Because the mean deviation, age, global thickness, and OCT clock-hour data are all continuous values, we used a mean squared error (MSE) loss function for all of the auxiliary outputs.

$$BCE = -(y \log(p) + (1 - y) \log(1 - p))$$
$$MSE = \sum_{i=1}^{D} (x_i - y_i)^2$$
$$LOSS = (-(y \log(p) + (1 - y) \log(1 - p))) * \lambda_1 + (\sum_{i=1}^{D} (x_i - y_i)^2) * \lambda_2)$$

To combine the auxiliary loss with the main progression task loss, we simply summed each of the individual losses before computing the backwards propagation. Each loss is weighted with λ, a floating point value between 0 and 1 that weighs the importance of the task. In previous research, it has been shown that structural glaucoma findings might have a greater effect on determining glaucoma progression [15]. Knowing this, we weighted the auxiliary losses of age and mean deviation (0.3) to have a higher loss weight than (0.2) to apply more "attention" to these tasks when computing the loss. The values 0.2 and 0.3 are given so that we can maintain a larger emphasis on the main glaucoma progression loss (0.7 or 0.8). As shown in the equation above, we multiply the main BCE loss with λ_1, which should hold the highest loss weight. The second half of the formula represents the specific auxiliary task we are dealing with, and it is a MSE loss function with λ_2 being the weight of the auxiliary loss. The sum of λ_1 and λ_2 should always equate to 1.

3   Experiments and Results

In this study, we ran a comparative analysis amongst the baseline model of predicting glaucoma progression and the models with age, mean deviation, global thickness, and OCT clock-hour data to see which auxiliary outputs show an improvement in the main glaucoma progression task. To evaluate each model's performance, we used the area under the receiver operating characteristic curve to gain insight on how well our model is predicting true positives and true negatives. We first experimented with the random forest, support vector machine (SVM), Naïve Bayes, and logistic regression classifiers to predict glaucoma progression as justifications for the need for deep learning. These four approaches are commonly used in medical imaging [16,17]. In this study, the baseline models are used to justify the need for utilizing deep learning and our auxiliary domain learning. In order to ensure a fair comparison between all of our models, we instantiated a seeding algorithm for reproducible weight initializations and repeatable augmentations. The baseline model trained for only 19 epochs at a learning rate of 1×10^{-4} before the validation ROC-AUC stopped improving. At this stage, the ROC-AUC result for the test set was 84.8%. When we added age as an auxiliary loss with a weight $\lambda = 0.3$, the validation ROC-AUC reached its peak at 74 epochs allowing for longer training, and in result a better ROC-AUC on the test set (87.3%). Although the MD auxiliary output converged even faster than the baseline model, it is evident that the features of mean deviation were learned through the 16 epochs because the testing ROC-AUC increased to 89.1%. The features that improved the ROC-AUC performance the most on the testing set was the OCT data. Just including one continuous output (global thickness) improved the baseline model to 90.8% ROC-AUC, and finally when concatenating the global thickness to the twelve-clock-hour vector as an additional output, the network yielded an ROC-AUC of 91.3%. To obtain an error margin for each of our model, we utilized a bootstrapping sampling method, where a random observation is chosen from our dataset and scored using ROC-AUC.

Table 1. ROC-AUC scores for each auxiliary output. Each loss was weighted with λ shown on the third column. We illustrate the strong regularization that each auxiliary output provides.

Auxiliary Output(s)	ROC-AUC	Loss Weight (λ)	Epoch Converged
Baseline Siamese Neural Network	$84.8 \pm 4.9\%$	N/A	19
Age	$87.3 \pm 4.3\%$	0.3	74
Mean Deviation	$89.1 \pm 3.8\%$	0.3	16
Global Thickness	$90.8 \pm 3.3\%$	0.2	102
Global Thickness + Clock Hours	$\mathbf{91.3 \pm 2.6\%}$	**0.2**	**72**
Baseline Models	**ROC-AUC**	**Loss Weight (λ)**	**Epoch Converged**
Random Forest [18]	$86.6 \pm 4.6\%$	N/A	N/A
SVM [19]	$81.8 \pm 4.6\%$	N/A	N/A
Naïve Bayes [20]	$81.9 \pm 3.8\%$	N/A	N/A
Logistic Regression	$84.1 \pm 4.3\%$	N/A	N/A

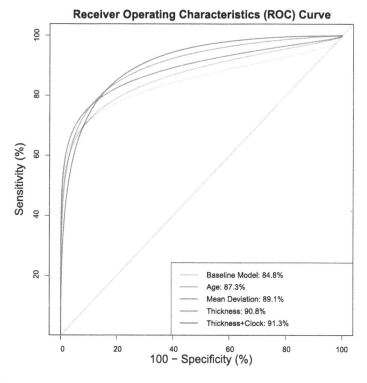

Fig. 3. Illustration of the receiver operating characteristic (ROC) curve for our baseline and multi-output networks. We performed a binormal fitting to smoothen each ROC curve.

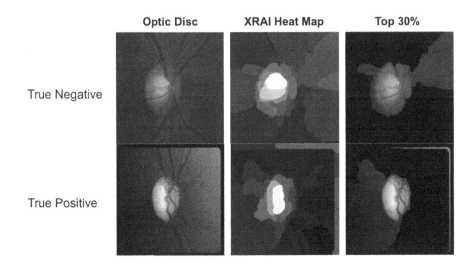

Fig. 4. XRAI heat maps depicting true positive and true negative glaucoma progression predictions. This ensures that our model is learning relevant features to glaucoma progression.

4   Discussion

The end goal for this project was to train a convolutional neural network to capture relevant features to detecting glaucoma progression through multi-domain learning, where auxiliary tasks are solved alongside the main task. We noticed that when giving the network ground truth values such as the age, mean deviation, and OCT data, there was a significant increased in ROC-AUC. As shown in the ROC-AUC curves in Fig. 3, the ROC-AUC improved from 84.8% to 91.3% after adding relevant output labels. This is crucial because the neural network captured relevant information of the auxiliary labels without needing any input other than the optic disc photographs. To ensure that our deep learning model captured the relevant features to predict glaucoma progression, we generated "heat-maps" based on the region based attribution method (XRAI) [21] to localize the areas of the neural network with the steepest gradients in respect to the second optic disc photograph (Fig. 4). In application, the auxiliary-domain neural network can be directly implemented by clinicians by inputting the first three optic disc photographs into the model, and it will predict glaucoma progression by utilizing already learned features from OCT, age, and MD data. We also noticed that auxiliary outputs act as a heavy regularization method that helps the model train for more epochs without overfitting. As shown in Table 1, the baseline no auxiliary output network converged after just 19 epochs. However, a majority of the auxiliary outputs took more than fifty epochs to reach the optimum solution. For example, the progression + global thickness model was trained for 102 epochs before reaching an optimum solution. We did not include all auxiliary outputs combined in one model to ensure that the majority of the loss was still allocated to the main progression prediction task.

There are several methods to further improve our multi-output neural network. One potential method is implementing is an encoder-decoder U-Net [22] model that learns to segment the optic disc and vessels from each optic disc photograph. By doing so, we hope that the model encapsulated important structural information related to glaucoma that is found in the optic disc and vessel. Because manually labeling the masks for vessels and optic discs is a timely task, we plan to pre-train a segmentation model from the open source FIVES dataset [23] and Refuge Challenge [24] dataset, and apply the pre-trained model on our dataset for pseudo ground truth labels.

5 Conclusion

This paper describes a new training pipeline for auxiliary-domain learning for an improved prediction of glaucoma progression. We used hard parameter sharing between the final fully connected layers for each task, and created a combined loss function that weights both the main task, and each auxiliary task with different values of λ scaled between 0 and 1 to balance the importance of the task during back propagation. One limitation to our study may be a lack of clinical data such as pattern standard deviation, gender, and the visual field count that can even further improve the main glaucoma progression prediction. Our model performs well on non-progressing eyes; however, there are still a few false positives due to our weighted loss function that can be fixed by using other class-balancing methods such as random under or oversampling [25]. We conclude that an auxiliary-domain network leads to a significant increase in ROC-AUC for the main classification task when learning to predict relevant auxiliary features. The auxiliary tasks provide a strong regularization to a convolutional neural network, allowing the model to train for more epochs and generalize better on external test data.

The training pipeline we constructed can handle any form of pairwise or sequential image data for a classification task. We expect that our auxiliary-domain pipeline is a novel contribution that can be used by many to solve machine learning problems from a wide range of research topics across various disciplines, including biology, physics, and medicine. The auxiliary-domain learning that we demonstrated in this study shows promise to have a large impact for medical diagnosis in regions around the globe that may not have access to state of the art machinery such as an OCT scanner to assess the health of a patient. Rather than needing expensive machinery, researchers and clinicians can simply pre-train a multi-output convolutional neural network similar to ours, and deploy the model on readily available data.

References

1. Quigley, H.A., Broman, A.T.: The number of people with glaucoma worldwide in 2010 and 2020 (2006)

2. Allison, K., Patel, D., Alabi, O.: Epidemiology of glaucoma: the past, present, and predictions for the future (2020)

3. Ting, D.S., et al.: Deep learning in ophthalmology: the technical and clinical considerations. Prog. Retin. Eye Res. **72**, 100759 (2019)

4. Abràmoff, M.D., et al.: Improved automated detection of diabetic retinopathy on a publicly available dataset through integration of deep learning. Invest. Ophthalmol. Visual Sci. **57**, 5200–5206 (2016)

5. Shibata, N., et al.: Development of a deep residual learning algorithm to screen for glaucoma from fundus photography. Sci. Rep. **8**, 14665 (2018)

6. Christopher, M., et al.: Deep learning approaches predict glaucomatous visual field damage from oct optic nerve head EN face images and retinal nerve fiber layer thickness maps. Ophthalmology **127**, 346–356 (2020)

7. Dixit, A., Yohannan, J., Boland, M.V.: Assessing glaucoma progression using machine learning trained on longitudinal visual field and clinical data. Ophthalmology **128**, 1016–1026 (2021)

8. Hemelings, R., Elen, B., Barbosa-Breda, J., Blaschko, M.B., De Boever, P., Stalmans, I.: Deep learning on fundus images detects glaucoma beyond the optic disc. Sci. Rep. **11**, 20313 (2021)

9. Sun, Y., Zhu, L., Wang, G., Zhao, F.: Multi-input convolutional neural network for flower grading. J. Electr. Comput. Eng. **2017**, 9240407 (2017)

10. Koch, G., Zemel, R., Salakhutdinov, R., et al.: Siamese neural networks for one-shot image recognition. In: ICML Deep Learning Workshop, vol. 2, Lille (2015)

11. He, K., Zhang, X., Ren, S., Sun, J.: Deep residual learning for image recognition. CoRR abs/1512.03385 (2015)

12. Deng, J., Dong, W., Socher, R., Li, L.J., Li, K., Fei-Fei, L.: Imagenet: a large-scale hierarchical image database. In: 2009 IEEE Conference on Computer Vision and Pattern Recognition, pp. 248–255 (2009)

13. Caruana, R.: Multitask learning: a knowledge-based source of inductive bias1. In: Proceedings of the Tenth International Conference on Machine Learning, pp. 41–48. Citeseer (1993)

14. Zhang, Z., Sabuncu, M.R.: Generalized cross entropy loss for training deep neural networks with noisy labels. CoRR abs/1805.07836 (2018)

15. Nouri-Mahdavi, K., Mohammadzadeh, V., Rabiolo, A., Edalati, K., Caprioli, J., Yousefi, S.: Prediction of visual field progression from oct structural measures in moderate to advanced glaucoma. Am. J. Ophthalmol. **226**, 172–181 (2021)

16. Sarica, A., Cerasa, A., Quattrone, A.: Random forest algorithm for the classification of neuroimaging data in Alzheimer's disease: a systematic review. Front. Aging Neurosci. **9**, 329 (2017)

17. Lo, C.S., Wang, C.M.: Support vector machine for breast MR image classification. Comput. Math. Appl. **64**, 1153–1162 (2012)

18. Breiman, L.: Random forests. Mach. Learn. **45**, 5–32 (2001)

19. Hearst, M.A., Dumais, S.T., Osuna, E., Platt, J., Scholkopf, B.: Support vector machines. IEEE Intell. Syst. Appl. **13**, 18–28 (1998)

20. Rish, I., et al.: An empirical study of the Naive Bayes classifier. In: IJCAI 2001 Workshop on Empirical Methods in Artificial Intelligence, vol. 3, pp. 41–46 (2001)

21. Kapishnikov, A., Bolukbasi, T., Viégas, F., Terry, M.: Xrai: better attributions through regions. In: Proceedings of the IEEE/CVF International Conference on Computer Vision, pp. 4948–4957 (2019)

22. Ronneberger, O., Fischer, P., Brox, T.: U-net: convolutional networks for biomedical image segmentation. CoRR abs/1505.04597 (2015)

23. Jin, K., et al.: Fives: a fundus image dataset for artificial intelligence based vessel segmentation. Sci. Data **9**, 475 (2022)
24. Orlando, J.I., et al.: Refuge challenge: a unified framework for evaluating automated methods for glaucoma assessment from fundus photographs. Med. Image Anal. **59**, 101570 (2020)
25. Mohammed, R., Rawashdeh, J., Abdullah, M.: Machine learning with oversampling and undersampling techniques: overview study and experimental results. In: 11th International Conference on Information and Communication Systems (ICICS). IEEE 2020, pp. 243–248 (2020)

QuickQual: Lightweight, Convenient Retinal Image Quality Scoring with Off-the-Shelf Pretrained Models

Justin Engelmann[1,2(✉)], Amos Storkey[2], and Miguel O. Bernabeu[1,3]

[1] Centre for Medical Informatics, Usher Institute, University of Edinburgh, Edinburgh, Scotland, UK
`justin.engelmann@ed.ac.uk`
[2] Institute for Adaptive and Neural Computation, School of Informatics, University of Edinburgh, Edinburgh, Scotland, UK
[3] The Bayes Centre, University of Edinburgh, Edinburgh, Scotland, UK

Abstract. Image quality remains a key problem for both traditional and deep learning (DL)-based approaches to retinal image analysis and identifying poor quality images can be time consuming and subjective. Thus, automated methods for retinal image quality scoring (RIQS) are needed. The current state-of-the-art is MCFNet, composed of three Densenet121 backbones each operating in a different colour space. MCFNet, and the EyeQ dataset released by the same authors, was a huge step forward for RIQS. We present QuickQual, a simple approach to RIQS, consisting of a single "off-the-shelf" ImageNet-pretrained Densenet121 backbone plus a Support Vector Machine (SVM). QuickQual performs very well, setting a new state-of-the-art for EyeQ (Accuracy: 88.50% vs 88.00% for MCFNet; AUC: 0.9687 vs 0.9588). This suggests that RIQS can be solved with generic "perceptual" features learned on natural images, as opposed to requiring DL models trained on large amounts of fundus images. Additionally, we propose a Fixed Prior linearisation scheme, that converts EyeQ from a 3-class classification to a continuous logistic regression task. For this task, we present a second model, QuickQual MEga Minified Estimator (QuickQual-MEME), that consists of only 10 parameters on top of an off-the-shelf Densenet121 and can distinguish between gradable and ungradable images with an accuracy of 89.18% (AUC: 0.9537). Code and model are available on GitHub. QuickQual is so lightweight, that the entire inference code (and even the parameters for QuickQual-MEME) is already contained in this paper.

Keywords: Retinal imaging · Deep learning · Retinal quality scoring

1 Introduction

Retinal colour fundus images are used in ophthalmology for detecting and grading of retinal diseases like diabetic retinopathy, and also capture a detailed picture of the blood vessels, which could be informative about systemic health

---

A. Storkey and M. O. Bernabeu—Equal supervision.

© The Author(s), under exclusive license to Springer Nature Switzerland AG 2023
B. Antony et al. (Eds.): OMIA 2023, LNCS 14096, pp. 32–41, 2023.
https://doi.org/10.1007/978-3-031-44013-7_4

[9, 11, 12]. However, image quality is a key problem even when data is specifically collected for research purposes. For example, in UK Biobank, recent studies discarded 26% [14] to 43% [11] of the available images due to quality issues and only about 60% of participants were found to have at least one good quality image [8]. However, Retinal Image Quality Scoring (RIQS) can be subjective and even graders with medical backgrounds only have moderate to substantial agreement [7]. Thus, automated RIQS methods are needed to provide objective and reproducible quality scores. Reproducibility is especially as image quality-based exclusions can introduce selection bias by excluding older, male, less-healthy, and non-White subjects more frequently [3]. Even work that develops retinal image improvement [10] or robust retinal image analysis methods [4] depends on reliable quality scores.

Fu et al. [5] introduced an automated RIQS method called MultiColourspace-FusionNetwork (MCFNet) and the EyeQ dataset, a re-annotation of the publicly available Kaggle Diabetic Retinopathy dataset that provides quality annotations on a 3 class scale (Good, Usable, Reject). This work was a huge step forward for the field of RIQS with both MCFNet and the EyeQ dataset being very important contributions in their own right. The authors made the code, model weights, and data annotations publicly available, enabling others to both use and build on their work. However, MCFNet requires specific colourspace data transformation steps and consists of 3 Densenet121 backbones. Thus, MCFNet requires a specific dataloader and model weights, and is a somewhat large model. Recent work showed that "off-the-shelf" DL models pretrained on ImageNet might be able to capture salient information such as age from retinal fundus images even without fine-tuning [2]. Inspired by that, we set out to investigate whether we can develop a simpler yet effective automated RIQS method that uses such an off-the-shelf model with a classical machine learning classifier.

Our main contributions are:

- **QuickQual**, a simple RIQS method based on an "off-the-shelf" Densenet121 and an SVM, that achieves state-of-the-art on EyeQ while requiring only standard libraries and 14 lines of code;
- **Fixed Prior linearisation**, a simple method for converting EyeQ into a continuous task while retaining information about the Usable class;
- **QuickQual-MEME**, an even simpler version of QuickQual with a linear layer instead of an SVM that produces a continuous quality score. In fact, QuickQual-MEME is so lightweight, that the entire code and model parameters are contained in Fig. 5.

2 Methods

2.1 EyeQ Dataset

We use the EyeQ dataset introduced by [5], which provides quality annotations for a subset of the EyePacs Diabetic Retinopathy dataset on Kaggle, with three classes: Good, Usable, Bad. We preprocess the images by removing black areas

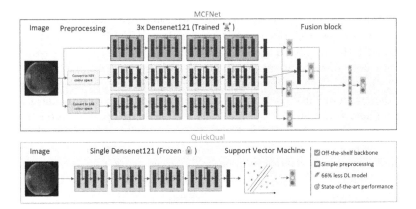

Fig. 1. Comparison between MCFNet (top) and QuickQual (bottom). QuickQual-MEME uses a linear layer instead of SVM.

and then padding the images to square in case they would be non-square otherwise.

2.2 QuickQual

With QuickQual, we aim to develop a method that is quick and convenient to use. By that, we do not merely mean processing speed but also ease of implementation. Our goal is that with less than 20 lines of code and only standard Python libraries, a researcher could apply this method to their own images to obtain quality scores. Thus, we avoid complex preprocessing schemes and non-standard DL architecture code. We use a pretrained DL model from a standard Python DL library and instead of fine-tuning this on the EyeQ dataset, we simply keep it fixed and learn a Support Vector Machine (SVM) on top (Fig. 1).

To enable an easier comparison with MCFNet, we also use Densenet121 [6] as our DL model, but with pre-trained ImageNet [1] weights from the pytorch image models (timm) [13] library. We use a SVM from scikit-learn with standard parameters, except setting "probability=True" to obtain probability scores from the SVM. To obtain discrete class labels, we take the class with the highest probability. We process images at a resolution of 512×512 and simply normalise all channels with mean and standard deviation parameters of 0.5.

2.3 RIQS Beyond 3-Way Classification: Fixed Prior Linearisation

In practice, individual probabilities for three separate classes can be inconvenient to use. Thus, previous work [15] focused on the binary task Gradable (Good or Usable) vs Bad (Reject) instead. This produces a single, continuous score where a simple cut-off for excluding images can be selected. However, this approach treats Good images exactly the same as Usable ones, losing the information that Usable images are at least slightly poorer quality. To remedy this, we propose a simple linearisation scheme with a fixed prior, i.e. that Usable images are in-between Good and Bad images in terms of quality. During model fitting, we set the optimal output p(Bad) that minimises the loss function to be 0 for Good images, 1 for Bad images, and our fixed prior p for Usable images. In present work, we simply set $p = 0.5$ and thus ask our model to map Usable images in-between Good and Bad ones, thus retaining the information in the labels. This should produce a smooth and desirable quality score but might reduce accuracy for the binary task.

2.4 QuickQual MEga Minified Estimator (QuickQual-MEME)

QuickQual-MEME is an even more lightweight, easy-to-use RIQS model consisting of a pretrained Densenet121 and only 10 parameters for a linear layer. QuickQual-MEME only needs standard python libraries and 15 lines of code. Instead of a SVM, QuickQual-MEME uses a Logistic Regression (Logit) with 10 parameters (9 weights, 1 bias) as classifier. To find these parameters, we proceeded as follows: First, we fit a Logit on the whole EyeQ training set with an L1 penalty ("Lasso") with the default regularisation $C = 1$ and the SAGA optimiser. We then examined the histogram of absolute coefficient magnitudes and chose a cut-off of 0.2 to select 288 of the 1,024 Densenet121 variables. Next, we did forward step-wise features selection using 2-fold crossvalidation on the training set and the AUC as criterion to select the 9 most useful features. Finally, we rounded the parameters to two decimal places so they are easier to report and copy, which led to an insubstantial change in accuracy.

2.5 Evaluation

For the standard EyeQ 3-way classification task, we use standard metrics like Accuracy, F1 score, area under the receiver operating characteristic curve (AUC), logistic loss also known as cross-entropy (LogLoss), cohen's unweighted Kappa (Kappa) and quadratic weighted Kappa (QuadKappa). AUC is a ranking metric that evaluates the model across all possible decision thresholds, whereas LogLoss provides a measure of calibration. Kappa captures how well the model agress with the labels compared to random chance, and QuadKappa penalises errors by more than one class much more, i.e. confusing Good with Bad is worse than confusing Good with Usable. For the binary Gradable vs. Ungradable, we use the same metrics except for Kappa/QuadKappa, which are only suitable for multi-class problems. We calculate all metrics using scikit-learn and use the predicted probabilities for MCFNet provided by the authors to ensure a fair and accurate comparison.[1]

---

[1] Note that for MCFNet, the original accuracy scores provided were not entirely accurate due to a bug in the evaluation code. See the note here on the Github for MCFNet: https://github.com/HzFu/EyeQ#-reference *"Note: The corrected accuracy score of MCF-Net is 0.8800."* We thank the authors of MCFNet for their exceptional transparency in sharing not just code, model weights and data, but also their model's test set predictions.

Table 1. Performance for MCFNet and QuickQual on the test set of EyeQ (n=16,249). Note: All metrics are calculated from per-sample predictions using identical code to ensure an accurate comparison. See Sect. 2.5 and footnote 1.

Model	Accuracy	AUC	F1	LogLoss	Kappa	QuadKappa	Filesize
MCFNet [5]	0.8800	0.9588	0.8606	0.3632	0.8017	0.8955	112 MB
QuickQual (ours)	**0.8863**	**0.9687**	**0.8675**	**0.3049**	**0.8107**	**0.9019**	**31 + 25 = 56 MB**

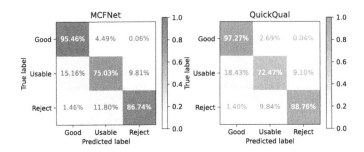

Fig. 2. Confusion matrices for MCFNet and QuickQual, normalised per row.

3   Results

3.1   QuickQual Performance on EyeQ

Table 1 shows the results for QuickQual and MCFNet. QuickQual performs better in every metric. Accuracy, F1 and QuadKappa are slightly better, whereas AUC, LogLoss and Kappa are substantially better. QuadKappa penalises large errors (i.e. confusing Good with Reject) more than Kappa. Thus, QuickQual having a larger improvement in Kappa than in QuadKappa suggests that it is particularly good at distinguishing between the Usable and Good/Reject classes. The confusion matrix (Fig. 2) shows that QuickQual is also better at avoiding large errors (top right and bottom left corners). The only category where Quick-Qual makes more errors than MCFNet is confusing Usable with Good (middle left). In our opinion, this error is the least concerning type of error - in fact previous work has even combined these two categories [15].

LogLoss is the metric with the largest difference, suggesting that QuickQual is much better calibrated. Fig. 3 shows the distributions of predicted probabilities for both models. Interestingly, MCFNet - unlike QuickQual - never predicts the Usable or Reject classes with large confidence. This might be a by-product of class imbalance and batch training. The QuickQual approach projects the images to small 1,024 dimensional vectors first, which then allows us to fit the SVM to all training images at once.

3.2   QuickQual-MEME Performance on Binary Task

Table 2 shows the results for the binarised task. For comparison, we also evaluate MCFNet and QuickQual on this task, using the predictions for the Reject class,

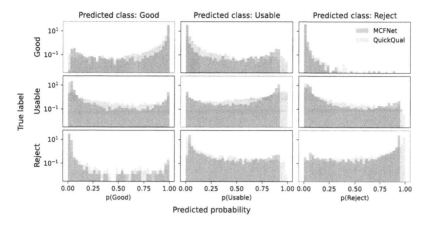

Fig. 3. Distributions of predictions on EyeQ test set for each class, stratified by ground-truth class. Note that y-axis is on a log-scale. This plot is a "soft" version of a confusion matrix. For the diagonal (highlighted red) plots, predictions closer to 1 are better; whereas for the off-diagonal plots, predictions closer to 0 are better. (Color figure online)

Table 2. Performance for binary task Gradable (Good/Usable) vs. Ungradable (Reject).

	Accuracy	AUC	F1	LogLoss
MCFNet [5] (Using p(Reject))	0.9459	0.9819	0.8640	0.1445
QuickQual (Using p(Reject))	**0.9520**	**0.9870**	**0.8799**	**0.1162**
QuickQual-MEME	0.8918	0.9537	0.7602	0.2742
QuickQual-Binary	0.9404	0.9787	0.8505	0.1650

as well as a QuickQual model trained on the binary task. The models trained on the original task perform best, with QuickQual offering slightly better performance in terms of Accuracy and AUC, and a large improvement for F1 and LogLoss over MCFNet. As expected, QuickQual-Binary using the SVM and all 1,024 Densenet121 features outperforms QuickQual-MEME which only uses 9 features.

Interestingly, QuickQual-Binary is outperformed by QuickQual trained on the original task, suggesting that the fixed Prior Linearisation scheme reduces accuracy for Bad vs Good/Usable. However, QuickQual-MEME produces very smooth and desirable quality scores (Fig. 4): The Good and Bad classes have modes on either extremes, while the Usable class is smoothly distributed in-between, with a mode closer to the Good class. This matches the class names: Usable is conceptually closer to Good than to Bad. Images from the Usable class with very low p(Bad) appear to be good quality, while those with high p(Bad) appear poor. Where the distributions of Good and Usable overlap, images are

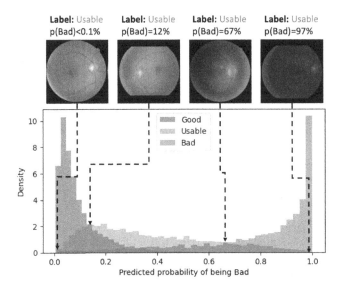

Fig. 4. QuickQual-MEME predicted p(Bad) on the EyeQ test set, stratified by ground-truth class, with example images belonging to the Usable class shown above.

```
import torch
from torchvision.transforms import functional as F
from PIL import Image
import timm
img = Image.open('[DATAFOLDER]/10036_left.jpeg')
model = timm.create_model('densenet121.tv_in1k',
                          pretrained=True, num_classes=0)
model.eval().cuda()
w = torch.tensor([-1411.32, 517.09, 342.41, -707.9,
                  1442.09, -23.25, -541.64, -8.44, 5.44])
b = torch.tensor([5.18])
img = F.to_tensor(F.resize(img, 512))
img = F.normalize(img, [0.5]*3, [0.5]*3).cuda().unsqueeze(0)
with torch.no_grad():
    feats = model(img).squeeze().cpu().reshape(1, -1)
feats = feats[:, [71, 109, 121, 53, 55, 123, 29, 133, 84]]
pred = torch.sigmoid(feats @ w + b)
```

Fig. 5. Entire inference code to run QuickQual-MEME, including the model parameters themselves. The code can be copied from the figure above.

imperfect but still generally good; and where Usable and Bad overlap, they are poor.

Although this evaluation is not comprehensive, this suggests QuickQual-MEME's quality score for the Usable class might align well with actual quality. Giving a very low p(Bad) score to all the Usable images, including the ones that look quite poor, would increase accuracy on the binarised task. However, in our opinion, the current behaviour of QuickQual-MEME appears preferable to that. Thus, accuracy might be an imperfect measure and more fine-grained expert evaluation is needed.

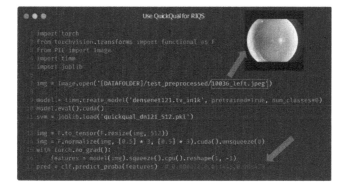

Fig. 6. Entire inference code needed for QuickQual. Arrows highlight the example image which is of poor quality; and the prediction for p(Bad)≈ 99%.

3.3 Convenience and Speed

QuickQual (Fig. 6) and QuickQual-MEME (Fig. 5) need about 15 lines of code to be used together with standard, widely used libraries like PyTorch, scikit-learn and timm. QuickQual-MEME only need 10 parameters to be used, QuickQual needs a 25MB pretrained scikit-learn SVM. This means that QuickQual is very easy to implement and thus very convenient to use for researchers.

Inference times for a single images were measured across 1,000 repetitions, with times reported being mean and standard deviation. QuickQual processed the image in 16.6 ms ± 602 µs on a GPU and 79.5 ms ± 2.45 ms on a CPU. QuickQual-MEME took 14.5 ms ± 536 µs on a GPU and 79.3 ms ± 1.88 ms on a CPU. These times suggest that the SVM only adds minimal overhead compared to a linear model when the Densenet121 is GPU-accelerated and no noticable overhead when no GPU is used. Note that batched inference for multiple images in parallel will likely be even faster per image, but even when processing images one-by-one, 767 images could be processed per minute on a CPU. A time of less than a tenth of a second on a CPU also means that QuickQual could conceivably be deployed in practice to assess images in real time as they are taken.

4 Discussion

We presented QuickQual, which achieves state-of-the-art on EyeQ with only 14 lines of inference code, and QuickQual-MEME which produces a single continuous quality score and fits in Fig. 5. We hope that these will be an easy-to-use, convenient method for other researchers in the field.

We also introduced a Fixed Prior linearisation scheme that better preserves information about the Usable class. While quantitatively this reduced accuracy, limited qualitative evaluation suggests that it might produce a smooth, desirable quality score.

In the future, we plan to evaluate this in more detail by having experts rank images in terms of quality and examining the correlation with QuickQual-MEME's quality score. We also plan evaluate other pretrained DL models to see whether a similarly performant yet more light-weight model could be found that enables even faster computation of quality scores. Additionally, even higher performance might be achieved by training DL models with state-of-the-art architectures for this task. Finally, we plan to externally validate QuickQual and QuickQual-MEME on images from UK Biobank.

Acknowledgements. We thank our friends and colleagues for their help and support. J.E. and this work was supported by the United Kingdom Research and Innovation (grant EP/S02431X/1), UKRI Centre for Doctoral Training in Biomedical AI at the University of Edinburgh, School of Informatics. For the purpose of open access, the author has applied a creative commons attribution (CC BY) licence to any author accepted manuscript version arising.

References

1. Deng, J., Dong, W., Socher, R., Li, L.J., Li, K., Fei-Fei, L.: ImageNet: a large-scale hierarchical image database. In: 2009 IEEE Conference on Computer Vision and Pattern Recognition, pp. 248–255. IEEE (2009)
2. Engelmann, J., Storkey, A., Bernabeu, M.O.: Deep learning (dl) identifies age as key axis of perceptual variation in fundus images-without training on fundus images. Investigat. Ophthalmol. Vis. Sci. **64**(9), PB004 (2023)
3. Engelmann, J., Storkey, A., LLinares, M.B.: Exclusion of poor quality fundus images biases health research linking retinal traits and systemic health. Investigat. Ophthalmol. Vis. Sci. **64**(8), 2922 (2023)
4. Engelmann, J., Villaplana-Velasco, A., Storkey, A., Bernabeu, M.O.: Robust and efficient computation of retinal fractal dimension through deep approximation. In: International Workshop on Ophthalmic Medical Image Analysis, pp. 84–93. Springer, Cham (2022). https://doi.org/10.1007/978-3-031-16525-2_9
5. Fu, H., et al.: Evaluation of retinal image quality assessment networks in different color-spaces. In: Shen, D., et al. (eds.) MICCAI 2019. LNCS, vol. 11764, pp. 48–56. Springer, Cham (2019). https://doi.org/10.1007/978-3-030-32239-7_6
6. Huang, G., Liu, Z., Van Der Maaten, L., Weinberger, K.Q.: Densely connected convolutional networks. In: Proceedings of the IEEE Conference on Computer Vision and Pattern Recognition, pp. 4700–4708 (2017)
7. Laurik-Feuerstein, K.L., Sapahia, R., Cabrera DeBuc, D., Somfai, G.M.: The assessment of fundus image quality labeling reliability among graders with different backgrounds. PLoS One **17**(7), e0271156 (2022)
8. MacGillivray, T.J., et al.: Suitability of UK biobank retinal images for automatic analysis of morphometric properties of the vasculature. PLoS One **10**(5), e0127914 (2015)
9. MacGillivray, T., Trucco, E., Cameron, J., Dhillon, B., Houston, J., Van Beek, E.: Retinal imaging as a source of biomarkers for diagnosis, characterization and prognosis of chronic illness or long-term conditions. Br. J. Radiol. **87**(1040), 20130832 (2014)
10. Shen, Z., Fu, H., Shen, J., Shao, L.: Modeling and enhancing low-quality retinal fundus images. IEEE Trans. Med. Imag. **40**(3), 996–1006 (2020)

11. Velasco, A.V., et al.: Decreased retinal vascular complexity is an early biomarker of mi supported by a shared genetic control. medRxiv (2021)
12. Wagner, S.K., et al.: Insights into systemic disease through retinal imaging-based oculomics. Transl. Vis. Sci. Technol. **9**(2), 6 (2020)
13. Wightman, R.: PyTorch Image Models (2019). https://github.com/rwightman/pytorch-image-models. https://doi.org/10.5281/zenodo.4414861
14. Zekavat, S.M., et al.: Deep learning of the retina enables phenome-and genome-wide analyses of the microvasculature. Circulation **145**(2), 134–150 (2022)
15. Zhou, Y., et al.: Automorph: automated retinal vascular morphology quantification via a deep learning pipeline. Transl. Vis. Sci. Technol. **11**(7), 12 (2022)

Recurrent Self Fusion: Iterative Denoising for Consistent Retinal OCT Segmentation

Shuwen Wei[1]([📧])[ID], Yihao Liu[1][ID], Zhangxing Bian[1][ID], Yuli Wang[2],
Lianrui Zuo[1,3][ID], Peter A. Calabresi[4][ID], Shiv Saidha[4], Jerry L. Prince[1][ID],
and Aaron Carass[1][ID]

[1] Department of Electrical and Computer Engineering, Johns Hopkins University,
Baltimore, MD 21218, USA
`swei14@jhu.edu`
[2] Department of Biomedical Engineering, Johns Hopkins University School of
Medicine, Baltimore, MD 21287, USA
[3] Laboratory of Behavioral Neuroscience, National Institute on Aging, National
Institutes of Health, Baltimore, MD 21224, USA
[4] Department of Neurology, Johns Hopkins University School of Medicine,
Baltimore, MD 21287, USA

Abstract. Optical coherence tomography (OCT) is a valuable imaging technique in ophthalmology, providing high-resolution, cross-sectional images of the retina for early detection and monitoring of various retinal and neurological diseases. However, discrepancies in retinal layer thickness measurements among different OCT devices pose challenges for data comparison and interpretation, particularly in longitudinal analyses. This work introduces the idea of a recurrent self fusion (RSF) algorithm to address this issue. Our RSF algorithm, built upon the self fusion methodology, iteratively denoises retinal OCT images. A deep learning-based retinal OCT segmentation algorithm is employed for downstream analyses. A large dataset of paired OCT scans acquired on both a Spectralis and Cirrus OCT device are used for validation. The results demonstrate that the RSF algorithm effectively reduces speckle contrast and enhances the consistency of retinal OCT segmentation.

Keywords: Optical coherence tomography · Denoise · Segmentation

1 Introduction

Optical coherence tomography (OCT) is a non-invasive imaging technique that utilizes low-coherence interferometry to generate high-resolution, cross-sectional images [7]. In the field of ophthalmology, OCT provides detailed visualization of the retina, facilitating the early detection and continuous monitoring of various retinal diseases, including age-related macular degeneration (AMD) [18] and diabetic macular edema (DME) [1,4]. In neurological diseases like multiple sclerosis (MS) [14,15], OCT has provided additional insights and potential biomarkers of disease, specifically the thinning of key retinal layers, such as

B. Antony et al. (Eds.): OMIA 2023, LNCS 14096, pp. 42–51, 2023.
https://doi.org/10.1007/978-3-031-44013-7_5

the retinal nerve fiber layer (RNFL) and the ganglion cell and inner plexiform layer (GCIPL) [16,17]. Retinal OCT images offer precise thickness measurements of each retinal layer, enabling the identification of subtle changes over time and providing valuable guidance for treatment decisions [19].

However, discrepancies in retinal layer thickness measurements arise due to variations in image quality such as noise levels and speckle patterns produced by different OCT devices, posing challenges in the consistent comparison and interpretation of data across studies or clinical settings. Studies have demonstrated that RNFL thickness measured using Spectralis OCT (Heidelberg Engineering, Heidelberg, Germany) tends to be thicker than measurements obtained from Cirrus OCT (Carl Zeiss Meditec, Dublin, CA, USA) [3,9,12]. Similar discrepancies have been observed for other retinal layers [3] and across different pairs of OCT devices [9]. Consequently, standardization efforts are crucial in establishing harmonized measurements and minimizing disparities among OCT devices. These ensure a more reliable and consistent assessment of retinal layer thicknesses in both clinical practice and research endeavors.

In this paper, we propose the recurrent self fusion (RSF) algorithm aimed at reducing speckle contrast and improving the consistency of retinal OCT segmentation. The RSF algorithm builds upon the self fusion approach of Oguz *et al.* [11] and iteratively denoises retinal OCT images. In the downstream segmentation task, we use a deep learning-based retinal OCT layer segmentation algorithm [5,6]. To validate our approach, we utilize a substantial dataset comprising paired Spectralis and Cirrus OCT scans. Our findings reveal that the RSF algorithm effectively reduces speckle contrast in retinal OCT images and enhances the consistency of the resulting segmentation.

2 Method

The RSF algorithm is based on the self fusion method [11], which incorporates the concept of joint label fusion (JLF) [20], as shown in Fig. 1. The retinal OCT volume contains a set of B-scans $\{f_n^{(0)} | n = 0, 1, ..., N-1\}$, where the superscript 0 refers to the original B-scans and n is an index over the N B-scans. In the $(t+1)^{\text{th}}$ iteration, we register the neighboring m^{th} B-scans $f_m^{(t)}$ to the nth B-scan $f_n^{(t)}$, by seeking the deformation field $\phi_{m,n}^{(t)}$ given by:

$$\phi_{m,n}^{(t)} = \arg\min_{\phi} \mathcal{L}_{\text{NCC}}(f_n^{(t)}, f_m^{(t)} \circ \phi) + \mathcal{R}(\phi), \qquad (1)$$

where $\mathcal{L}_{\text{NCC}}$ is the normalized cross correlation (NCC) loss that penalizes low NCC values, $\mathcal{R}$ is a regularization term on ϕ that penalizes discontinuities in ϕ, and $\phi_{m,n}^{(t)}$ is the identity if $m = n$. To solve Eq. 1, we use the `greedy reg` package[1] [21]. An affine transformation is performed first, followed by a deformable registration. A window size of 5×5 is chosen for the NCC calculation, and the default regularization parameters are used.

---

[1] https://github.com/pyushkevich/greedy.

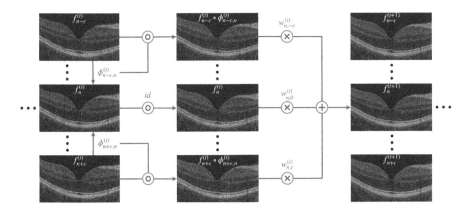

Fig. 1. Diagram of the RSF algorithm for iterative denoising. The operations ∘, ×, and + represent composition, pixel-wise multiplication and pixel-wise summation, respectively.

After registration, we perform a weighted summation to obtain updated denoised images. For the weights, we utilize the concept of JLF, to compute:

$$(M_n^{(t)})_{ij}(x,y) = \sum_{p=x-\gamma}^{x+\gamma} \sum_{q=y-\gamma}^{y+\gamma} d_{n+i,n}^{(t)}(p,q) \cdot d_{n+j,n}^{(t)}(p,q) + \alpha \delta_{ij}, \qquad (2)$$

where $M_n^{(t)}$ is a matrix with entries $i,j \in \{-\epsilon, \ldots, \epsilon\}$ at the tth iteration, (x,y) is a pixel location, γ defines a local patch size, $\delta_{ij} = 1$ when $i = j$ or otherwise $\delta_{ij} = 0$, α is a regularization term which controls the weight similarity, and d is an intensity distance measure expressed as:

$$d_{m,n}^{(t)}(x,y) = \left| f_m^{(t)} \circ \phi_{m,n}^{(t)}(x,y) - f_n^{(t)}(x,y) \right|^{\beta}, \qquad (3)$$

where β is a parameter that controls the measure, and $d_{m,n}^{(t)}(x,y) = 0$ if $m = n$. The weight parameter is then calculated as:

$$w_{n,i}^{(t)}(x,y) = \frac{\displaystyle\sum_{j=-\epsilon}^{\epsilon} (M_n^{(t)})_{ij}^{-1}(x,y)}{\displaystyle\sum_{i=-\epsilon}^{\epsilon} \sum_{j=-\epsilon}^{\epsilon} (M_n^{(t)})_{ij}^{-1}(x,y)}, \qquad (4)$$

where $w_{n,i}^{(t)}$ is the weight for the warped B-scan $f_{n+i}^{(t)} \circ \phi_{n+i,n}^{(t)}$. The updated n^{th} B-scan $f_n^{(t+1)}$ is obtained through the weighted summation:

$$f_n^{(t+1)}(x,y) = \sum_{i=-\epsilon}^{\epsilon} w_{n,i}^{(t)}(x,y) \cdot f_{n+i}^{(t)} \circ \phi_{n+i,n}^{(t)}(x,y), \qquad (5)$$

where $2\epsilon + 1$ is the number of wrapped B-scans used in weighted summation. In this paper, we set $\alpha = 30$, $\beta = 2$, $\gamma = 2$, $\epsilon = 1$, and we explore up to a total of $T = 10$ iterations.

3   Results

Dataset.   Our dataset consists of 59 MS participants that were scanned contemporaneously on both a Spectralis and Cirrus OCT device with institutional review board (IRB) approval. For all 59 participants and the two OCT devices, both the left and right eye were imaged. Thus our evaluations will be on the 118 eyes, comparing Spectralis to Cirrus. Spectralis scans comprise 49 B-scans with dimensions of 496×1024 and Cirrus scans consist of 128 B-scans with dimensions of 1024×512. Both sets of scans cover an approximate field of view of 6 mm $\times$ 6 mm around the central fovea. The Spectralis and Cirrus scans have axial resolutions of $3.87\,\mu$m and $1.96\,\mu$m, respectively.

Speckle Contrast.   By applying the RSF algorithm, we observe a continuous reduction in speckle patterns of both OCT devices as iterations progress as shown in Fig. 2(a). To assess the quantitative reduction in speckle patterns at each iteration, we evaluate the speckle contrast, K_l, in each retinal layer and across the entire retina in each B-scan:

$$K_l = \frac{\sigma_l}{\mu_l}, \tag{6}$$

where μ_l and σ_l are the mean and standard deviation of intensities in the lth layer, respectively, and the segmentation of each retinal layer is explained in the next paragraph. The speckle contrast for both OCT devices over 10 iterations is shown in Fig. 2(b). We observe that the speckle contrast for all layers decreases initially, before stabilizing for both devices. From Eq. 6, there is an inverse relationship between speckle contrast and the signal to noise ratio (SNR). Therefore, as the iterations progress, the SNR in each retinal layer increases. Furthermore, we notice that the decreasing rate of the speckle contrast is much higher for Cirrus scans than Spectralis scans. This is expected since Spectralis scans possess better initial image quality. It is interesting to note that while the original Spectralis and Cirrus scans exhibit different speckle contrast, their speckle contrast converges to similar values for the GCIPL, INL, OPL, ONL and OS after denoising; see Fig. 2 for the layer names.

Segmentation Convergence. To investigate the impact of the RSF algorithm on downstream segmentation, we use a deep learning-based retinal OCT segmentation algorithm, to generate smooth and continuous surfaces that accurately represent the retinal layers with the correct topology [5,6]. This network was trained with 394 Spectralis and 321 Cirrus retinal OCT volumes. The ground truth for layer segmentation in these OCT volumes was obtained using AURA, a well-established retinal OCT segmentation software [8]. Manual corrections were

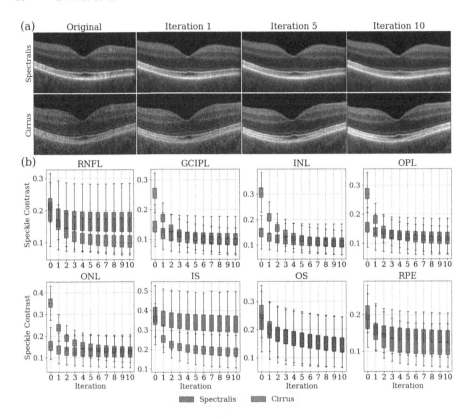

Fig. 2. (a) Original and denoised retinal OCT images after one, five and ten iterations on paired Spectralis and Cirrus scans for a similar cross section. (b) Speckle contrast across the 118 Spectralis scans (red) and the 118 Cirrus scans (green) over ten iterations. The value at iteration '0' is the speckle contrast of the original images. **Key:** RNFL: retinal nerve fiber layer; GCIPL: ganglion cell layer and inner plexiform layer; INL: inner nuclear layer; OPL: outer plexiform layer; ONL: outer nuclear layer; IS: inner segment; OS: outer segment; RPE: retinal pigment epithelium complex. (Color figure online)

made to the initial segmentation results obtained from AURA to ensure precise and accurate delineation of the retinal layers. It is important to note that none of the training data for the deep learning-based OCT segmentation algorithm were included in the paired scans used in the validation of the RSF method. We apply the deep learning-based retinal OCT segmentation algorithm to the paired Spectralis and Cirrus scans. We calculate both the unsigned (blue) and signed (yellow) differences between the segmentation results of consecutive iterations, as shown in Fig. 3, for both Spectralis and Cirrus scans. This allows us to evaluate the magnitude and direction of changes in the segmentation outcomes throughout the RSF iterations. These plots demonstrate a convergence in the segmentation results for the majority of retinal layers.

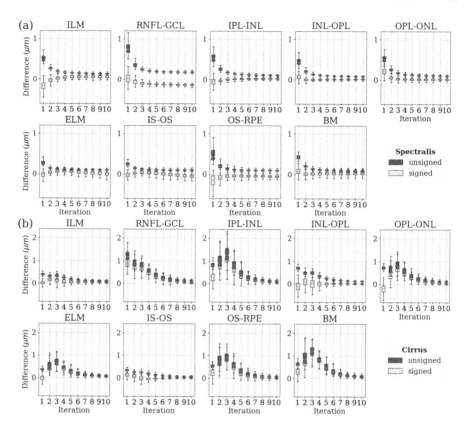

Fig. 3. (a) Boxplots of the unsigned (blue) and signed (yellow) differences between the segmentation results of consecutive iterations across the 118 Spectralis scans. (b) Boxplots of the unsigned (blue) and signed (yellow) differences between the segmentation results of consecutive iterations across the 118 Cirrus scans. **Key:** ILM: internal limiting membrane; ELM: external limiting membrane; BM: Bruch's membrane; see Fig. 2 for the other layer names. (Color figure online)

Average Thickness Comparison. After analysing the convergence of the independent segmentation results, we proceed to analyse the paired segmentation results between Spectralis and Cirrus scans. However, directly comparing their segmentation results requires OCT image registration [13] between the two scan types as the images are not aligned, see Fig. 2(a) for example. OCT image registration can be challenging due to the interpolation issues arising from the sparseness of OCT B-scans. To circumvent the registration problem, we calculate the average thickness within a circular area centered at the fovea, with a diameter of 5 mm, for both Spectralis and Cirrus scans. Then, we compare the difference in the averaged thickness for each retinal layer by subtracting the Spectralis thickness from the Cirrus thickness. The overall results for the average thickness difference between the paired scans at different iteration steps are shown in

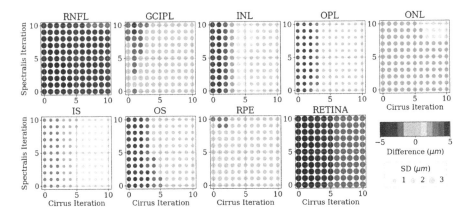

Fig. 4. Difference of the averaged thickness for each retinal layer by subtracting the Spectralis thickness from the Cirrus thickness at different denosing iteration steps for each device. The color and the size of each circle represent the mean and the standard deviation, respectively, of the thickness difference between the paired OCT scans across 118 paired scans. The value of the mean is shown in the color bar. The value of the standard deviation is proportional to the circle size, with the unit circle representing a standard deviation of $3\,\mu m$.

Fig. 4. We observe that in comparison to Spectralis thickness measurements, the initial thickness measurements obtained from Cirrus scans tend to be smaller in RNFL, GCIPL, OPL, OS, RPE and the overall retina, but tend to be larger in INL, ONL and IS. After applying the RSF algorithm, the thickness measurements for all retinal layers from the paired scans converge to a smaller value. Moreover, it is noteworthy that the RSF algorithm applied to Spectralis scans does not noticeably reduce the thickness difference, as opposed to its impact on Cirrus scans. This outcome is expected due to the inferior initial image quality of Cirrus scans, thus benefit more from the RSF algorithm.

Thickness Distribution Comparison. To gain a more comprehensive understanding, it is valuable to analyse the differences in thickness distributions, as they capture the overall statistics of retinal layer thickness. To quantify the dissimilarity between the Spectralis and Cirrus thickness distributions, we employ the Jensen-Shannon Distance (JSD):

$$JSD(p_1||p_2) = \sqrt{\frac{D(p_1||q) + D(p_2||q)}{2}}, \tag{7}$$

where p_1 and p_2 are two probability density functions, D is the Kullback-Leibler divergence, and $q = \frac{1}{2}(p_1 + p_2)$. The JSD between the paired thickness distributions at different iteration steps are shown in Fig. 5. These results align with the findings from Fig. 4. Specifically, we observe a reduction in the JSD between the thickness distributions of each retinal layer as the denoising iterations progress.

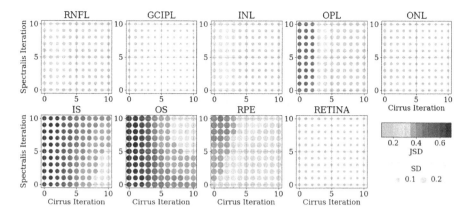

Fig. 5. JSD of the thickness distributions for each retinal layer between the Spectralis and the Cirrus OCT scans at different denosing iteration steps for each device. The color and the size of each circle represent the mean and the standard deviation, respectively, of the JSD between the paired OCT scans across the 118 paired scans. The value of the mean is shown in the color bar. The value of the standard deviation is proportional to the circle size, with the unit circle representing a standard deviation of 0.2.

Furthermore, it is evident that the RSF algorithm has a more pronounced impact on the Cirrus scans than the Spectralis scans.

4 Discussion and Conclusions

Spectralis and Cirrus OCT devices are widely used in ophthalmology, but they differ in terms of their hardware and imaging algorithms, which impact their image quality. Spectralis scans tend to exhibit smoother images with reduced noise and fewer speckle patterns. These disparities in image quality can contribute to domain discrepancies between the two OCT scans and potentially lead to variations in retinal layer thickness measurements following segmentation. Our hypothesis is that by applying the RSF algorithm, the two distinct OCT scans gradually become more similar, resulting in improved consistency in retinal layer thickness measurements. This hypothesis is supported by the results obtained in this study.

However, the proposed method has certain limitations. First, the processing speed of the current RSF is relatively slow due to its reliance on a classical registration method, which requires a longer processing time. Second, the validation of the proposed method is limited to a single deep learning-based retinal OCT segmentation algorithm and lacks comparison with other denoising algorithms. Third, the proposed method is evaluated on a cross-sectional study and its impact on longitudinal OCT data remains unexplored. To address these limitations, future work involves exploring the implementation of deep learning-based registration methods such as Voxelmorph [2] or Coordinate Translator [10] to improve processing speed, validating the consistency of thickness measurements after denoising using a broader range of OCT segmentation and denoising algorithms, and investigating the RSF algorithm in longitudinal OCT data for identifying subtle retinal layer thickness changes over time.

In this paper, we propose the RSF algorithm for iteratively denoising retinal OCT images. Each RSF iteration effectively reduces speckle contrast and improves SNR across various retinal OCT layers and on both investigated devices. Moreover, by applying a deep learning-based retinal OCT segmentation algorithm to the paired OCT volumes from different OCT devices, we observe a significant improvement in the consistency of the segmentation results. These findings underscore the potential of the proposed RSF algorithm as a valuable pre-processing step for retinal OCT images, facilitating more consistent and reliable retinal OCT segmentation.

Acknowledgements. This work was supported by the NIH under NEI grant R01-EY024655 (PI: J.L. Prince), NEI grant R01-EY032284 (PI: J.L. Prince) and in part by the Intramural Research Program of the NIH, National Institute on Aging.

References

1. Alsaih, K., Lemaitre, G., Rastgoo, M., Massich, J., Sidibé, D., Meriaudeau, F.: Machine learning techniques for diabetic macular edema (DME) classification on SD-OCT images. Biomed. Eng. Online **16**, 1–12 (2017)
2. Balakrishnan, G., Zhao, A., Sabuncu, M.R., Guttag, J., Dalca, A.V.: Voxelmorph: a learning framework for deformable medical image registration. IEEE Trans. Med. Imag. **38**(8), 1788–1800 (2019)
3. Bhargava, P., et al.: Applying an open-source segmentation algorithm to different OCT devices in multiple sclerosis patients and healthy controls: implications for clinical trials. Multiple Sclerosis Int. **2015** (2015)
4. Chiu, S.J., Allingham, M.J., Mettu, P.S., Cousins, S.W., Izatt, J.A., Farsiu, S.: Kernel regression based segmentation of optical coherence tomography images with diabetic macular edema. Biomed. Opt. Express **6**(4), 1172–1194 (2015)
5. He, Y., et al.: Structured layer surface segmentation for retina OCT using fully convolutional regression networks. Med. Image Anal. **68**, 101856 (2021)
6. He, Y., et al.: Fully convolutional boundary regression for retina OCT segmentation. In: Shen, D., et al. (eds.) MICCAI 2019. LNCS, vol. 11764, pp. 120–128. Springer, Cham (2019). https://doi.org/10.1007/978-3-030-32239-7_14
7. Huang, D., et al.: Optical coherence tomography. Science **254**(5035), 1178–1181 (1991)
8. Lang, A., et al.: Retinal layer segmentation of macular oct images using boundary classification. Biomed. Opt. Express **4**(7), 1133–1152 (2013)
9. Leite, M.T., et al.: Agreement among spectral-domain optical coherence tomography instruments for assessing retinal nerve fiber layer thickness. Am. J. of Ophthalmol. **151**(1), 85–92 (2011)

10. Liu, Y., Zuo, L., Han, S., Xue, Y., Prince, J.L., Carass, A.: Coordinate translator for learning deformable medical image registration. In: Multiscale Multimodal Medical Imaging: Third International Workshop, MMMI 2022, Held in Conjunction with MICCAI 2022, Singapore, 22 September 2022, Proceedings, MICCAI 2022. LNCS, vol. 13594, pp. 98–109. Springer, Cham (2022). https://doi.org/10.1007/978-3-031-18814-5_10

11. Oguz, I., Malone, J.D., Atay, Y., Tao, Y.K.: Self-fusion for OCT noise reduction. In: Medical Imaging 2020: Image Processing, vol. 11313, pp. 45–50. SPIE (2020)

12. Patel, N.B., Wheat, J.L., Rodriguez, A., Tran, V., Harwerth, R.S.: Agreement between retinal nerve fiber layer measures from Spectralis and Cirrus spectral domain OCT. Optomet. Vis. Sci. **89**(5), E652 (2012)

13. Reaungamornrat, S., Carass, A., He, Y., Saidha, S., Calabresi, P.A., Prince, J.L.: Inter-scanner variation independent descriptors for constrained diffeomorphic Demons registration of retinal OCT. In: Proceedings of SPIE Medical Imaging (SPIE-MI 2018), Houston, 10–15 Feb. 2018, vol. 10574, p. 105741B (2018)

14. Rothman, A., et al.: Retinal measurements predict 10-year disability in multiple sclerosis. Annal. Clin. Transl. Neurol. **6**(2), 222–232 (2019)

15. Saidha, S., et al.: Primary retinal pathology in multiple sclerosis as detected by optical coherence tomography. Brain **134**(2), 518–533 (2011)

16. Saidha, S., et al.: Visual dysfunction in multiple sclerosis correlates better with optical coherence tomography derived estimates of macular ganglion cell layer thickness than peripapillary retinal nerve fiber layer thickness. Multip. Scleros. J. **17**(12), 1449–1463 (2011)

17. Saidha, S., et al.: Microcystic macular oedema, thickness of the inner nuclear layer of the retina, and disease characteristics in multiple sclerosis: a retrospective study. Lancet Neurol. **11**(11), 963–972 (2012)

18. Sotoudeh-Paima, S., Jodeiri, A., Hajizadeh, F., Soltanian-Zadeh, H.: Multi-scale convolutional neural network for automated AMD classification using retinal OCT images. Comput. Biol. Med. **144**, 105368 (2022)

19. Talman, L.S., et al.: Longitudinal study of vision and retinal nerve fiber layer thickness in multiple sclerosis. Annal. Neurol. **67**(6), 749–760 (2010)

20. Wang, H., Suh, J.W., Das, S.R., Pluta, J.B., Craige, C., Yushkevich, P.A.: Multi-atlas segmentation with joint label fusion. IEEE Trans. Patt. Anal. Mach. Intell. **35**(3), 611–623 (2012)

21. Yushkevich, P.A., Pluta, J., Wang, H., Wisse, L.E., Das, S., Wolk, D.: IC-P-174: fast automatic segmentation of hippocampal subfields and medial temporal lobe subregions in 3 Tesla and 7 Tesla T2-weighted MRI. Alzheimer's Dementia **12**, P126–P127 (2016)

UAU-Net: United Attention U-Shaped Network for the Segmentation of Pigment Deposits in Fundus Images of Retinitis Pigmentosa

Jingcheng Xu[1], Zhuoshi Wang[2], Weifang Zhu[1], Yi Zhou[1], Yan Sun[3], Zhuang Li[3], Ming Liu[1], Wenhao Tan[1], Ling Xu[3(✉)], and Xinjian Chen[1,4(✉)]

[1] School of Electronics and Information Engineering,
Soochow University, Suzhou, China
xjchen@suda.edu.cn
[2] Gene Center of Precision Medicine Innovation Institute,
He University, Shenyang, China
[3] Genetic Counseling Clinic, He Eye Specialist Hospital, Shenyang, China
xuling@hsyk.com.cn
[4] State Key Laboratory of Radiation Medicine and Protection,
Soochow University, Suzhou, China

Abstract. Retinitis Pigmentosa (RP) is a retinal disease with high rate of blindness. Retinal pigment deposits are a typical symptom of RP, whose automatic segmentation is crucial to the early diagnosis of RP. In fundus images, pigment deposits have various shapes and sizes and are scattered randomly, which makes the automatic segmentation very challenging. In this paper, we propose a United Attention U-shaped Network (UAU-Net) for segmentation of pigment deposits in fundus images, comprising four parts: encoder, decoder, Multi-scale Global Attention Module (MsGAM), and Spatial-enhanced Attention Module (SEAM). The MsGAM is proposed to extract multi-scale spatial and channel information in constructing associations between different locations of pigment deposits, and the SEAM is proposed to preserve detailed features and enhance the model's ability to segment small targets. Comprehensive experiments on 215 fundus images show that UAU-Net outperforms other state-of-the-art methods with Dice and Intersection-over-Union of 60.25% and 44.91%, respectively.

Keywords: Retinitis pigmentosa · Pigment deposits segmentation · United attention mechanism · Deep neural network

1 Introduction

Retinitis Pigmentosa (RP) is an inherited retinal dystrophy caused by loss of photoreceptors with a global prevalence of approximately 0.025% [8], which is irreversible and has high risk of blindness. Therefore, it is significant for RP

B. Antony et al. (Eds.): OMIA 2023, LNCS 14096, pp. 52–61, 2023.
https://doi.org/10.1007/978-3-031-44013-7_6

patients to be promptly diagnosed at an early stage. Retinal pigment deposits are a classic RP feature observable in fundus images, and a method that automatically and accurately segments retinal pigment deposits would be important for the early diagnosis of RP as well as for grading studies. However, pigment deposits in fundus images have various shapes and sizes and are scattered randomly, and blurring of the image also leads to reduced contrast of pigment deposits, all of which bring challenges to segmentation.

At this stage, there are many methods to segment small targets like pigment deposits, such as diabetic retinal exudates. Sambyal et al. [12] proposed a new upsampling technique to improve segmentation performance. Wang et al. [16] proposed a Contextual and local collaborative network (CLC-Net), using a collaborative architecture that comprises a contextual branch and a local branch. For segmenting pigment deposits, currently, most methods for segmenting pigmentation are based on traditional machine learning. Brancati et al. [3] proposed a supervised segmentation method for pigment signs detection in fundus images using an integrated classifier with Random Forests and Adaptive Boosting, and they also proposed another method [2] based on the relationship between adjacent region features. These methods rely on manually designed features and cannot achieve automatic end-to-end segmentation. With the development of deep learning (DL), neural network-based methods have also started to emerge. Brancati et al. [4] first applied a U-Net [11] based network to segment pigment deposits in retinal fundus images. Arsalan et al. [1] proposed an automatic RP Segmentation Network (RPS-Net) that is able to enhance the ability to segment pigment deposits through multiple dense connections between convolutional layers. However, these DL-based methods do not efficiently extract semantic information, which tend to negatively affect the final segmentation results.

To tackle these problems and improve the ability to segment small and dispersed targets, in this paper, we propose a novel end-to-end learning framework UAU-Net. Our main contributions include: 1) Proposing a Multi-scale Global Attention Module (MsGAM) to capture multi-scale global semantic features from encoder to enable model to ignore the problem of scattered randomly pigment deposits. 2) Introducing a Spatial-enhanced Attention Module (SEAM) to guide model in learning contextual information to preserve detailed features against small target segmentation. 3) Combining MsGAM and SEAM, a U-shaped structure-based model UAU-Net is proposed to achieve good pigment deposits segmentation performance on all three different fundus image data.

2 Method

2.1 Proposed Model

Overall Architecture: The diagram of proposed UAU-Net is shown in Fig. 1, with an overall U-shaped network consisting of encoder, decoder, MsGAM, and SEAM. The MsGAM is inserted at the top of the encoder to capture multi-scale global semantic information. And the SEAM is placed between the encoder and the decoder at each layer as a skip connection to extract more contextual

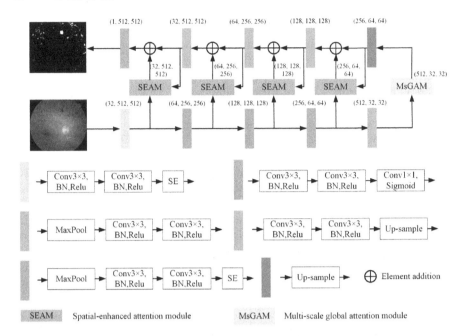

Fig. 1. Diagram of the proposed UAU-Net. Above each block is the number of output channels and the output feature map size. Fundus images are fed into the network, passed through encoder to extract high-level features, then through MsGAM to capture multi-scale global semantic information. Finally, these features are recovered by decoder and meanwhile the contextual semantic information flows are introduced by SEAM.

semantic information. Our goal is to obtain an end-to-end pigment deposits segmentation model by feeding fundus images into the network.

Backbone for Image Segmentation: The backbone of the proposed segmentation model is a U-Net [11] based network with Squeeze-and-Excitation (SE) block added to first four layers of encoder. Compared with U-Net encoder, adding the SE block enhances the ability of the encoder in extracting semantic features.

Multi-scale Global Attention Module: Due to the complexity of pigment deposits in fundus images, segmentation model needs to enhance the extraction of multi-scale global features. Inspired by convolutional block attention module [17] and Self-attention [14], a novel MsGAM is designed and inserted to top layer of encoder, which is illustrated in Fig. 2. Unlike the traditional self-attention, three inputs Key (K), Query (Q), and Value (V) each have different input information. The feature map X_{in} obtained from the encoder is fed into 1×1 convolution as input of Q. The feature map X_m is obtained by multi-scale information fusion on X_{in}, then X_m is passed through a global averag pooling

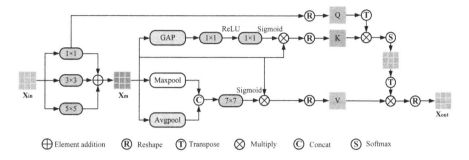

Fig. 2. The illustration of Multi-scale Global Attention Module (MsGAM).

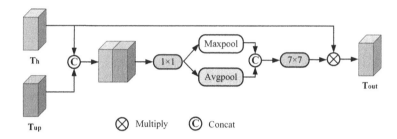

Fig. 3. The illustration of Spatial-enhanced Attention Module (SEAM).

and two 1×1 convolutions as input of K. After X_m undergoes a Spatial Attention Module (SAM) [17], it serves as input of V. The proposed MsGAM allows model to capture local spatial and channel information at multiple scales by compressing the channel dimension and spatial dimension, respectively, while obtaining global long-range information. This results in a higher discriminative power of model, which is suitable for segmenting widely distributed lesion regions like pigment deposits.

Spatial-Enhanced Attention Module: The simple skip connection in U-Net combines local information with different levels indiscriminately, ignoring semantic information and may be disturbed by unrelated features [13]. To solve this problem, we design a SEAM to take the place of the skip connection in U-Net, whose structure is shown in Fig. 3. The feature map T_h with high-resolution weak semantic features from encoder is combined with the up-sampled T_{up} with low resolution strong semantic features from decoder [15]. Subsequently, the obtained features are normalized by a 1×1 convolution and a SAM to get the weight information, which is then multiplied with T_h and finally the final feature map T_{out} is obtained. This allows the model to fully account for the contextual information to retain more semantic information, achieving a good segmentation of smaller targets.

Loss Function: We utilize a joint loss function of Dice loss and binary cross entropy (BCE) loss. Dice loss can effectively alleviate the data imbalance problem, which facilitates the segmentation of pigment deposits with varying size and random scatter, and the addition of BCE loss could stabilize the training of the model. The joint loss can be expressed as follows:

$$L_{joint} = L_{Dice} + L_{BCE}$$
$$= 1 - \frac{2\sum_{i=1}^{C} g_i \times p_i}{\sum_{i=1}^{C} g_i + p_i} - \frac{1}{C}\sum_{i=1}^{C} g_i \log p_i + (1 - g_i)\log(1 - p_i), \tag{1}$$

where $0 \leq g \leq 1$ and $0 \leq p \leq 1$ are segmentation ground truth and predicted probability, respectively. C is the sum of output results in pixels, i is per pixel.

2.2 Dataset

An in-house dataset consisting of 215 fundus images with RP are used to evaluate the proposed UAU-Net, which was approved by IRB of the University and informed consent was obtained from all subjects. The corresponding segmentation ground truth was manually annotated by professional ophthalmologists. The dataset contains seven different sizes of fundus images, which are 3100×2848, 2592×1944, 2528×2036, 2048×1536, 1600×1216, 884×818 and 874×957, acquired by two types of cameras. For each original image, a crop of the smallest outer rectangle of the retinal region was used to remove useless background and mitigate its negative impact on segmentation performance. We roughly group the dataset randomly by 6:2:2 for training, validation, and testing, specifically 132, 42, and 41.

2.3 Evaluation Metrics

The evaluation metrics used in this paper include Dice, Intersection-over-Union (IoU), Accuracy (Acc), and Specificity (Spec), where Dice is regarded as the most important metric. These metrics are defined as:

$$Dice = \frac{2 \times TP}{2 \times TP + FP + FN}, IoU = \frac{TP}{TP + FP + FN}, \tag{2}$$

$$Acc = \frac{TP + TN}{TP + FP + TN + FN}, Spec = \frac{TN}{TN + FN}, \tag{3}$$

where TP, FN, FP, and TN are the pixel number of true positive, false negative, false positive, and true negative, respectively.

3 Experiments and Results

3.1 Implementation Details

We use Adam optimizer with an initial learning rate of 1.0×10^{-4} and a momentum of 0.9. The batch size is set to 4 and 350 epochs are trained. All images

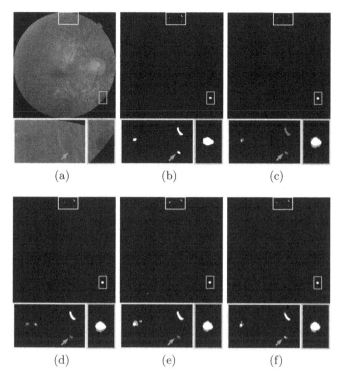

Fig. 4. Examples results of ablation study. (a) Original Fundus image (b) Ground truth (c) Baseline (d) Baseline+SEAM (e) Baseline+MsGAM (f) Baseline+MsGAM+SEAM (Proposed UAU-Net). Red, green, and white color represent FN, FP, and TP, respectively. The blue arrows point to the hard-to-segment pigment deposits. Best view in color and zoom in. (Color figure online)

are first resized to 1024×1024, then divided into 4 patches, i.e. 512×512 each, and then they are enhanced by flipping horizontally and vertically respectively, after which they are served as input to the model. The proposed UAU-Net is implemented using Pytorch and is trained with one NVIDIA RTX 3060 GPU of 12 GB memory.

3.2 Ablation Study

To investigate the contribution of each proposed module to segmentation performance, we conduct ablation experiments in four cases: 1) the first four layers of U-Net encoder join the SE module as Baseline, 2) combination of Baseline and SEAM, 3) combination of Baseline and MsGAM, and 4) the Baseline combines both SEAM and MsGAM, i.e., the segmentation model UAU-Net proposed in this paper. The experimental results are shown in Table 1.

The visualization results of the ablation study are shown in Fig. 4, with yellow and pink rectangular boxes representing two manually selected regions of

Table 1. Results of ablation study (mean ± standard deviation).

Method	Dice (%)	IoU (%)	Acc (%)	Spec (%)
Baseline	58.87±17.07	43.64±16.14	99.07±1.24	99.51±0.69
Baseline+SEAM	59.60±17.47	44.46±16.37	98.90±1.64	99.26±1.39
Baseline+MsGAM	59.96±16.10	44.62±15.87	98.92±1.79	99.31±1.48
UAU-Net (Proposed)	**60.25±16.11**	**44.91±15.73**	**99.09±1.27**	**99.53±0.73**

interest for better comparison. It can be clearly seen that the pigment deposits in the yellow box are smaller and the edges are more blurred, and they are more difficult to be segmented compared to those in the pink box. The addition of SEAM (Fig. 4(d)) and MsGAM (Fig. 4(e)) makes the pigment deposits segmentation more comprehensive compared to the Baseline (Fig. 4(c)). When both modules are used (Fig. 4(f)), the model accurately segmented the pigment deposits pointed by blue arrows, demonstrating that the proposed UAU-Net is able to successfully segment difficult small targets regardless of the variation in size and random scatter of pigment deposits. This is also demonstrated by the results listed in Table 1. Due to the fusion of contextual information, the addition of SEAM alone more efficiently enhances the feature selection ability of the model, with Dice increasing from 58.87% to 59.60% and IoU increasing from 43.64% to 44.46%. The multi-scale information fusion and global attention brought by the MsGAM allows the model to more accurately capture important features, with Dice and IoU rising further to 59.96% and 44.62%, respectively. When the two modules are combined with the Baseline, Acc, IoU, Dice, and Spec all achieve the best. The proposed segmentation model UAU-Net improves Dice by 1.38% and IoU by 1.27% compared to the Baseline.

3.3   Comparison Study

For a more comprehensive demonstration of the superiority of UAU-Net, we compare seven state-of-the-art methods, including U-Net [11], U-Net++ [18], Context Encoder Network (CE-Net) [7], Context Pyramid Fusion Network (CPFNet) [6], Attention U-Net (Att-UNet) [10], Curvilinear Structure Segmentation Network (CS^2-Net) [9], Unet-like pure Transformer for medical image segmentation (Swin-Unet) [5]. The hyperparameters of all competing methods are set the same as the proposed UAU-Net to ensure fairness.

The qualitative results in Fig. 5 show that the proposed UAU-Net achieves the best segmentation performance (Fig. 5(j)). It can be seen from Fig. 5(a) that the pigment deposits to be segmented are widely distributed and vary greatly in size, making it extremely difficult to identify and segment them. When comparing all segmentation results, we can see that the sum of the red and green regions of the UAU-Net (Fig. 5(j)) proposed in this paper is the smallest, which demonstrates the best segmentation performance.

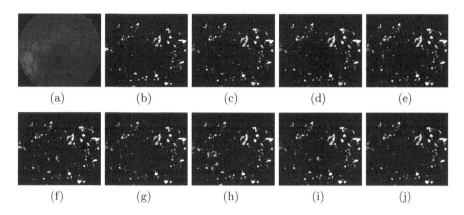

Fig. 5. Examples results of comparison experiments. (a) Original Fundus image (b) Ground truth (c) U-Net [11] (d) U-Net++ [18] (e) CE-Net [7] (f) CPFNet [6] (g) Att-UNet [10] (h) CS^2-Net [9] (i) Swin-Unet [5] (j)UAU-Net (Proposed). Red, green, and white color represent FN, FP, and TP, respectively. (Color figure online)

The comparison of quantitative performance is presented in Table 2, and the results demonstrate that our model achieves optimal results on Dice, IoU, and Acc, and also ranks second on Spec. Comparing to the best U-Net++ among competing methods, which has 58.51% and 43.62% on Dice and IoU, respectively, our UAU-Net still has a 1.74% and 1.29% boost on these two metrics. What's more, compared to Att-UNet, which has the highest computational cost (see the GFLOPs in Table 2), Dice and IoU improve 2.14% and 1.54%, respectively. With the exception of CS^2-Net and Swin-Unet, none of other methods focus on global attention, i.e., they ignore the long-distance dependence of features. For pigment deposit, which is a more widely distributed and variable-sized target, global attention allows long-distance features to be correlated with each other, making it easier to determine whether features at different distances are the same target. Although CS^2-Net and Swin-Unet also use a Self-attention related module and their computational cost is comparable to that of UAU-Net, they ignore the information of small targets and thus fail to segment the pigment deposits of small size. This leads to a Dice metric that are 8.17% and 6.28% respectively lower than the proposed model. It is worth noting that our method obtains the smallest standard deviation in both Dice and IoU, indicating that it obtains the most stable segmentation performance.

Table 2. Results of comparison experiments (mean ± standard deviation).

Method	Dice (%)	IoU (%)	Acc (%)	Spec (%)	GFLOPs
U-Net [11]	57.75±18.69	42.83±17.20	99.03±1.33	99.48±0.88	124.47
U-Net++ [18]	58.51±18.98	43.62±17.16	98.99±1.30	99.33±0.97	139.61
CE-Net [7]	58.11±18.48	43.10±16.77	99.01±1.27	99.37±0.94	35.60
CPFNet [6]	56.91±19.43	42.07±17.18	99.00±1.27	99.41±0.83	**32.28**
Att-UNet [10]	58.11±19.81	43.37±17.61	99.02±1.44	99.53±0.82	333.37
CS^2-Net [9]	52.08±20.19	37.57±17.53	98.87±1.59	99.47±0.97	56.02
Swin-Unet [5]	53.97±18.93	39.13±16.98	98.88±1.44	99.29±1.00	45.43
UAU-Net (Proposed)	**60.25±16.11**	**44.91±15.73**	**99.09±1.27**	**99.53±0.73**	83.02

4   Conclusion

In this paper, we propose a novel end-to-end segmentation network, UAU-Net, which can significantly improve the retinal pigment deposits segmentation performance in fundus images. The model proposes two modules, MsGAM and SEAM, for solving the problems of pigment deposits with random scatter and large size variation, respectively. The MsGAM is able to fuse multi-scale long-range spatial and channel information to construct associations of the same segmentation target at different locations. The SEAM enables combining contextual information to retain detailed features well and improve the segmentation accuracy of small targets. The experimental results show that the proposed model has good performance and great potential in segmenting retinal pigment deposits.

References

1. Arsalan, M., Baek, N.R., Owais, M., Mahmood, T., Park, K.R.: Deep learning-based detection of pigment signs for analysis and diagnosis of retinitis pigmentosa. Sensors **20**(12), 3454 (2020)
2. Brancati, N., Frucci, M., Gragnaniello, D., Riccio, D., Di Iorio, V., Di Perna, L.: Automatic segmentation of pigment deposits in retinal fundus images of retinitis pigmentosa. Comput. Med. Imag. Graph. **66**, 73–81 (2018)
3. Brancati, N., et al.: Learning-based approach to segment pigment signs in fundus images for retinitis pigmentosa analysis. Neurocomputing **308**, 159–171 (2018)
4. Brancati, N., Frucci, M., Riccio, D., Di Perna, L., Simonelli, F.: Segmentation of pigment signs in fundus images for retinitis pigmentosa analysis by using deep learning. In: Ricci, E., Rota Bulò, S., Snoek, C., Lanz, O., Messelodi, S., Sebe, N. (eds.) ICIAP 2019. LNCS, vol. 11752, pp. 437–445. Springer, Cham (2019). https://doi.org/10.1007/978-3-030-30645-8_40
5. Cao, H., et al.: Swin-unet: unet-like pure transformer for medical image segmentation. In: European Conference on Computer Vision, pp. 205–218. Springer, Cham (2022). https://doi.org/10.1007/978-3-031-25066-8_9
6. Feng, S., et al.: Cpfnet: context pyramid fusion network for medical image segmentation. IEEE Trans. Med. Imag. **39**(10), 3008–3018 (2020)

7. Gu, Z., et al.: Ce-net: context encoder network for 2d medical image segmentation. IEEE Trans. Med. Imag. **38**(10), 2281–2292 (2019)
8. Hamel, C.: Retinitis pigmentosa. Orphanet J. Rare Dis. **1**(1), 1–12 (2006)
9. Mou, L., et al.: Cs2-net: deep learning segmentation of curvilinear structures in medical imaging. Med. Image Anal. **67**, 101874 (2021)
10. Oktay, O., et al.: Attention u-net: learning where to look for the pancreas. arXiv preprint arXiv:1804.03999 (2018)
11. Ronneberger, O., Fischer, P., Brox, T.: U-Net: convolutional networks for biomedical image segmentation. In: Navab, N., Hornegger, J., Wells, W.M., Frangi, A.F. (eds.) MICCAI 2015. LNCS, vol. 9351, pp. 234–241. Springer, Cham (2015). https://doi.org/10.1007/978-3-319-24574-4_28
12. Sambyal, N., Saini, P., Syal, R., Gupta, V.: Modified u-net architecture for semantic segmentation of diabetic retinopathy images. Biocybernet. Biomed. Eng. **40**(3), 1094–1109 (2020)
13. Song, J., et al.: Global and local feature reconstruction for medical image segmentation. IEEE Trans. Med. Imag. **41**(9), 2273–2284 (2022)
14. Vaswani, A., et al.: Attention is all you need. Adv. Neural Inf. Process. Syst. **30** (2017)
15. Wang, M., et al.: Mstganet: automatic drusen segmentation from retinal oct images. IEEE Trans. Med. Imag. **41**(2), 394–406 (2021)
16. Wang, X., et al.: Clc-net: contextual and local collaborative network for lesion segmentation in diabetic retinopathy images. Neurocomputing **527**, 100–109 (2023)
17. Woo, S., Park, J., Lee, J.Y., Kweon, I.S.: Cbam: convolutional block attention module. In: Proceedings of the European Conference on Computer Vision (ECCV), pp. 3–19 (2018)
18. Zhou, Z., Rahman Siddiquee, Md.M., Tajbakhsh, N., Liang, J.: UNet++: a nested U-net architecture for medical image segmentation. In: Stoyanov, D., et al. (eds.) DLMIA/ML-CDS -2018. LNCS, vol. 11045, pp. 3–11. Springer, Cham (2018). https://doi.org/10.1007/978-3-030-00889-5_1

Glaucoma Progression Detection and Humphrey Visual Field Prediction Using Discriminative and Generative Vision Transformers

Ye Tian[1]([✉]), Mingyang Zang[1], Anurag Sharma[1], Sophie Z. Gu[2], Ari Leshno[2], and Kaveri A. Thakoor[1,2]

[1] Department of Biomedical Engineering, Columbia University,
New York, NY 10027, USA
yt2793@columbia.edu
[2] Department of Ophthalmology, Columbia University Irving Medical Center,
New York, NY 10032, USA

Abstract. Glaucoma is one of the top causes of blindness worldwide. Assessing its progression is critical to determine potential visual impairment and to design sound treatment plans. Standard automated perimetry tests, commonly known as visual field (VF) tests, are clinically used to evaluate the state of functional vision. To provide an accurate and automatic diagnostic tool for clinical decision making in glaucoma progression, we utilize the predictive power of artificial intelligence (AI) and propose two vision transformer (ViT)-based deep learning (DL) networks. First, we optimize a spatiotemporal ViT to classify a subject's rate of glaucoma progression (GP) using only 3 baseline VFs; we explore threshold mean deviation (MD) rate of change from -0.3 to $-1.5\,\mathrm{dB/year}$ and achieve up to 89% GP detection accuracy. Second, we develop a VF-to-VF generation architecture via a diffusion model with a ViT backbone. The model predicts future VFs with Pointwise Mean Absolute Error (PMAE) as low as 2.15 dB for mild VF deficits and is the first to extend VF prediction up to 10 years into the future. Our models are trained and validated on our '62K+' dataset, the largest available of VFs to-date including at-risk, minority populations, thus ensuring our models' generalizability. We establish our computational methods and compare testing results on the publicly available UWHVF dataset. In short, our study utilizes novel AI methods for predicting future rates and patterns of glaucoma progression in order to expedite timely treatment for better patient quality of life. The code is available at https://github.com/AI4VSLab/GP-Detection-VF-Prediction.

Keywords: Glaucoma · Visual Field · Vision Transformer

Supplementary Information The online version contains supplementary material available at https://doi.org/10.1007/978-3-031-44013-7_7.

1   Introduction

Glaucoma impacts more than 76 million people worldwide and is expected to affect nearly 112 million people by 2040. [1] Accurate assessment of glaucoma progression (GP) is critical as it determines the potential for future impairment to functional vision and enables the design of a timely treatment plan. [2] GP is typically assessed using a combination of optical coherence tomography (OCT) measurements, which are used to evaluate structural damage to retinal layers, and standard automated perimetry tests (commonly known as visual field [VF] tests), which are used to evaluate the state of functional vision. The grayscale values in the VF depict the patient's functional sensitivity to light at various positions in their visual field. The darker shades correspond to lower visual sensitivity. The interaction between structural and functional changes in the retina serves as a crucial biomarker for GP [3].

Clinicians use OCT and VF data together to attempt to predict a patient's rate of VF change with time; they determine if this rate of change is acceptable given the patient's age, other risk factors, and the likelihood of development of visual impairment during the patient's lifetime. [3] VF assessment, however, is subjective to expertise and requires consecutive data collection over months or years. Furthermore, there is disagreement, even among experts, about which VF tests to use, i.e., those that capture a wider field (24-2) versus those that focus on the central field in greater detail (10-2). We use the 24-2 VF which measures $24°$ temporally and $30°$ nasally and tests 54 points; it is the most common VF test repeated for patients at routine intervals.

Multiple algorithms are used to detect progression mathematically in clinical practice, including the slope of the mean deviation (MD) (average of total deviation from age-matched controls at each VF test point, measured in decibels [dB/year]) and Guided Progression Analysis. Past studies [4,5] have found that when machine learning (ML) algorithms were used to classify VFs as either 'stable', 'progressing', or 'unclear' compared to the majority vote of 4 or more of the above mathematical scores (with the ground truth generated by a panel of glaucoma specialists), the ML algorithms were 'more balanced' than the mathematical algorithms. In other words, the ML algorithms tended to achieve equivalent or sometimes better accuracy than existing mathematical approaches without 'overcalling' progression, thus making ML approaches potentially generalizable to a wider range of datasets.

Given the observed benefits of using ML algorithms for GP detection, a next step toward employing AI to aid clinicians in GP decision-making is to use the power of detection-based and generative deep learning approaches. For automating detection, a potential starting criteria used clinically is an MD rate of change of worse than -0.3 dB/year on the 24-2 VF. Past DL-based approaches using generative models have successfully predicted VF appearance from OCT image inputs [6], reducing the number of VF tests required, and another approach has used a U-Net-inspired model to predict VF appearance up to 5 years after a baseline VF test. [7]

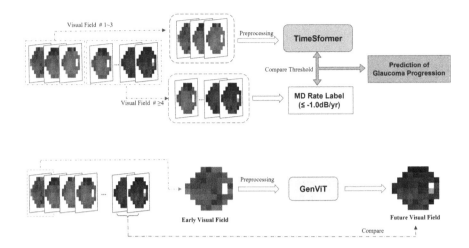

Fig. 1. Study Pipeline. The first stream at top illustrates our first task: Glaucoma Progression Detection using a spatiotemporal ViT (TimeSformer). The second stream at bottom showcases our second task: Visual Field Prediction using a diffusion model with ViT-base backbone (GenViT).

In this paper, we design a novel deep learning system to aid clinicians in predicting future rates and patterns of GP. We utilize AI to detect GP and predict future VF appearance. Our study pipeline is shown in Fig. 1. Furthermore, we utilize the largest available dataset of VFs to-date including minority populations (e.g., of African, Hispanic, Asian descent) to train our models, thus ensuring our models' robustness to new test patient data from minority populations.

2   Methods

2.1   Datasets

62K+ dataset: the largest available dataset of VFs to-date including minority populations (e.g., of African, Hispanic, Asian descent). The dataset includes raw retrospective visual field test data of up to 5,167 patients (62,000+ visual fields) collected between October 2010 through October 2023 (IRB-approval-required). More information is included in Table S1.

University of Washington Humphrey Visual Field (UWHVF): The UWHVF dataset [8] is an open-source (publicly-available) VF dataset from the Department of Ophthalmology at the University of Washington. It contains 28,943 VF tests from 3,871 patients and 7,428 eyes.

For both UWHVF and 62K+ datasets, the laterality of all visual field images was altered to OD (right eyes) for analysis and consistent storage. The VF-test year was stored to compute time difference between tests and glaucoma progression rate. Each 24-2 VF was stored in an 8×9 matrix (and zero-padded

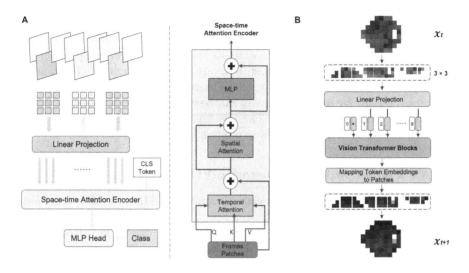

Fig. 2. Model Architecture of Glaucoma Progression TimeSformer and GenViT. A: the schematic of TimeSformer and Space-time attention; B: the backbone of GenViT.

to 9×9 for ease of computation), with a total of 54 informative perimetry points (the rest valued to zero as non-noise background). We trained and validated models using the 62K+ data and tested on the UWHVF dataset.

2.2 GP Detection Using TimeSformer

To detect glaucoma progression using longitudinal visual field images from each patient, we design the task as multi-frame image classification. Glaucoma progression is reflected by the rate of change of mean deviation (MD) in visual fields. For all VFs from a given subject, we used the first 3 VFs to detect any progressive MD change in future VFs. In other words, starting from the fourth VF, if any MD changes between consecutive VFs surpassed the defined threshold, the subject was labelled as positive for GP. We explored model performance at clinically important thresholds of -0.5, -1.0 and -1.5 dB/year, respectively. The strategy of using only the 3 earliest VFs as input minimizes the number of VF tests required from a patient, and maintains AI's predictive power with the lowest computational cost.

We propose our Glaucoma Progression TimeSformer (GPTS), a 3D transformer-based spatiotemporal deep learning model. Transformer [9] originated from the field of natural language processing (NLP) in 2017, and was pioneered in the field of computer vision (CV) starting from the emergence of Vision Transformer (ViT) [10] in 2021. Compared with convolutional neural networks (CNN), transformers have achieved better performance on multiple benchmarks such as ImageNet [11] and COCO [12] datasets. To fit our 3D VF data with temporal information, we implemented and modified the TimeSformer [13]. The convolution-free TimeSformer was originally developed for video understanding and treats each VF image as a single input frame. As is shown in Fig. 2A, its space-time attention mechanism extends the self-attention to spatiotemporal 3D space, allows efficient training, and also provides accurate classification results. Due to limited image size (8×9) of visual fields, it is not feasible to use pre-trained weights by upsampling. Alternatively, we trained TimeSformer from scratch with patch size equal to 3. The loss function used was Binary CrossEntropy with 0.3 positive weight because of class imbalance in our datasets.

2.3   VF Prediction Using Generative ViT

Global measurements of GP risk, such as monitoring MD rate of change, have limitations, as glaucomatous changes can occur in a small portion of VF points. To achieve pointwise VF-to-VF generation, we use the first VF as the only input to predict future VFs in 1–2 years, 3–5 years, and over 5 years, respectively. Our method is less data-expensive than conventional linear regression models [14], only requiring one model to yield prediction for 54 perimetry points, and more robust than previous CNN-based deep learning approaches [7] because of its superiority in model performance and independence to additional predictors other than the initial VF of a subject. Though VFs become more unpredictable as time differences increase, we design our AI model to extend its predictive power to up to 10 years in the future, as shown in the visualization results in Fig. 3.

For VF prediction, we utilized and modified GenViT, a combination of a ViT and a diffusion model [15]. Diffusion Models (so called diffusion probabilistic models, DPM) are generative models using a U-Net [16] backbone to enhance image synthesis and have demonstrated higher output quality [17,18] than generative adversarial networks (GANs). GenViT substitutes U-Net with a ViT. The ViT architecture used as its backbone differs from standard ViT only at the decoding stage: instead of learning a 'class token' to further apply a multi-layer perceptron for image classification, GenViT reconstructs patch projections based on positional embeddings and encoder outputs from the transformer block. As is shown in Fig. 2B, this structure enables GenViT to generate a VF with the same size and dimension as the input VF. The direct connection between DPM and ViT has proven to be computationally efficient and scalable to growing model and data sizes [15,16]. The loss function and performance metrics used are both masked pointwise-mean-absolute-error (masked PMAE).

3   Results and Discussion

3.1   GP Detection

We report results on the validation set - a subset (20%) of the 62K+ data, and the test set - the entire UWHVF dataset. The results are separated for three MD rate of change thresholds: -0.5 (GP: non-GP ratio, 62K+: $\approx 14 : 1$, UWHVF:

Table 1. Glaucoma Progression Detection Results using CNN, ViT, and GPTS

| | | −0.5 dB/yr | | | −1 dB/yr | | | −1.5 dB/yr | | |
	Dataset	CNN	ViT	GPTS	CNN	ViT	GPTS	CNN	ViT	GPTS
Accuracy	62K	**0.918**	0.918	0.889	0.822	0.800	0.796	0.711	0.664	0.723
	UWHVF	**0.886**	0.873	0.845	0.689	0.666	0.708	0.555	0.533	0.646
Precision	62K	0.538	0.568	0.568	0.548	0.594	0.609	0.630	0.595	**0.641**
	UWHVF	0.457	0.451	0.521	0.421	0.541	0.612	0.533	0.534	**0.631**
Recall	62K	0.512	0.525	0.569	0.522	0.592	0.623	0.651	0.619	**0.661**
	UWHVF	0.489	0.491	0.513	0.477	0.534	0.601	0.532	0.535	**0.624**
F1-score	62K	0.512	0.531	0.568	0.521	0.593	0.615	0.636	0.597	**0.647**
	UWHVF	0.470	0.469	0.513	0.428	0.534	0.605	0.532	0.530	**0.625**
AUC	62K	**0.769**	0.719	0.662	0.692	0.703	0.692	0.724	0.689	0.702
	UWHVF	0.395	0.362	0.597	0.513	0.547	0.657	0.563	0.553	**0.659**

$\approx 8 : 1$), -1.0 (GP: non-GP ratio, 62K+: $\approx 6 : 1$, UWHVF: $\approx 3 : 1$), and -1.5 dB/year (GP: non-GP ratio, 62K+: $\approx 3 : 1$, UWHVF: $\approx 1.5 : 1$). All models are trained on the 62K+ dataset with the validation set excluded. The definition and explanation of metrics are: $Accuracy = \frac{(TP+TN)}{(TP+TN+FP+FN)}$, $precision = \frac{(TP)}{(TP+FP)}$, $Recall = \frac{(TP)}{(TP+FN)}$, F1 score is the harmonic mean of precision and recall, and AUC is the area under the receiver operating characteristic. Table 1 shows results of all metrics for the GP detection task.

Glaucoma Progression TimeSformer (GPTS) achieves better Precision, Recall, F1-Score, and AUC than the CNN with 2 convolutional layers and 2 fully-connected layers, and the vanilla Vision Transformer [7]. Though the CNN seems to perform the best in terms of Accuracy and AUC at a slower progression rate (-0.5 dB/yr), the CNN actually failed to predict the non-GP (minor) class at all; the relatively good results of the CNN were due to the highly-imbalanced GP: non-GP ($\approx$13:1) class-size distribution (especially at low MD threshold).

When testing on the whole UWHVF dataset, performance decreased slightly but remained comparable with validation results on the 62K+ subset. Possible reasons include that the UWHVF dataset has lower average MD and a different data collection protocol. The testing result on the UWHVF dataset showcases the strong generalizability of our GPTS model.

3.2   VF Prediction Results

The VF prediction results using an initial VF for three time interval groups (1–2, 3–5, and over 5 years in the future) are shown in Table 2. For each group, we compare the results on the 62K+ and UWHVF datasets, and also compare our model's capacity for predicting mild, moderate and severe VF deficits. We defined mild VF deficits as a MD of −6 dB or better, moderate VF deficits as a

Table 2. VF Prediction results (MAE) reported in dB: unmasked 72-point MAE (masked 54-point MAE). Results from Wen et al. [7] (masked 54-point MAE only) on UWHVF are shown for comparison in the second column.

Group	Wen et al.	62K+		UWHVF	
years	Val	Val	VF Deficit	Test	VF Deficit
¿5	NA	2.75 (3.67)	Mild: 1.82 (2.42) Moderate: 3.65 (4.88) Severe: 5.67 (7.56)	2.80 (3.74)	Mild: 1.98 (2.64) Moderate: 3.79 (5.05) Severe: 4.94 (6.59)
3–5	2.71	2.37 (3.17)	Mild: 1.63 (2.17) Moderate: 3.41 (4.55) Severe: 5.13 (6.84)	2.64 (3.53)	Mild: 1.63 (2.57) Moderate: 3.60 (4.80) Severe: 4.81 (6.42)
1–2	2.68	2.30 (3.07)	Mild: 1.61 (2.15) Moderate: 3.30 (4.40) Severe: 4.45 (5.93)	2.54 (3.39)	Mild: 1.57 (2.50) Moderate: 3.39 (4.53) Severe: 4.76 (6.35)

MD of -6 to -12 dB, and severe VF deficits as a MD of -12 dB or worse [19] (Table 2).

Our model outperforms a previous convolution-based approach (Wen et al. [7]), extends predictive power to over 5 years in the future, and generalizes well on the unseen UWHVF dataset. Also, our approach does not require additional demographic information for prediction; it uses only a baseline VF input. When time interval increases, all PMAE scores become slightly higher but still remain lower than 3.8 dB. The prediction results are better when target VFs show mild or moderate deficits rather than severe deficits. Example AI-predicted VFs vs. ground truth VFs are shown in Fig. 3.

4   Discussion, Conclusions, and Future Directions

Our study uses AI models to detect glaucoma progression and predict future visual fields. In conclusion,

(1) We are the first to solve the GP Detection challenge in 3D space, using GPTS with a spatiotemporal attention mechanism.

(2) We explored significant glaucoma MD rates of change from -0.3 to -1.5 dB/year, with -1.0 db/year considered fast progression [20]. Smaller rates such as -0.5 dB/year can also be harmful, such as in juvenile glaucoma patients [21].

(3) Our method achieves VF prediction up to 10 years in the future, as shown in the 3rd row of Fig. 3 with no additional predictors, channels, or demographic data needed. Our model uses only a single VF as input to generate robust and generalizable VF prediction. When the baseline is a moderate VF, GenViT pre-

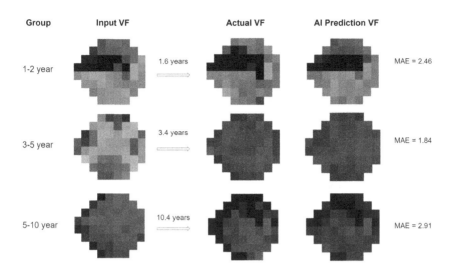

Fig. 3. Visualization of GenViT output VF prediction examples at each time interval (MAE reported in dB).

dicts future mild and moderate changes better. The model can be iteratively applied (output used as new input) to generate VFs in the late future.

(4) We trained models on the 62K+ dataset including minority populations. It is well-established that there is a higher risk of development and progression of glaucoma in certain ethnic populations, such as a higher risk of primary open-angle glaucoma (POAG) in those of African descent [22]. However, systematic reviews and meta-analyses have shown poor representation of those ethnic populations in glaucoma studies, including both clinical trials and machine learning studies [23–25]. Within machine learning studies, it is vital to both report on the demographic distribution of imaging datasets and ensure that the datasets are representative of a variety of populations, including those most at risk of disease in order to increase the generalizability of these algorithms [26].

One review of open access datasets containing ophthalmic imaging found that most originated from Asia, North America, and Europe and 74% failed to report any demographic data at all [25]. Another review found that 59% of machine learning studies published since 2016 did not report on race or ethnicity [24]. Of the 6 studies that reported race or ethnicity and included patient data solely from North America, Black or African descent representation varied between 17.7% and 45.5% and only a single study even reported Hispanic representation at just 1.5% [24]. The UK Biobank is another example of a large dataset with imaging data that has been used for machine learning purposes in glaucoma, but most subjects are of European descent [27,28]. By contrast, our 62K+ dataset consists of 6.7% of African descent, 6.8% of Asian descent, and 3.7% of Hispanic descent. This dataset thus includes the greatest Hispanic representation of existing glaucoma datasets containing ophthalmic imaging. This may explain why our models generalize well to the publicly available UWHVF dataset and suggests an ability to maintain robustness to other unseen data.

In future work, we plan to combine OCT inputs with VF inputs to capture structure and function correlations in model training. Multiple studies have proved the feasibility of OCT-to-VF conversion [18,29]. We instead propose to use structural OCT as a prior to create weighted, 'region-aware' VFs as input to GenViT. Overall, our AI models exhibit superior performance compared to existing state-of-the-art approaches, showcasing their potential to aid in clinical decision-making of GP detection and future VF appearance prediction to expedite glaucoma treatment for the broadest patient populations.

Acknowledgements. The authors would like to thank Dr. Jeffrey M. Liebmann, Dr. George A. Cioffi, and Dr. Aaki G. Shukla for their guidance on clinical issues related to GP. This work was supported in part by an Unrestricted Grant from Research to Prevent Blindness awarded to Columbia Ophthalmology.

References

1. Allison, K., Patel, D., Alabi, O.: Epidemiology of glaucoma: the past, present, and predictions for the future. Cureus **12**(11), e11686 (2020)
2. Anderson, R.S.: The psychophysics of glaucoma: improving the structure/function relationship. Prog. Retin. Eye Res. **25**(1), 79–97 (2006)
3. Wollstein, G., et al.: Optical coherence tomography (oct) macular and peripapillary retinal nerve fiber layer measurements and automated visual fields. Am. J. Ophthalmol. **138**(2), 218–225 (2004)
4. Saeedi, O., et al.: Development and comparison of machine learning algorithms to determine visual field progression. Transl. Vision Sci. Technol. **10**(7), 27–27 (2021)
5. Yousefi, S., et al.: Detection of longitudinal visual field progression in glaucoma using machine learning. Am. J. Ophthalmol. **193**, 71–79 (2018)
6. Lazaridis, G., et al.: Predicting visual fields from optical coherence tomography via an ensemble of deep representation learners. Am. J. Ophthalmol. **238**, 52–65 (2022)
7. Wen, J.C., et al.: Forecasting future humphrey visual fields using deep learning. PLoS ONE **14**(4), e0214875 (2019)
8. Montesano, G., Chen, A., Lu, R., Lee, C.S., Lee, A.Y.: UWHVF: a real-world, open source dataset of perimetry tests from the humphrey field analyzer at the university of washington. Transl. Vision Sci. Technol. **11**(1), 2–2 (2022)
9. Vaswani, A.: Attention is all you need. In: Advances in Neural Information Processing Systems, vol. 30 (2017)
10. Dosovitskiy, A., et al.: An image is worth 16x16 words: transformers for image recognition at scale. arXiv preprint arXiv:2010.11929 (2020)
11. Deng, J., Dong, W., Socher, R., Li, L.-J., Li, K., Fei-Fei, L.: Imagenet: a large-scale hierarchical image database. In: 2009 IEEE Conference on Computer Vision and Pattern Recognition, pp. 248–255. IEEE (2009)
12. Fleet, D., Pajdla, T., Schiele, B., Tuytelaars, T. (eds.): ECCV 2014, Part I. LNCS, vol. 8689. Springer, Cham (2014). https://doi.org/10.1007/978-3-319-10590-1
13. Bertasius, G., Wang, H., Torresani, L.: Is space-time attention all you need for video understanding? In: ICML, vol. 2, p. 4 (2021)

14. Caprioli, J., et al.: A method to measure and predict rates of regional visual field decay in glaucoma. Invest. Ophthalmol. Visual Sci. **52**(7), 4765–4773 (2011)
15. Yang, X., Shih, S.-M., Fu, Y., Zhao, X., Ji,, S.: Your vit is secretly a hybrid discriminative-generative diffusion model. arXiv preprint arXiv:2208.07791 (2022)
16. Bao, F., Li, C., Cao, Y., Zhu, J.: All are worth words: a vit backbone for score-based diffusion models. arXiv preprint arXiv:2209.12152, 2022
17. Dhariwal, P., Nichol, A.: Diffusion models beat GANs on image synthesis. Adv. Neural. Inf. Process. Syst. **34**, 8780–8794 (2021)
18. Müller-Franzes, G., et al.: Diffusion probabilistic models beat GANs on medical images. arXiv preprint arXiv:2212.07501 (2022)
19. Mills, R.P., et al.: Categorizing the stage of glaucoma from pre-diagnosis to end-stage disease. Am. J. Ophthalmol. **141**(1), 24–30 (2006)
20. Jackson, A.B., et al.: Fast progressors in glaucoma: Prevalence based on global and central visual field loss. Ophthalmology **130**, 462–468 (2023)
21. Saunders, L.J., Medeiros, F.A., Weinreb, R.N., Zangwill, L.M.: What rates of glaucoma progression are clinically significant? Expert Rev. Ophthalmol. **11**(3), 227–234 (2016)
22. Tielsch, J.M., Sommer, A., Katz, J., Royall, R.M., Quigley, H.A., Javitt, J.: Racial variations in the prevalence of primary open-angle glaucoma: the baltimore eye survey. JAMA **266**(3), 369–374 (1991)
23. Allison, K., Patel, D.G., Greene, L.: Racial and ethnic disparities in primary open-angle glaucoma clinical trials: a systematic review and meta-analysis. JAMA Netw. Open **4**(5), e218348–e218348 (2021)
24. Sekimitsu, S., Zebardast, N.: Glaucoma and machine learning: a call for increased diversity in data. Ophthalmol. Glaucoma **4**(4), 339–342 (2021)
25. Khan, S.M., et al.: A global review of publicly available datasets for ophthalmological imaging: barriers to access, usability, and generalisability. Lancet Digital Health **3**(1), e51–e66 (2021)
26. Lee, E.B., Wang, S.Y., Chang, R.T.: Interpreting deep learning studies in glaucoma: unresolved challenges. Asia-Pacific J. Ophthalmol. **10**(3), 261–267 (2021)
27. Mehta, P., et al.: Automated detection of glaucoma with interpretable machine learning using clinical data and multimodal retinal images. Am. J. Ophthalmol. **231**, 154–169 (2021)
28. Phene, S., et al.: Deep learning and glaucoma specialists: the relative importance of optic disc features to predict glaucoma referral in fundus photographs. Ophthalmology **126**(12), 1627–1639 (2019)
29. Shin, J., Kim, S., Kim, J., Park, K.: Visual field inference from optical coherence tomography using deep learning algorithms: a comparison between devices. Transl. Vision Sci. Technol. **10**(7), 4–4 (2021)

Utilizing Meta Pseudo Labels for Semantic Segmentation of Targeted Optic Nerve Features

Ashelyn Mann[1]([⊠]), Adam Hedberg-Buenz[2,3], Michael G. Anderson[2,3], and Mona K. Garvin[1,3]([⊠])

[1] Department of Electrical and Computer Engineering,
The University of Iowa, Iowa City, IA, USA
{ashelyn-mann,mona-garvin}@uiowa.edu
[2] Department of Molecular Physiology and Biophysics,
The University of Iowa, Iowa City, IA, USA
{adam-hedberg-buenz,michael-g-anderson}@uiowa.edu
[3] Iowa City VA Center for the Prevention and Treatment of Visual Loss,
Iowa City VA Health Care System, Iowa City, IA, USA

Abstract. Evaluating optic nerve cross-sectional images requires significant time and effort by experts to perform. Autonomous systems using deep learning can help to reduce this workload by performing the evaluation automatically, though they tend to require labeled images to train, which can be time and effort intensive to produce. This work utilizes a semi-supervised training algorithm based on the Meta Pseudo Labels (MPL) model, combined with the feature pyramid network architecture used by AxonDeep, to create a highly adaptable network model that can leverage large amounts of unlabeled data and minimal labeled data to train. This opens up the possibility of being able to quickly retrain the network to adapt to different contexts. This method was applied for semantic segmentations of axons within optic nerve cross-sectional images of mice. The tests performed in this work utilized the same network architecture, training data, and post-processing as an existing deeplearning approach, AxonDeep, to establish a fair comparison. The evaluations performed involved training four models using 10%, 25%, 50%, and 100% of the labeled images (n = 26) alongside unlabeled images (n = 50). Results from the test set (n = 18) show that with 10% of the labeled training data, the MPL model was able to achieve a similar Dice score as the AxonDeep model when trained with 100% of the labeled training data, though the axon-count results calculated during post-processing did not achieve a similar level of accuracy from minimal labeled training data.

1 Introduction

Quantitative analyses of image data from optic nerve histology represent the gold-standard in measuring the anatomic damage that confers visual loss and blindness in animal models of various disorders of the optic nerve, including

B. Antony et al. (Eds.): OMIA 2023, LNCS 14096, pp. 72–81, 2023.
https://doi.org/10.1007/978-3-031-44013-7_8

glaucoma and optic nerve atrophy, among others. In particular, quantitative analyses of the abundance and morphometry of axons within the nerve will contribute to our understanding of the etiology and mechanisms of damage in these disorders. However, it is difficult to produce good segmentation results for axons through traditional image processing techniques due to the shape, density, and variance of the axons. For example, first-generation approaches based on more traditional image-processing approaches, such as AxonJ [12] and AxonMaster [9], often begin to perform poorly in cases of diseased nerves and thus have not been widely adopted.

More recently, second-generation deep-learning methods have been proposed, such as AxoNet [10], AxoNet 2.0 [5], and AxonDeep [4]. However, these approaches also have their own limitations. For example, AxoNet [10] only provides an axon count and both AxoNet and AxoNet 2.0 were not trained to detect damaged nerves. While axon counts are a useful metric (and the only practical one for manual measurements), other measures based on the segmentation themselves (such as area) would be important in disease understanding. AxoNet 2.0 [5] and AxonDeep [4] both present deep-learning approaches that directly provide axon segmentations rather than just a prediction of the counts and address many of the limitations of prior approaches. However, while these approaches show great promise and can work very well on images similar to those in their training sets, the variety of imaging techniques and animal models of optic nerve disease available makes an approach that is easily trainable with limited data and adaptable across labs still of great interest. AxonDeep [4] does provide a generative-adversarial-network (GAN) training framework [involving a feature-pyramid-like (FPN) architecture with a deep ResNeXt-50 encoder and more lightweight decoder for both the segmentation/generator network and discriminator network] for reducing the need for large training sets; however, in practice, this framework can sometimes be challenging to train and fine-tune and relying even less on manually labeled data would be desirable.

As an important step in this direction for reducing the training effort, in this work, we applied a novel deep learning technique, Meta Pseudo Labels [8], to train a neural network to provide semantic segmentations of axons within optic nerve cross-sectional images. This work builds upon and expands the capabilities of previous works, such as AxonDeep [4], to decrease the dependency on labeled data and provide a flexible system to retrain a neural network to fit new contexts through transfer learning. We utilize many of the same training and testing parameters as used by AxonDeep [4], as well as the same underlying FPN segmentation network architecture, so that the performance of AxonDeep can be used as a metric for comparison.

The motivation of this work is to reduce the manual work experts need to perform to produce labeled training data by providing a method that can be trained and fine-tuned with minimal labeled training data [2,7]. This would allow for a neural network model to more easily adapt to new contexts as it would not require as much labeled data to fine-tune its weights. This ultimately could lead to a pre-trained network that could be re-trained with a few images in order to account for differences in the new dataset, such as alternative staining techniques, camera-based variables, or even detecting different objects of interest (such as glial cells).

2   Meta Pseudo Labels

The Meta Pseudo Labels (MPL) method is designed as a way to build upon self-supervised concepts to reduce the dependency on labeled data during the training process [8]. Supervised learning is the process of using labeled training data to learn targeted features [6]. Self-supervised methods train from unlabeled data by creating self-imposed labels to learn generalized feature information [11]. MPL combines these concepts to train in a semi-supervised fashion where it utilizes a larger amount of unlabeled data to learn generalized features and a small batch of labeled data so that it can learn targeted features. This process is achieved through a collaborative system between two networks: a teacher who produces fake labels for the unlabeled dataset, and a student who trains from these fake labels. The performance of the student is then used to update the teacher model, allowing for the teacher to learn meta-information about how to best help the student network learn. The labeled training data is utilized to facilitate the teacher's capacity for producing feature-specific pseudo labels, not for training the student directly [8].

2.1   Implementation

This work utilizes the Meta Pseudo Labels (MPL) method to train its network. MPL creates a feedback loop between two networks, as seen in Fig. 1, working collaboratively to improve their results [8]. This differs from AxonDeep's Generative Adversarial Network (GAN), which has two networks attempting to outperform each other. Further information on how the GAN method is implemented can be found in [4]. Note that the FPN segmentation network used in this work is the same as in AxonDeep [4].

Because Meta Pseudo Labels has two networks, there are two loss functions that work in tandem. The student network (θ_S) learns exclusively from the pseudo labels generated ($T(x_u; \theta_T)$, where x_u is the unlabeled data) by the teacher (θ_T). The loss function for the student is described in Eq. (1), where $\mathcal{L}_u(\theta_T, \theta_S)$ is the BCE loss between the student's prediction and the pseudo label generated by the teacher (Eq. (2)) [8].

$$\theta_S^{PL} = \arg\min_{\theta_S} \mathbb{E}_{X_u}[\mathcal{L}_u(\theta_T, \theta_S)] \tag{1}$$

$$\mathcal{L}_u(\theta_T, \theta_S) = BCE(T(x_u; \theta_T), S(x_u; \theta_S)) \tag{2}$$

The step function detailed in Eq. (3) shows how the gradient determined by the loss function is applied to the student weights, with η_S as the student network's learning rate [8].

$$\theta_S' = \theta_S - \eta_S \nabla_{\theta_S} \mathcal{L}_u(\theta_T, \theta_S) \tag{3}$$

The teacher network's step function, Eq. (4), details how the combination of gradients from the teacher model, and the student model, are utilized to update the weights of the teacher network [8].

$$\theta'_T = \theta_T - \eta_T \nabla_{\theta_S} \mathcal{L}_l(\theta_S - \nabla_{\theta_S} \mathcal{L}_u(\theta_T, \theta_S)) \tag{4}$$

A more detailed breakdown of the steps involved in this process and how the various losses are combined is visualized in Fig. 1.

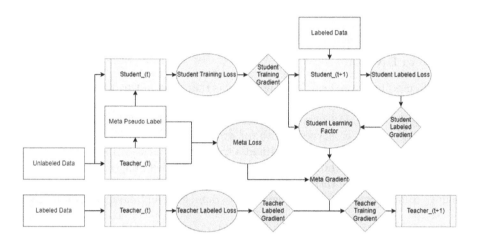

Fig. 1. A flow diagram showing the training process of MPL, including how gradients are calculated and applied. White boxes represent image tensors; orange double-edged boxes represent models (the FPN architecture used by AxonDeep); blue ovals represent losses or singular numerical values; green diamonds represent gradients. Detailed equations for each step of the flow diagram can be found in [8] (Color figure online)

3   Experimental Methods

3.1   Data Collection

The data used in this work is the same dataset used by AxonDeep [4], which used mice as an animal model. All of the mice in this study were originally purchased from The Jackson Laboratory (Bar Harbor, ME). All animals were treated in accordance with the ARVO Statement for the Use of Animals in Ophthalmic and Vision Research. All experiment protocols were approved by the Institutional Animal Care and Use Committee of the University of Iowa. Further information can be found in [4].

3.2 Data Acquisition

A detailed description of how the optic nerves were extracted can be found in [7,12]. A brief overview of this process is as follows: the mice were euthanized with carbon dioxide inhalation, decapitated, and skulls were opened and immersion-fixed in half-strength Karnovsky's fixative. Optic nerves were subsequently dissected, rinsed, dehydrated, infiltrated, and embedded in resin (Eponate-12; Ted Pella, Redding, CA), and polymerized in a 65° C oven. Semithin (1-µm) cross sections were cut, transferred to glass slides, stained with 1% paraphenylenediamine, mounted with cover slips, and imaged by light microscopy.

3.3 Data Division

The data used in AxonDeep [4] is the same as that used in this work. In brief, 56 optic nerves from 38 mice were split into a training (28 nerves), validation (10 nerves), and testing (18 nerves) set. One image (1024×1024) was taken from each of the non-severe nerves to use for ground truth results. The 28 training nerves included 2 severe nerves and had a total of 50 images (4140×3096) gathered as unlabeled data (note that the 1024×1024 labeled images for the training set were sub-samples of these 4140×3096 images) [4]. The labeled datasets had a roughly equal amount of no-damage, mildly damaged, and moderately damaged nerves.

This work used the same experimental datasets as AxonDeep to provide an accurate model for comparison. The four experiments utilized different quantities of the 26 labeled training images: 10% (2 images), 25% (6 images), 50% (13 images), and 100% (26 images) [4]. For this work, we used the same randomly sampled image sets as used in the AxonDeep paper. The division of the four experimental training datasets were as follows: 10% (2 labeled, 50 unlabeled), 25% (6 labeled, 50 unlabeled), 50% (13 labeled, 50 unlabeled), 100% (26 labeled, 50 unlabeled) [4].

4 Results

4.1 Segmentation Results

The results of the experiment were compared using a Dice score, measuring the overlap between the predicted segmentation and the ground truth [3]. Table 1 shows the Dice values of each model when trained with various percentages of the labeled data. Meta Pseudo Labels provides consistently good Dice scores, providing similar results to the best of the AxonDeep models even with only 10% of the labeled training data. Visual outputs for grade 2 (moderate damage) and grade 1 (mild or no damage) corresponding to the Dice results can be seen in Fig. 2. When trained on 100% of the labeled data, the MPL approach demonstrated significantly larger Dice coefficients than AxonDeep ($n = 18$, paired t-test, $p = 0.0011$).

Table 1. The average Dice scores on the manually traced contours of the test set (n = 18), and the segmentation results of AxonDeep (FCN), AxonDeep (GAN), and Meta Pseudo Labels. This calculation is repeated for each experiment, where 10%, 25%, 50%, and 100% of the labeled data was used in training. Results for FCN and GAN AxonDeep are as found in the AxonDeep paper [4].

Dice Coefficient Scores			
% Labeled Data	AxonDeep(FCN)	AxonDeep(GAN)	MPL
100%	0.80	0.81	0.84
50%	0.79	0.80	0.81
25%	0.78	0.78	0.81
10%	0.57	0.71	0.81

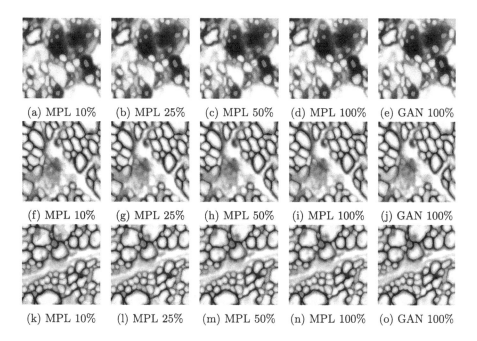

(a) MPL 10%   (b) MPL 25%   (c) MPL 50%   (d) MPL 100%   (e) GAN 100%

(f) MPL 10%   (g) MPL 25%   (h) MPL 50%   (i) MPL 100%   (j) GAN 100%

(k) MPL 10%   (l) MPL 25%   (m) MPL 50%   (n) MPL 100%   (o) GAN 100%

Fig. 2. Example results using variations of the models for grade 2 (moderate damage, row 1) and grade 1 (mild or no damage, rows 2–3) images. Each row (a–e), (f–j), (k–o) shows the results on the same image with a changing model, as designated by the subcaption. Each column (a, f, k), (b, g, l), (c, h, m), (d, i, n), and (e, j, o) show the results of the same model on three different images. The foreground is made up of 3 colors: correctly classified pixels are green, false positive classifications are cyan, and false negative classifications are magenta. (Color figure online)

Further details of the Dice results when trained with 100% of the training data, as well as the additional expert, can be found in Table 2. This table separates the Dice score averages between the grade 1 and grade 2 test images, allow-

ing for insight into the performance based on the level of damage to the optic
nerve [4]. Using a paired t-test, the MPL approach demonstrated significantly
larger Dice coefficients over AxonDeep for grade 2 images ($n = 6$, $p = 0.0026$),
but not for grade 1 images ($n = 12$, $p = 0.3025$). Figure 3 shows visual segmentations from Expert 2 as well as AxonDeep (GAN) and the Meta Pseudo Labels
method.

Table 2. A breakdown of the Dice segmentation results for AxonDeep when trained
as a Fully Connected Network (FCN), Generative Adversarial Network (GAN), and
Meta Pseudo Labels (MPL), with 100% of the available labeled data. 'Healthy' refers
to grade-1 images, having mild or no damage, and 'Damaged' refers to grade-2 images,
having moderate damage. Results for FCN and GAN AxonDeep are as found in the
AxonDeep paper [4].

	Expert 2	AxonDeep (FCN)	AxonDeep (GAN)	Meta Pseudo Labels
Dice (All)	0.78	0.80	0.81	0.84
(Healthy)	0.77	0.82	0.83	0.83
(Damaged)	0.82	0.75	0.77	0.85

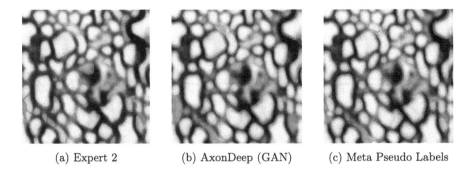

(a) Expert 2   (b) AxonDeep (GAN)   (c) Meta Pseudo Labels

Fig. 3. Example results with respect to the ground truth: (a) Expert 2, (b) AxonDeep
(GAN), (c) Meta Pseudo Labels. The foreground is made up of 3 colors: correctly
classified pixels are green, false positive classifications are cyan, and false negative
classifications are magenta. (Color figure online)

4.2   Axon Counts

A secondary metric for comparing the performance of the models is based on
the number of axons counted in the segmentation. The axons were counted
using a post-processing script that removed small objects, filled small holes, and
applied a watershed algorithm to provide final counts [4]. The results provided

for MPL used the same script that provided the AxonDeep results. This was done to reduce the differences between the original AxonDeep experiments and the MPL experiment; a post-processing script that is more mindful of the outputs the MPL model provides may have improved axon count results.

Two metrics were performed for the axon count results, a Pearson R Correlation Coefficient, and an average absolute percent difference [1]. For these two metrics, the AxonDeep model did perform better than the MPL model. Axon-Deep (GAN) has R values of 0.83, 0.90, 0.96, and 0.97 when trained with 10%, 25%, 50%, and 100% of labeled training data, respectively. The MPL model has R values of 0.86, 0.90, 0.89, and 0.94 when trained with each respective amount of labeled training data. The absolute percent difference between the AxonDeep counts and the ground truth counts were 9.4%, 6.2%, 4.3%, and 4.4%, compared to MPL's 9.6%, 8.6%, 8.8%, and 6.1% respectively [4]. A second expert was used as a baseline in the original AxonDeep experiment, who achieved an R correlation coefficient of 0.93 and an absolute percent difference of 6.6%, where the reference was expert 1. While the axon count results of MPL were slightly worse than AxonDeep (GAN) with respect to expert 1, the MPL method did achieve a similar level to that of expert 2, at least matching the baseline skill of an expert.

5   Discussion

Meta Pseudo Labels has shown that it yields excellent segmentation results, even with access to extremely limited labeled training data. MPL was able to match the Dice score of AxonDeep with access to 10% of the training data. With 100% of the training data, MPL has shown statistically significant improvement over AxonDeep for moderately damaged optic nerves. These segmentation results provide meaningful shape and area data that is not practical to produce through manual methods.

5.1   Limitations

A limitation of the current method and results is its dependence on a post-processing script in order to provide the axon count of the output. The experiments performed in this work utilized the same axon counting script used for AxonDeep. AxonDeep produces a probability map where there is only a high degree of certainty, establishing a high contrast between axon regions and non-axon regions; making thresholding relatively easy. The results produced by MPL have a lower contrast probability, including regions of high confidence and lower confidence. This leads to a situation where the thresholding process may include partial segmentations due to the lower confidence regions and potentially have an adverse effect on the number of axons within the output. Figure 4 shows a visual of this difference for a moderately damaged optic nerve.

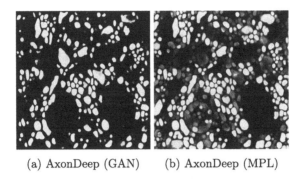

(a) AxonDeep (GAN)   (b) AxonDeep (MPL)

Fig. 4. An overlay of the final segmentation (green) on the probability map output generated by AxonDeep (GAN) and MPL models when trained with 100% of labeled training data on a moderately damaged nerve demonstrating a current challenge/limitation of applying the same AxonDeep-post-processing step to the MPL results. The background is the probability map provided by each model, with 0-valued (black) regions indicating non-axons and 1-valued (white) indicating axons. The foreground (semi-transparent green) is the resulting segmentation after post-processing occurs. Note the green from the foreground covers most of the white from the background. (a) Probability map and segmentation from AxonDeep (GAN), (b) Probability map and segmentation from MPL. (Color figure online)

6   Conclusion

Applying a Meta Pseudo Labels (MPL) algorithm to train a neural network architecture to accurately segment axons in optic nerve images has shown good results overall. The results of the Dice scores in Table 1 show that MPL was able to yield improved segmentations with limited access to labeled data. This provides a solid foundation for establishing the MPL training method as a way to fine-tune a pre-trained model on a new data modality with significantly reduced labeled training data.

Acknowledgements. This study was supported, in part, by the U.S. Department of Veterans Affairs (I50RX003002, I01RX003797, and I01 RX001481), and the National Institutes of Health (T32DK112751, P30 EY025580, and R21 EY029991).

References

1. Akoglu, H.: User's guide to correlation coefficients. Turkish J. Emergency Med. **18**(3), 91–93 (2018)
2. Anderson, M.G., et al.: Genetic context determines susceptibility to intraocular pressure elevation in a mouse pigmentary glaucoma. BMC Biol. **4**, 1–11 (2006)
3. Bertels, J., et al.: Optimizing the Dice score and Jaccard index for medical image segmentation: theory and practice. In: Shen, D., et al. (eds.) MICCAI 2019. LNCS, vol. 11765, pp. 92–100. Springer, Cham (2019). https://doi.org/10.1007/978-3-030-32245-8_11

4. Deng, W., et al.: AxonDeep: automated optic nerve axon segmentation in mice with deep learning. Transl. Vision Sci. Technol. **10**(14), 22–22 (2021)
5. Goyal, V., et al.: AxoNet 2.0: a deep learning-based tool for morphometric analysis of retinal ganglion cell axons. Transl. Vision Sci. Technol. **12**(3), 9–9 (2023)
6. LeCun, Y., Bengio, Y., Hinton, G.: Deep learning. Nature **521**(7553), 436–444 (2015)
7. Mao, M., Hedberg-Buenz, A., Koehn, D., John, S.W., Anderson, M.G.: Anterior segment dysgenesis and early-onset glaucoma in nee mice with mutation of Sh3pxd2b. Invest. Ophthalmol. Visual Sci. **52**(5), 2679–2688 (2011)
8. Pham, H., Dai, Z., Xie, Q., Le, Q.V.: Meta pseudo labels. In: Proceedings of the IEEE/CVF Conference on Computer Vision and Pattern Recognition, pp. 11557–11568 (2021)
9. Reynaud, J.: Automated quantification of optic nerve axons in primate glaucomatous and normal eyes—method and comparison to semi-automated manual quantification. Investi. Ophthalmol. Visual Sci. **53**(6), 2951–2959 (2012)
10. Ritch, M.D., et al.: AxoNet: a deep learning-based tool to count retinal ganglion cell axons. Sci. Rep. **10**(1), 1–13 (2020)
11. Wang, Y., Zhang, J., Kan, M., Shan, S., Chen, X.: Self-supervised equivariant attention mechanism for weakly supervised semantic segmentation. In: Proceedings of the IEEE/CVF Conference on Computer Vision and Pattern Recognition, pp. 12275–12284 (2020)
12. Zarei, K., et al.: Automated axon counting in rodent optic nerve sections with AxonJ. Sci. Rep. **6**(1), 26559 (2016)

Privileged Modality Guided Network for Retinal Vessel Segmentation in Ultra-Wide-Field Images

Xuefei Li[1,2], Huaying Hao[1], Huazhu Fu[3], Dan Zhang[4], Da Chen[5], Yuchuan Qiao[6], Jiang Liu[7], Yitian Zhao[1(✉)], and Jiong Zhang[1(✉)]

[1] Institute of Biomedical Engineering, Ningbo Institute of Materials Technology and Engineering, Chinese Academy of Sciences, Ningbo, China
{yitian.zhao,zhangjiong}@nimte.ac.cn
[2] University of Chinese Academy of Sciences, Beijing, China
[3] Institute of High Performance Computing, A*STAR, Singapore, Singapore
[4] School of Cyber Science and Engineering, Ningbo University of Technology, Ningbo, China
[5] Shandong Artificial Intelligence Institute, Jinan, China
[6] Institute of Science and Technology for Brain-Inspired Intelligence, Fudan University, Shanghai, China
[7] Department of Computer Science and Engineering, Southern University of Science and Technology, Shenzhen, China

Abstract. Retinal vessel segmentation in ophthalmic images is an essential task to support the computer-aided diagnosis of eye-related diseases. As a non-invasive imaging technique, ultra-wide-field (UWF) fundus imaging provides a large field-of-view (FOV) of 200° with full coverage of the retinal territory, making it a suitable modality for vessel analysis. However, imaging the large FOV may result in low-contrast vascular details and background artifacts, which pose challenges to the accurate segmentation of retinal microvasculature. To address these issues, a privileged modality guided multi-scale location-aware fusion network is proposed for vessel segmentation in UWF images. We first perform style transfer on the UWF images to generate the corresponding FFA image with higher contrast. Afterwards, we employ cross-modal coherence loss to segment the vessels guided by the FFA image. Additionally, a multi-scale location-aware fusion module is proposed and embedded into the segmentation network for reducing the boundary artifacts. Finally, experiments are performed on a dedicated UWF dataset, and the evaluation results demonstrate that our method achieves competitive vessel segmentation performance with a Dice score of around 78.13%. This indicates that our method is potentially valuable for subsequent vessel analysis to support disease diangosis.

Keywords: UWF · Vessel segmentation · Privileged modality · Location-aware

ⓒ The Author(s), under exclusive license to Springer Nature Switzerland AG 2023
B. Antony et al. (Eds.): OMIA 2023, LNCS 14096, pp. 82–91, 2023.
https://doi.org/10.1007/978-3-031-44013-7_9

1   Introduction

The morphological changes of retinal vessels are crucial markers for guiding oph-thalmic disease diagnosis and treatment planning. In clinical practice, color fun-dus photography and fundus fluorescence angiography (FFA) are commonly used retinal imaging techniques [1]. Among these, FFA is typically considered as the golden standard for observing pathological alterations in vessel flow. However, FFA is invasive, difficult to acquire, and can have serious side effects. Therefore, color fundus photography has been extensively analyzed in numerous computer-aided diagnosis tasks [2,3]. Conventional color fundus images typically have a limited field-of-view (FOV) of 45°, providing only the central retina morphology to assist ophthalmologist. In contrast, UWF fundus imaging, as a non-invasive imaging technique, allows for a complete visualization of retinal fundus struc-tures with a FOV over 200° [4]. UWF images provide superior observation of ves-sels and lesions in the retinal periphery with rich pathological features, and are thus of great value to support clinical analysis. Over the past decade, numerous efforts have been dedicated to fundus vessel segmentation, including filtering [3], morphological [5], statistical [6] and deep learning algorithms [7]. However, these methods focus on vessel segmentation based on color fundus images. Limited studies [8,9] have explored the potential of extracting comprehensive vascular structures from UWF images. Pellegrini et al. [8] proposed a supervised method using multi-scale matched filters for vessel segmentation in UWF of view scan-ning laser ophthalmoscope (UWFoV SLO) images. Ding et al. [9] proposed a deep learning framework for efficient vessel detection in UWF fundus photog-raphy (FP). Although these methods are capable of extracting primary vessel structures from UWF images, they still face challenges in accurately segmenting low-contrast details and mitigating background artifacts. In comparison, FFA image offers a high-contrast reference for vessel structures, making it a potential tool to aid vessel segmentation in UWF images.

Style transfer learning [10] has been developed to facilitate the translation of samples between different domains. It has been demonstrated to be useful for image enhancement and the subsequent segmentation task. This techinique has been applied to domain adaption of multi-modal medical images to assist downstream tasks. For instance, Peng et al. [10] employed StyleGAN to perform translation between OCT and OCT-A images for precise vessel segmentation. Ju et al. [4] proposed a novel modification to the CycleGAN model, aiming to bridge the gap between color fundus images and UWF images. Their objective was to generate UWF images specifically for downstream task training. These applica-tions have motivated our investigation into cross-modal assisted vessel segmen-tation using style transfer. Consequently, in this paper, we propose to utilize a style transfer model to perform the translation from ultra-wide-field (UWF) images to fundus fluorescence angiography (FFA) images for the enhancement of vascular details.

Moreover, the ultra-high resolution of UWF images poses challenges for vessel segmentation performance. Currently, most segmentation networks use patch-based techniques to mitigate the computational demands of high-resolution images. However, such methods primarily focus on local features and may over-look the global relationship between vessels and their surrounding tissue. Recent works [11,12] have proposed multi-stream networks that extract and merge global and local features, thereby enhancing the contextual association informa-tion of local patches. These works effectively address the issue of context omission during local patch training. Motivated by these advancements, we introduce a local-aware context fusion module into the UWF vessel segmentation network to alleviate vessel breakage caused by missing contexts.

In this paper, we propose a privileged guided multi-scale position-aware fusion network framework for vessel segmentation of UWF images. We aim to generate FFA images using higher contrast FFA images aided by UWF images and train a more accurate fundus vessel segmentation model by the generated FFA images with consistency loss guided by UWF images. Additionally, we employ the local perception fusion module (LPFM) to improve the local seg-mentation accuracy. The main contributions are summarized as follows:

(a) We propose to perform a style transfer strategy to transform UWF image to FFA image, aiming to enhance the visibility of vessel details;
(b) Considering the large scale variations within UWF images, we propose to embed a multi-scale local perception fusion module into the segmentation network to improve the ability for perceiving local context;
(c) Our work presents the attempt to incorporate privileged modality consis-tency loss to guide the vessel segmentation in UWF images.

2   Methodology

2.1   Overall Architecture

Our objective is to incorporate FFA images into the network to facilitate the training of the segmentation network and enhance vessel segmentation accuracy through privileged modality consistency loss. The core of our proposed frame-work is a cross-modal fundus vessel segmentation framework, comprising a local perception fusion module and two contrast consistency losses. Additional FFA images are generated using a CycleGAN-based UWF-FA converter. The overall architecture is illustrated in Fig. 1.

We utilize a paired UWF dataset X_i and an FFA dataset C_i. By employing the CycleGAN model, we transform the UWF sample domain into the FFA sample domain, resulting in a new image set Y_i. This conversion enables the enhancement of vessel contrast and improves the capability of assisting in the segmentation of UWF images.

Afterwards, we feed X_i and Y_i into E_x and E_y to obtain the hidden space feature maps Z_x and Z_y, respectively, where E_y is a ResNet [13] block-based encoder and E_x is an encoder with a local perception fusion module. These feature maps are then passed through two shared decoders, resulting in seg-mentation predictions M_x and M_y. Finally, M_x is fed into a pooling refinement module and a small U-shaped network to obtain the final segmentation results

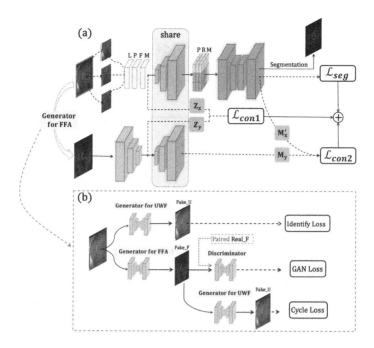

Fig. 1. The attainment of the final result involves a two-step procedure. Initially, FFA images are generated through the utilization of method (b). Subsequently, both the FFA and UWF images are fed as inputs into method (a).(a) The framework of the proposed method; (b) The training process of the generator network of FFA.

M_x'. During the training process, the consistent regularization module is introduced to align the hidden spaces Z_x and Z_y as well as M_x' and M_y. This module enhances the network's ability to detect minute blood vessels by leveraging the high-contrast characteristics of vessels in the enhanced images. During testing, we omit the need for the enhancement model and solely output more precise vessel segmentation results through network segmentation. In the subsequent sections, we will primarily focus on presenting the vessel extraction network and the consistent regularization loss.

2.2 Consistency Regularization Loss

In the generative model, we transform the UWF image domain into the FFA image domain, resulting in synthetic FFA images. However, it is important to note that the generated FFA images might not be able to precisely represent the realistic FFA images. Thus, the utilization of the generated FFA images for direct segmentation may not yield significant improvements in accuracy.

Semi-supervised learning usually enhances the generalization capability of a model by incorporating unsupervised regularized loss terms [14–16]. These loss terms compare the prediction results obtained by perturbing unlabeled data with

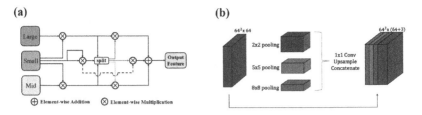

Fig. 2. (a) The architecture of the LPFM; (b) The architecture of the PRM.

the normal prediction results. In our research, the synthetic FFA images and the UWF images contain the same vessel information, ensuring consistency in the prediction results. To enhance the segmentation of low-contrast vessels in UWF images, we introduce a consistency regularization module guided by FFA images. This module aims to improve the model's ability to recognize low-contrast vessel information in UWF images without sacrificing valuable information.

The structure of this module is presented in Fig. 1. Firstly, the UWF images and the generated FFA images are separately fed into the encoder in a chunking manner. Subsequently, the UWF images are processed by the local perception fusion module to optimize local features. Then, we obtain the high-dimensional information Z_x and Z_y which are passed through the shared decoder to obtain the preliminary segmentation results M_x and M_y. Finally, M_x is fed into a pooling refinement module and a small U-shaped network to obtain the final segmentation results $M_x^{'}$. To enforce consistency, we employ the SmoothL1loss [17] to control the distances of Z_x and Z_y, as well as between $M_x^{'}$ and M_y. The overall loss function combines the final segmentation loss and the consistency regularization loss:

$$\mathcal{L}_{all} = \mathcal{L}_{seg} + \alpha\mathcal{L}_{con1} + \beta\mathcal{L}_{con2}, \tag{1}$$

where $\mathcal{L}_{seg}$ represents the distance between the final segmentation result and label, and where $\mathcal{L}_{con1}$ and $\mathcal{L}_{con2}$ represent the distance between Z_x and Z_y, $M_x^{'}$ and M_y, respectively. After experimentation, we found that assigning values of 0.6 for α and 0.4 for β yielded the most suitable results.

2.3   Vessel Extraction Network

Due to the relatively large size of UWF images, vessel segmentation networks require a trade-off between accuracy and computational resources. Common strategies such as down-sampling, patch cropping, and cascade models, can hardly solve the balance between accuracy and computational cost. Therefore, we introduce an efficient cropping method [11] to randomly crop the original image size of 3900×3072 to obtain a patch size of 256×256, which we define as small patch. A contextual location-aware fusion module is employed to enhance the contextual location features of local patches of different scales. The specific steps are shown in Fig. 2. Based on the small patches, we cut two medium patches and large patches of different scales, with sizes of 512×512 and 768×768, respectively. Then we scale the three patches into the same size and input them into three feature extractors (ResNet) to obtain the respective high-dimensional features of different scales. After that, we separately calculate the inner product of the small patch and the other two patches, and get the attention graph by Softmax. Then, the attention graph and the small patch are inner product to get the new feature graph. We regularize the three feature maps and reassign weights to them, followed by a fusion step among them to obtain the hidden vector Z_x. Through this module, the vessel segmentation network can enhance the relevant features of the local patches and refine the vessel edges. Finally, we input Z_x into the decoder to obtain the preliminary segmentation results.

In order to optimize the segmentation of fine vessels, the initial segmentation results are fed into the spatial pooling refinement module (PRM). The specific structure is shown in Fig. 2. We utilize three maximal pooling layers with respective kernel sizes of 2, 5, and 8 to enhance the network's perceptual field in the feature map. The specific definition of the module is given by:

$$y = V(C(P_1(x) + P_2(x) + P_3(x) + x)), \tag{2}$$

where P_i represents the different pooling layers and V represents the convolutional layers. x represents the input information of the module, C represents the concat layer, while y represents the final output information. Furthermore, to extract deeper semantic information, we employed a compact encoder-decoder architecture to effectively optimize the segmentation of fine vessels. It is composed of encoder-decoder blocks inspired by ResNet. We finally use Dice loss to optimize the training process of the network.

3   Experiments and Results

3.1   Data Description

We evaluate the proposed method using an in-house UWF dataset comprising 65 fundus images captured from a local hospital using an Optos 200Tx device. These images have an imaging resolution of 3900×3072 pixels and include patients with venous obstruction as well as healthy individuals. Additionally, we utilized a corresponding FFA dataset consisting of 65 FFA images acquired using Heidelberg Eye Version 10.2.0, representing the same population as the UWF dataset. The vessel labels of UWF images were completely annotated by experienced ophthalmologists using the ITK-snap annotation tool. All images were acquired with regulatory approvals and patient consents as appropriate.

3.2   Implementation Details

Prior to the experiments, we preprocessed the UWF images using contrast adaptive histogram equalization method to initially enhance the image contrast. In our implementation, the dataset consisted of 65 images, with 20 images allocated for the test set and the remaining 45 images used for training. To ensure consistency, all images were resized to a dimension of 1024×1024 pixels, and the input patches were further resized to 256×256 pixels. During the experimental process, data augmentation techniques such as random flipping and rotation were employed. For optimization, we utilized the Adam optimizer with recommended parameters. The batch size and sub-batch size were set to 15. We set the training process with a maximum of 100 epochs that allows the model to converge and capture the underlying patterns in the data.

3.3   Ablation Study

We conducted experiments to evaluate the performance of our vessel segmentation method and the effectiveness of each module. Different baselines were compared in these experiments using the same image cropping method and exclusively tested on UWF images. Net_1: ResUnet segmentation model trained using UWF images. Net_1^*: Improved ResUnet-based vessel extraction network segmentation model trained on UWF images. Net_1^{**}: Net_1^* model with an addition of the local feature-aware fusion module, trained on UWF images only. $Ours$: Based on Net_1^{**}, we add the consistency regularization module and train the network using UWF images and FFA images. Four metrics, i.e., Dice coefficient, sensitivity (SEN), false discovery rate (FDR), and balanced accuracy (BACC) were employed to assess the network's performance in vessel segmentation.

Table 1 presents the segmentation performance of various experimental methods. Specifically, our final method obtains the highest scores among them. The Dice obtained using Net_1^* is 0.91% better than using Net_1, thus showing that the refinement module as well as the dual codec improves the network's segmentation performance on vessels. Furthermore, the sequential incorporation of the local perception fusion module and the consistency regularization module yields noticeable improvements in Dice, SEN, and BACC, while progressively optimizing the FDR. These findings highlight the positive impact of both the added local perception fusion module and the consistency regularization module on the model's segmentation performance. Our final method optimizes 3.42%, 6.63%, 6.63%, and 3.25% in Dice, FDR, SEN, and BACC over Resunet.

3.4   Comparisons with State-of-the-Art Methods

We evaluated the effectiveness of the following state-of-the-art vessel segmentation methods using Dice, sensitivity (SEN), FDR, and BACC as metrics: U-Net [18], CE-Net [19], CS-Net [20], TransUnet [21] and SwinUnet [22]. As shown in Table 1, the proposed method outperformed these methods in terms of metrics. Our proposed method demonstratded its superiority in vessel segmentation. Among the evaluated methods, CS-Net exhibited subpar segmentation results, potentially attributed to overfitting caused by the limited size of the dataset. On the other hand, among the remaining methods, CE-Net demonstrated superior overall performance. This could be attributed to its capability to capture

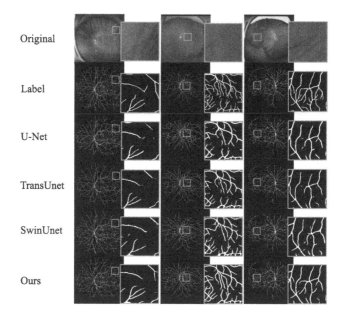

Fig. 3. Visualized results on the different methods.

Table 1. Vessel Performance of different segmentation methods on UWF Images.

Methods	Dice (%) ↑	FDR (%) ↓	SEN (%) ↑	BACC (%) ↑
Net_1	74.71 ± 0.48	26.67±2.56	73.33±2.56	86.05±1.17
Net_1^*	75.62±0.46	23.25±1.83	76.75±1.83	87.54±0.97
Net_1^{**}	76.38±0.52	24.14±2.38	75.85±2.38	87.24±1.11
U-Net [18]	73.14 ± 0.82	28.12 ± 2.62	71.88 ± 2.62	85.34 ± 1.22
CE-Net [19]	72.64 ± 0.55	29.20 ± 2.71	77.55 ± 3.35	87.71 ± 1.66
CS-Net [20]	68.50 ± 5.54	39.82 ± 7.54	60.18 ± 7.54	79.69 ± 3.66
TransUnet [21]	74.75 ± 0.76	31.18 ± 3.38	68.82 ± 3.39	83.95 ± 1.64
SwinUnet [22]	73.64 ± 0.94	28.20 ± 2.98	71.80 ± 2.98	85.24 ± 1.47
Ours	**78.13 ± 0.73**	**20.04 ± 2.57**	**79.96 ± 2.57**	**89.30 ± 1.22**

higher-level information and preserve the spatial details required for UWF image segmentation, which provides a competitive advantage.

Figure 3 depicts the results of our proposed method for vessel segmentation on UWF images. It can be seen from the images that the our methods can effectively segment the fine vessels of UWF images with low contrast. However, these comparison approaches cannot completely segment all the vessel regions when the peripheral vessel contrast of the images is too low. Nevertheless, even in such challenging scenarios, our method consistently outperforms other methods.

4 Conclusion

In this paper, we have presented an investigation of a cross-modal guided multi-scale local perception fusion network framework for vessel segmentation in UWF fundus images. Our proposed framework leverages high-contrast FFA images, i.e., the clinical golden standard, to aid in vessel segmentation of UWF images. Specifically, we have exploited the vessel segmentation from UWF images by using highlighted vessel features from the generated FFA images through consistent regularization loss. Furthermore, we have embed a multi-scale local perception fusion module in the network to capture contextual information for local feature extraction, thereby aiming to enhance the segmentation accuracy of high-resolution UWF images. Experimental validation has demonstrated the competitive performance of our approach in the vessel segmentation of UWF fundus images.

References

1. Kashani, A.H., et al.: Optical coherence tomography angiography: a comprehensive review of current methods and clinical applications. Prog. Retin. Eye Res. **60**, 66–100 (2017)
2. Dashtbozorg, B., Zhang, J., Huang, F., ter Haar Romeny, B.M.: Retinal microaneurysms detection using local convergence index features. IEEE Trans. Image Process. **27**(7), 3300–3315 (2018)
3. Zhang, J., Dashtbozorg, B., Bekkers, E.J., Pluim, J.P.W., Duits, R., Romeny, B.M.T.H.: Robust retinal vessel segmentation via locally adaptive derivative frames in orientation scores. IEEE Trans. Med. Imaging (2016)
4. Ju, L., Wang, X., Zhao, X., Bonnington, P., Drummond, T., Ge, Z.: Leveraging regular fundus images for training UWF fundus diagnosis models via adversarial learning and pseudo-labeling. IEEE Trans. Med. Imaging **40**(10), 2911–2925 (2021)
5. Fraz, M.M., Basit, A., Barman, S.: Application of morphological bit planes in retinal blood vessel extraction. J. Dig. Imaging **26**, 274–286 (2013)
6. Orlando, J.I., Prokofyeva, E., Blaschko, M.B.: A discriminatively trained fully connected conditional random field model for blood vessel segmentation in fundus images. IEEE Trans. Biomed. Eng. **64**, 16–27 (2017)
7. Wu, Y., Xia, Y., Song, Y., Zhang, Y., Cai, W.: Multiscale network followed network model for retinal vessel segmentation. In: Frangi, A.F., Schnabel, J.A., Davatzikos, C., Alberola-López, C., Fichtinger, G. (eds.) MICCAI 2018. LNCS, vol. 11071, pp. 119–126. Springer, Cham (2018). https://doi.org/10.1007/978-3-030-00934-2_14
8. Pellegrini, E., et al.: Blood vessel segmentation and width estimation in ultra-wide field scanning laser ophthalmoscopy. Biomed. Opt. Express **5**(12), 4329–4337 (2014)
9. Ding, L., Kuriyan, A.E., Ramchandran, R.S., Wykoff, C.C., Sharma, G.: Weakly-supervised vessel detection in ultra-widefield fundus photography via iterative multi-modal registration and learning. IEEE Trans. Med. Imaging **40**(10), 2748–2758 (2020)
10. Peng, L., Lin, L., Cheng, P., Huang, Z., Tang, X.: Unsupervised domain adaptation for cross-modality retinal vessel segmentation via disentangling representation style transfer and collaborative consistency learning. In: IEEE 19th International Symposium on Biomedical Imaging (ISBI). IEEE 2022, pp. 1–5 (2022)

11. Chen, W., Jiang, Z., Wang, Z., Cui, K., Qian, X.: Collaborative global-local networks for memory-efficient segmentation of ultra-high resolution images. In: Proceedings of the IEEE/CVF Conference on Computer Vision and Pattern Recognition, pp. 8924–8933 (2019)

12. Li, Q., Yang, W., Liu, W., Yu, Y., He, S.: From contexts to locality: ultra-high resolution image segmentation via locality-aware contextual correlation. In: Proceedings of the IEEE/CVF International Conference on Computer Vision, pp. 7252–7261 (2021)

13. Zhang, Z., Liu, Q., Wang, Y.: Road extraction by deep residual u-net. IEEE Geosci. Remote Sens. Lett. **15**(5), 749–753 (2018)

14. Wu, Y., Xu, M., Ge, Z., Cai, J., Zhang, L.: Semi-supervised left atrium segmentation with mutual consistency training. In: de Bruijne, M., et al. (eds.) MICCAI 2021. LNCS, vol. 12902, pp. 297–306. Springer, Cham (2021). https://doi.org/10.1007/978-3-030-87196-3_28

15. Verma, V., et al.: Interpolation consistency training for semi-supervised learning. Neural Netw. **145**, 90–106 (2022)

16. Zhao, X., Fang, C., Fan, D.J., Lin, X., Gao, F., Li, G.: Cross-level contrastive learning and consistency constraint for semi-supervised medical image segmentation. In: 2022 IEEE 19th International Symposium on Biomedical Imaging (ISBI), pp. 1–5. IEEE (2022)

17. Girshick, R.: Fast R-CNN. In: Proceedings of the IEEE International Conference on Computer Vision, pp. 1440–1448

18. Ronneberger, O., Fischer, P., Brox, T.: U-net: convolutional networks for biomedical image segmentation. In: Navab, N., Hornegger, J., Wells, W.M., Frangi, A.F. (eds.) MICCAI 2015. LNCS, vol. 9351, pp. 234–241. Springer, Cham (2015). https://doi.org/10.1007/978-3-319-24574-4_28

19. Gu, Z., et al.: Ce-net: context encoder network for 2d medical image segmentation. IEEE Trans. Med. Imaging **38**(10), 2281–2292 (2019)

20. Mou, L., Zhao, Y., Chen, L., Cheng, J., Gu, Z., Hao, H., Qi, H., Zheng, Y., Frangi, A., Liu, J.: CS-Net: Channel and Spatial Attention Network for Curvilinear Structure Segmentation. In: Shen, D., Liu, T., Peters, T.M., Staib, L.H., Essert, C., Zhou, S., Yap, P.-T., Khan, A. (eds.) MICCAI 2019. LNCS, vol. 11764, pp. 721–730. Springer, Cham (2019). https://doi.org/10.1007/978-3-030-32239-7_80

21. Chen, J., et al.: Transunet: transformers make strong encoders for medical image segmentation. arXiv preprint arXiv:2102.04306 (2021)

22. Cao, H., et al.: Swin-Unet: Unet-like pure transformer for medical image segmentation. In: Karlinsky, L., Michaeli, T., Nishino, K. (eds.) ECCV 2022, Part III. LNCS, vol. 13803, pp. 205–218. Springer, Cham (2022). https://doi.org/10.1007/978-3-031-25066-8_9

Adapting Segment Anything Model (SAM) for Retinal OCT

Botond Fazekas, José Morano, Dmitrii Lachinov, Guilherme Aresta,
and Hrvoje Bogunović$^{(\boxtimes)}$

Christian Doppler Laboratory for Artificial Intelligence in Retina, Department
of Ophthalmology and Optometry, Medical University of Vienna, Vienna, Austria
{botond.fazekas,hrvoje.bogunovic}@meduniwien.ac.at

Abstract. The Segment Anything Model (SAM) has gained significant attention in the field of image segmentation due to its impressive capabilities and prompt-based interface. While SAM has already been extensively evaluated in various domains, its adaptation to retinal OCT scans remains unexplored. To bridge this research gap, we conduct a comprehensive evaluation of SAM and its adaptations on a large-scale public dataset of OCTs from RETOUCH challenge. Our evaluation covers diverse retinal diseases, fluid compartments, and device vendors, comparing SAM against state-of-the-art retinal fluid segmentation methods. Through our analysis, we showcase adapted SAM's efficacy as a powerful segmentation model in retinal OCT scans, although still lagging behind established methods in some circumstances. The findings highlight SAM's adaptability and robustness, showcasing its utility as a valuable tool in retinal OCT image analysis and paving the way for further advancements in this domain.

1 Introduction

Optical coherence tomography (OCT) has become the gold-standard imaging modality in ophthalmology, in particular for retinal diseases affecting the macula and consequently the central vision, such as age-related macular degeneration (AMD), retinal vein occlusion (RVO), and diabetic macular edema (DME). Its ability to provide three-dimensional cross-sectional views of the retina in a fast and non-invasive manner has proven invaluable in the management of patients with neovascular AMD, RVO, and DME, characterized by the onset of fluid into the macula, and in guiding their treatment with anti-VEGF drugs [3]. However, in the current clinical practice, the clinical assessment of retinal fluid is still primarily qualitative, which is subjective, inaccurate, and time-consuming.

Deep learning has revolutionized the field of medical image analysis, with a high potential for empowering clinicians with robust second opinions, quantitative measures of biomarkers via image segmentation, and even (semi-)automation of the patient management workflow. The accurate segmentation of healthy and pathological biomarkers allows for quantitative analysis of these images, easing

B. Antony et al. (Eds.): OMIA 2023, LNCS 14096, pp. 92–101, 2023.
https://doi.org/10.1007/978-3-031-44013-7_10

early disease detection, monitoring, and patient follow-up. This made the self-configuring nnU-net [12] model especially popular as a go-to solution for training segmentation models for tasks in medical and ophthalmic imaging. However, the variety and complexity of the retinal anatomical structures and the low signal-to-noise ratio of OCT make this task still very challenging.

Recently, the deep learning community has focused on the development of foundation models [22]. These models leverage large-scale pre-training on massive datasets, enabling them to learn rich representations and capture intricate visual patterns. While the majority of such models were developed for the purpose of image interpretation, few targeted image segmentation task, likely the most important one for ophthalmic image analysis. This changed when Segment Anything Model (SAM) was introduced in April 2023 [17]. Trained on 11 million images and 1 billion masks, it demonstrated excellent capability in semantic segmentation of natural images, including *zero-shot* generalization. However, the potential of SAM for medical image segmentation is still unclear and is being extensively explored [32]. Specifically, SAM potential for retinal OCT segmentation, and how best to exploit it for this task is currently unknown.

In this paper, we examine the performance of SAM-based models for retinal OCT segmentation, for the purpose of measuring fluid volumes in an automated manner, the most important biomarkers for the management of patients with macular edema. We perform a large-scale evaluation of different SAM modalities on a public dataset originating from a MICCAI challenge [2]. We first analyze different SAM modalities, from a zero-shot setup to multi-click and box selection. Then, more importantly, we show that SAM can be effectively adapted and trained to become a powerful segmentation model in retinal OCT.

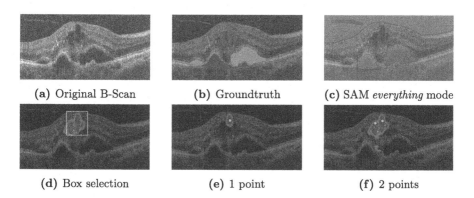

| (a) Original B-Scan | (b) Groundtruth | (c) SAM *everything* mode |
| (d) Box selection | (e) 1 point | (f) 2 points |

Fig. 1. An overview of the SAM segmentation modalities. In *everything* mode, the model returns the masks deemed by itself as the most important. By prompting it with a bounding box, the model reduces the search space within the box and returns the best-fitting mask from it. The model can be also prompted by providing positive positions (e.g. belonging to a region of interest (ROI)), or negative positions (not belonging to the ROI)

2   Background and Related Works

SAM Model. SAM is composed of three main components: an image encoder, a prompt encoder, and a mask decoder. The image encoder is a Vision Transformer (ViT) [6] that takes one image as input and outputs the image embedding. The prompt encoder has three different branches, one for each prompt type. The branch for mask prompts consists of a simple CNN; for points/boxes (Fig. 1), of a lightweight embedding module; and for text, of the text encoder of CLIP [25]. The mask decoder takes the embeddings from the image encoder and the prompt encoder as input and outputs the final segmentation mask. It consists of two modified Transformer decoder blocks followed by a segmentation head.

SAM for Medical Image Segmentation. Excelling at natural image segmentation, SAM provides a promising foundation for expert-level methods for analyzing medical data. However, its straightforward application encounters a number of challenges specific to medical image analysis. As discussed by Zhang et al. [32], structural complexity, low contrast and inter-observer variability limits zero-shot application of SAM. Furthermore, previous works [5, 11,14,15,27] confirm unsatisfactory performance for the majority of medical images, high dependence on the human prior knowledge (*i.e.*, the quality of the points/boxes) and unstable performance across different datasets. For these reasons, recent works have been focusing on fine-tuning SAM for fully automatic medical image segmentation.

Of the three components of SAM, most methods focus on adapting and fine-tuning the prompt encoder and the mask decoder, while keeping the image encoder frozen. Ma et al. [21] propose fine-tuning the mask decoder on a large set of multimodal medical images. Utilizing only box prompts, the method outperformed SAM by a large margin on 3D and 2D tasks. Although their fine-tuned models do not reach the level of specialized methods, the results highlight the potential of SAM for medical image analysis. Similarly, Hu et al. [10] propose to freeze SAM image encoder and train a lightweight task-specific prediction head, ignoring the prompt encoder. The method achieves promising results in a few-shot learning scenario. However, on a large dataset, the method proved to be inferior to U-Net [12]. SAMed [31] proposes to fine-tune the prompt encoder, its default input embedding, and the mask decoder of SAM, and apply a low-rank-based fine-tuning strategy (LoRA) [9] to the image encoder. Thus, only lightweight LoRA layers are fine-tuned, while the rest of the image encoder is kept frozen, highly reducing the training cost. SAMed comes close to the state of the art on Synapse multi-organ segmentation dataset. A similar approach is proposed by Wu et al. [29]. Following the popular NLP Adapter method [8], the authors propose to insert adapter modules at specific locations of the image encoder and the mask decoder of SAM. Moreover, the attention operation is split into two branches as 2D space + 1D depth to account for 3D images. Adapters are pre-trained using a self-supervised approach, and the model is trained using a combination of point and text prompts. The approach demonstrated competitive results on various medical tasks. DeSAM [7] proposes to fine-tune two modules added on top of the frozen image encoder and prompt encoder, to which random points or a full-size box are fed. The first module is a Transformer-based decoder that takes the outputs of both encoders and computes its embedding. Then, the second module, a U-Net-like decoder, processes this embedding and the features from the image encoder at different scales to produce the final segmentation. Authors reported that DeSAM surpassed other state-of-the-art methods on a cross-site private dataset. An extension of SAM to the domain of 3D medical images has been introduced by Lei et al. [19]. The method proposes a few-shot localization framework, MedLAM, for detecting 3D anatomical regions. The slices within selected region are then processed with SAM or MedSAM [21]. The method achieves moderate performance on a range of datasets.

3   Methods

Given an input image $\mathbf{x} \in \mathbb{R}^{H \times W}$, where H and W are the height and width of the image, respectively, we aim to obtain a segmentation mask $\mathbf{y} \in \mathbb{R}^{H \times W \times C}$, where C is the number of classes, using SAM-based models. In particular, we have chosen to focus on SAMed [31] for several reasons.

One key factor driving our decision is the lightweight image encoder fine-tuning solution of SAMed, which offers an efficient approach to adapt SAM for medical image segmentation. This allows us to fine-tune the model while keeping computational costs and storage requirements at a minimum.

Additionally, our decision was influenced by the limitations we encountered when attempting to achieve state-of-the-art results using some of the alternative models mentioned in the related works section. Despite our efforts, these models did not yield the desired performance levels on the retinal OCT fluid segmentation task we were addressing, or required extensive unsupervised pre-training [10,29]. Considering these factors, SAMed emerged as a promising adaptation method that addressed both the efficiency requirements and the need for improved performance. In the subsequent sections, we discuss the specific modifications introduced by SAMed and our training strategy.

SAM with LoRa. SAMed applies the LoRA technique [9] to the query and value projection layers of each transformer block in the image encoder of SAM. This technique serves as a bypass to achieve low-rank approximation in these layers. The authors of SAMed observed that applying LoRA only to these specific layers leads to improved performance.

To enable fast and automatic medical diagnosis during inference, SAMed eliminates the need for prompts. The default embedding utilized by the prompt encoder in SAM when no prompt is provided is retained and made trainable during the fine-tuning process. This ensures that the prompt encoder adapts and learns from the specific medical image segmentation tasks, enhancing its performance in handling different input scenarios.

SAMed introduces slight modifications to the segmentation head of the mask decoder in SAM. This modification customizes the output for each segmented semantic class, unlike the ambiguity prediction of SAM. SAMed predicts each semantic class of interest and the background in a deterministic manner, improving the interpretability and specificity of the segmentation results.

Training Strategy. SAMed utilizes both cross-entropy and dice losses to supervise the fine-tuning process. Similar to SAM, these losses are applied to the downsampled ground truth, as the output of SAMed has a lower spatial resolution compared to the input. During our experiments, we followed the training strategy suggested in SAMed, which involves using the AdamW optimizer with a warmup period, followed by an exponential learning rate decay.

4   Experimental Setup

To evaluate the enhancement achieved by the LoRA adaptation of the SAM model for retinal OCT scans, a comparative analysis was conducted against several baseline methods, including the original SAM model with point prompts, the SAM model with fine-tuned decoder, and state-of-the-art methods, including the methods participating in the MICCAI 2017 RETOUCH challenge [2], and the nnU-Net model [12].

Zero-Shot SAM with Point Prompts. To simulate the point prompts for the SAM model, centroids were computed for each connected component of the manual reference segmentation masks. For the simulation of n clicks per fluid class, the centroids of the n largest connected components were utilized. In cases where the total number of connected components was smaller than n, a random connected component was selected, and a random coordinate was generated from a 2D Gaussian distribution centered at the chosen component's centroid. The random selection process was repeated if the generated point fell outside the mask boundaries.

SAM Decoder Fine-Tuning. The SAM model was trained with the same settings as the SAMed model, but without incorporating the LoRA adaptations. The decoder component of the model was refined, while the encoder weights were kept frozen during the training process.

NnU-Net. We compared the SAMed against the current state-of-the-art on the RETOUCH dataset, the nnU-Net model [13], as it was described in [24].

4.1   Dataset and Evaluation

All methods were trained and tested on the public RETOUCH dataset [2]. The dataset consists of 112 macula-centered OCT volumes from 112 patients with macular edema secondary to AMD or to RVO. The training set consists of 70 OCT volumes and the test set of 42. There is an approx. equal number of OCT volumes acquired with each of three OCT devices: Cirrus HD-OCT (Zeiss Meditec), Spectralis (Heidelberg Engineering), and T-1000/T-2000 (Topcon). All volumes cover a macular area of 6×6 mm^2.

In RETOUCH, each B-scan was manually annotated pixel-wise (Fig. 1b) for intraretinal fluid (IRF), subretinal fluid (SRF), and pigment epithelial detachment (PED). The test set contained double annotations coming from two medical centers and only the pixels with consensus among the two annotations were used in the evaluation following the RETOUCH challenge protocol to facilitate the comparison with the results of the original challenge. In accordance with the challenge, two metrics were utilized for the evaluations: 1. *Dice coefficient*: to quantify the voxel overlap between the prediction (X) and the manual reference (Y). and 2. *Absolute volume difference* (AVD) in mm^3: This metric provides a clinically significant parameter by measuring the absolute difference between the volumes of X and Y: $AVD = abs(|X| - |Y|)$

Training Details. The training was carried out in a mixed-precision environment with an Nvidia A100 (80GB) GPU, in a Singularity [18] 3.7.3 environment based on the *pytorch:2.0.1-cuda11.7-cudnn8-devel* Docker image, with Python 3.10.11 and Pytorch 2.0.1. The training of SAMed took 16 h on this setup, while the training of the decoder-only configuration took 4 h.

5 Results

As shown in Table 1, the zero-shot performance of SAM is in general worse than those of the methods at least partially fine-tuned on the dataset. This aligns with findings from various studies conducted on different medical imaging modalities [5,11,14,15,27]. When examining SAM's performance with varying numbers of prompts, we observe a slight advantage for 3-point prompts over 1-point prompts, while 10-point prompts demonstrate a notable enhancement compared to the 3-point prompts. Fine-tuning the decoder led to a substantial

Table 1. Experiments for evaluating the segmentation performance of different SAM settings.

Experiment	Dice ↑			AVD ↓		
	IRF	SRF	PED	IRF	SRF	PED
SAM with 1 point	0.209	0.168	0.098	0.397	0.676	3.196
SAM with 3 points	0.260	0.184	0.148	0.650	0.821	2.526
SAM with 10 points	0.402	0.406	0.480	0.430	0.144	0.255
SAM with fine-tuned decoder	0.627	0.286	0.448	0.055	0.117	0.182
SAMed	**0.766**	**0.759**	**0.815**	**0.042**	**0.020**	**0.033**

98   B. Fazekas et al.

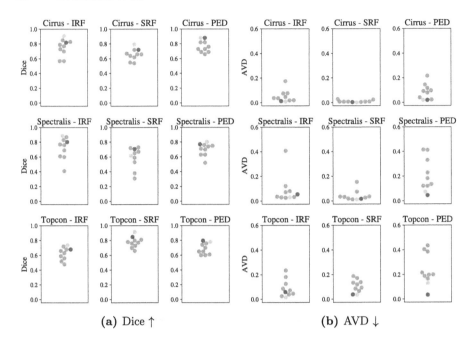

(a) Dice ↑   **(b)** AVD ↓

Fig. 2. Swarmplots of the detailed results per device vendor and fluid compartment. The SAMed model (red) performed worse than the best-performing baseline method (nnU-net, orange) but outperformed most of the other baseline methods (challenge participants, blue) both in terms of Dice and in AVD. The challenge participants are (in alphabetical order): Helios [30], MABIC [16], NJUST [4], RetinAI [1], RMIT [28], SFU [20], UCF [23] and UMN [26]. (Color figure online)

performance improvement, with an increase in Dice score of up to 50% compared to zero-short segmentation, however it lags behind the performance of the SAMed model with trained LoRA adapters.

The detailed results per device vendor and fluid compartment (Fig. 2) indicate that the SAMed model outperforms most of the baseline methods and would have been the winner of the 2017 RETOUCH challenge. However it performs worse than the nnU-net model in most of the device/disease configurations. Interestingly, the SAMed model demonstrates state-of-the-art performance on PED (Mean AVD SAMed: 0.033, nnU-net: 0.073). Likely due to the prominence of PED as typically the largest fluid compartment in the retina, which is often well-demarcated, it aligns more closely with the original SAM training set.

The qualitative results (Fig. 3), unveil both limitations and strengths of the SAMed method. While it excels in correctly segmenting serous PEDs even in challenging cases where Bruch's membrane is partially obscured (Rows 4, 8), it struggles with smaller fibrous PED cases (Rows 1, 5-6). Additionally, it occasionally produces anatomically implausible predictions for IRF (Rows 7, 9).

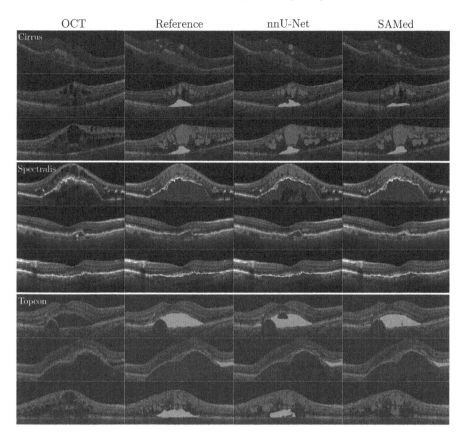

Fig. 3. Qualitative results grouped by OCT vendors. Columns (left to right): Sample B-Scan from the test set, manual reference segmentation, nnU-Net segmentation, SAMed segmentation. The fluid compartments displayed are: IRF (red), SRF (green) and PED (blue). (Color figure online)

6   Conclusion

This study assesses the applicability of SAM for biomarker segmentation in retinal OCT. Our results indicate that, despite achieving competitive performance, the adapted SAM slightly underperforms in comparison to networks specifically designed for medical image analysis. Nevertheless, this is still remarkable given that the SAM encoder was trained on natural images only. Further self-supervised fine-tuning of the encoder on OCT images is expected to boost the SAM performance even further, possibly beyond the one achieved with nnU-net. Finally, the semi-interactive nature of SAM makes it a particularly attractive approach in the clinical setting, as well as for semi-automated annotation procedures, as it allows to adjust segmentations in complex pathomorphological manifestations and account for user subjectivity.

Acknowledgements. The financial support by the Christian Doppler Research Association, Austrian Federal Ministry for Digital and Economic Affairs, the National Foundation for Research, Technology and Development is gratefully acknowledged.

References

1. Apostolopoulos, S., Ciller, C., Sznitman, R., De Zanet, S.: Simultaneous classification and segmentation of cysts in retinal oct. In: Proceedings of MICCAI Retinal OCT Fluid Challenge (RETOUCH), pp. 22–29 (2017)
2. Bogunovic, H., et al.: RETOUCH: the retinal OCT fluid detection and segmentation benchmark and challenge. IEEE Trans. Med. Imaging **38**(8), 1858–1874 (2019). https://doi.org/10.1109/TMI.2019.2901398
3. Campochiaro, P.A., Aiello, L.P., Rosenfeld, P.J.: Anti-vascular endothelial growth factor agents in the treatment of retinal disease: from bench to bedside. Ophthalmology **123**(10), S78–S88 (2016). https://doi.org/10.1016/j.ophtha.2016.04.056
4. Chen, Q., et al.: Automatic segmentation of fluid-associated abnormalities and pigment epithelial detachment in retinal sd-oct images. In: Proceedings of MICCAI Retinal OCT Fluid Challenge (RETOUCH), pp. 15–21 (2017)
5. Deng, R., et al.: Segment anything model (SAM) for digital pathology: assess zero-shot segmentation on whole slide imaging. In: MIDL (2023)
6. Dosovitskiy, A., et al.: An image is worth 16x16 words: transformers for image recognition at scale. arXiv preprint arXiv:2010.11929 (2020)
7. Gao, Y., Xia, W., Hu, D., Gao, X.: DeSAM: decoupling segment anything model for generalizable medical image segmentation, arxiv.org/abs/2306.00499 (2023)
8. Houlsby, N., et al.: Parameter-efficient transfer learning for nlp. In: International Conference on Machine Learning, pp. 2790–2799. PMLR (2019)
9. Hu, E.J., et al.: LoRA: low-rank adaptation of large language models. arXiv preprint arXiv:2106.09685 (2021)
10. Hu, X., Xu, X., Shi, Y.: How to efficiently adapt large segmentation model (SAM) to medical image (2023). https://doi.org/10.48550/arxiv.2306.13731, arxiv.org/abs/2306.13731
11. Huang, Y., et al.: Segment Anything Model for Medical Images? arXiv preprint arXiv:2304.14660 (2023)
12. Isensee, F., Jaeger, P.F., Kohl, S.A.A., Petersen, J., Maier-Hein, K.H.: nnU-Net: a self-configuring method for deep learning-based biomedical image segmentation. Nat. Methods **18**(2), 203–211 (2021). https://doi.org/10.1038/s41592-020-01008-z,www.nature.com/articles/s41592-020-01008-z
13. Isensee, F., Jaeger, P.F., Kohl, S.A.A., Petersen, J., Maier-Hein, K.H.: nnU-Net: a self-configuring method for deep learning-based biomedical image segmentation. Nat. Methods **18**(2), 203–211 (2021). https://doi.org/10.1038/s41592-020-01008-z, www.nature.com/articles/s41592-020-01008-z
14. Ji, G.P., Fan, D.P., Xu, P., Cheng, M.M., Zhou, B., Gool, L.V.: SAM Struggles in Concealed Scenes - Empirical Study on "Segment Anything". arXiv preprint arXiv:2304.06022 (2023)
15. Ji, W., Li, J., Bi, Q., Liu, T., Li, W., Cheng, L.: Segment anything is not always perfect: an investigation of SAM on different real-world applications. arXiv preprint arXiv:2304.05750 (2023)
16. Kang, S.H., Park, H.S., Jang, J., Jeon, K.: Deep neural networks for the detection and segmentation of the retinal fluid in oct images. In: MICCAI Retinal OCT Fluid Challenge (RETOUCH) (2017)

17. Kirillov, A., et al.: Segment Anything. arXiv (2023). https://doi.org/10.48550/arxiv.2304.02643, arxiv.org/abs/2304.02643

18. Kurtzer, G.M., Sochat, V., Bauer, M.W.: Singularity: scientific containers for mobility of compute. PLOS ONE **12**(5), e0177459 (2017) https://doi.org/10.1371/journal.pone.0177459, www.journals.plos.org/plosone/article?id=10.1371/journal.pone.0177459

19. Lei, W., Wei, X., Zhang, X., Li, K., Zhang, S.: MedLSAM: localize and segment anything model for 3D medical images (2023). https://doi.org/10.48550/arxiv.2306.14752, arxiv.org/abs/2306.14752

20. Lu, D., et al.: Deep-learning based multiclass retinal fluid segmentation and detection in optical coherence tomography images using a fully convolutional neural network. Med. Image Anal. **54**, 100–110 (2019)

21. Ma, J., Wang, B.: Segment anything in medical images. arXiv preprint arXiv:2304.12306 (2023)

22. Moor, M., et al.: Foundation models for generalist medical artificial intelligence. Nature **616**(7956), 259–265 (2023). https://doi.org/10.1038/s41586-023-05881-4,www.nature.com/articles/s41586-023-05881-4

23. Morley, D., Foroosh, H., Shaikh, S., Bagci, U.: Simultaneous detection and quantification of retinal fluid with deep learning. arXiv preprint arXiv:1708.05464 (2017)

24. Ndipenoch, N., Miron, A., Wang, Z., Li, Y.: nnUNet RASPP for Retinal OCT Fluid Detection, Segmentation and Generalisation over Variations of Data Sources. arXiv preprint arXiv:2302.13195 (2023)

25. Radford, A., et al.: Learning transferable visual models from natural language supervision. In: International Conference on Machine Learning, pp. 8748–8763. PMLR (2021)

26. Rashno, A., Koozekanani, D.D., Parhi, K.K.: Detection and segmentation of various types of fluids with graph shortest path and deep learning approaches. In: Proceedings of MICCAI Retinal OCT Fluid Challenge (RETOUCH), pp. 54–62 (2017)

27. Roy, S., et al.: SAM.MD: zero-shot medical image segmentation capabilities of the segment anything model. In: MIDL (2023)

28. Tennakoon, R., Gostar, A.K., Hoseinnezhad, R., Bab-Hadiashar, A.: Retinal fluid segmentation in OCT images using adversarial loss based convolutional neural networks. In: International Symposium on Biomedical Imaging (ISBI), pp. 1436–1440. IEEE Computer Society (May 2018). https://doi.org/10.1109/ISBI.2018.8363842

29. Wu, J., et al.: Medical SAM adapter: adapting segment anything model for medical image segmentation. arXiv preprint arXiv:2304.12620 (2023)

30. Yadav, S., Gopinath, K., Sivaswamy, J.: A generalized motion pattern and fcn based approach for retinal fluid detection and segmentation. arXiv preprint arXiv:1712.01073 (2017)

31. Zhang, K., Liu, D.: Customized Segment Anything Model for medical image segmentation (2023). https://doi.org/10.48550/arxiv.2304.13785, arxiv.org/abs/2304.13785

32. Zhang, Y., Jiao, R.: How Segment Anything Model (SAM) boost medical image segmentation: a survey (2023). https://doi.org/10.48550/arxiv.2305.03678, arxiv.org/abs/2305.03678

Dual-Modality Grading of Keratoconus Severity Based on Corneal Topography and Clinical Indicators

Xin Xu[1], Yingjie Chen[2], Fei Shi[1], Yi Zhou[1], Weifang Zhu[1], Song Gao[1], Muhammad Mateen[1,3], Xiaofeng Zhang[2(✉)], and Xinjian Chen[1,4(✉)]

[1] School of Electronics and Information Engineering,
Soochow University, Suzhou, China
xjchen@suda.edu.cn
[2] Department of Ophthalmology,
Dushu Lake Hospital Affiliated to Soochow University, Suzhou, China
zhangxiaofeng@suda.edu.cn
[3] Department of Computer Science,
Air University Multan Campus, Multan, Pakistan
[4] State Key Laboratory of Radiation Medicine and Protection,
Soochow University, Suzhou, China

Abstract. Keratoconus (KC) is a blinding eye disease characterized by corneal dilation, thinning, and conical protrusion. Currently, most studies just focus on KC screening and use only one modality. In this paper, we utilize two modalities of data, corneal topography and clinical indicators, to grade KC severity as normal, mild, moderate, and severe, rather than screening. Considering the data characteristics of each modality, we model their data in a targeted manner. For corneal topography, a Global Feature Extraction (GFE) block based on Self-Attention is designed as a parallel branch to obtain global information. In addition, a Feature Fusion (FF) module is proposed to better fuse local and global information. For clinical indicators, we utilize a tree model to grade KC and remove redundant information through feature selection. Finally, a trainable fusion model is used to make the final decision. Experimental results show that the proposed method outperforms all the competing methods and achieves 94.47% for weighted recall, improving the accuracy of KC grading effectively.

Keywords: keratoconus · dual-modality · fusion strategy

1 Introduction

Keratoconus (KC) is a non-inflammatory, chronic, progressive, and local corneal ectasia disease [21], which initially often causes highly irregular myopic astigmatism. If KC progresses to severe stages, it may trigger acute corneal edema and opacity and further reduce visual acuity. Therefore, an accurate grading of the KC severity is of great clinical significance.

X. Xu and Y.Chen—Equal contribution.

© The Author(s), under exclusive license to Springer Nature Switzerland AG 2023
B. Antony et al. (Eds.): OMIA 2023, LNCS 14096, pp. 102–111, 2023.
https://doi.org/10.1007/978-3-031-44013-7_11

Many previous work focused on the screening of KC. Kuo et al. [12] used three convolutional neural networks (CNNs) trained on corneal topography for identifying normal eyes from KC. Feng et al. [3] proposed an end-to-end deep learning method, called KerNet, which processed raw data of the anterior segment analysis system to detect KC and sub-clinical KC. Although these methods achieved good results, but they can only distinguish between normal eyes and KC. However, the initial presentation of KC is not obvious and often requires a more comprehensive analysis of corneal clinical indicators, which makes it more challenging to screen for KC at an early stage. A method that can determine the stage of KC in a timely and accurate manner is important to avoid further damage to the patient's vision. To grade KC, Gao et al. [5] proposed a lightweight KC grading network (LKG-Net). Alexandru et al. [13] used machine learning algorithms to evaluate the accuracy of corneal clinical indicators in KC detection and severity grading. These studies were successful in determining the stage of KC, but all utilized only single modality of information. In actual clinical practice, since each modality has its limitations, physicians usually consider both corneal topography and clinical indicators. To utilize on both modalities, Ali H et al. [1] proposed an ensemble of deep transfer learning (EDTL) method to combine corneal topographical maps and clinical indicators for KC screening, which did not accomplish the grading of KC severity. Therefore, there is an urgent clinical need for a KC grading method that can utilize both modalities, corneal topography and clinical indicators.

To solve this problem, we propose a dual-modality KC grading method, and the main contributions are summarized as: 1) The dual-modality data are used to grade the severity of KC, and two different classifiers are proposed based on the data characteristics of each modality. 2) For corneal topography, ResNet18 is used as baseline, and a branch module is proposed to obtain global features, with a feature fusion module designed to better fuse local and global features. For clinical features, a tree model and feature selection are used for training. 3) Using blending idea to train a fusion model for final decision.

2   Method

2.1   Overall Architecture

The diagram of the proposed framework is shown in Fig. 1 (a). Since images usually have high dimensional feature representation. In contrast, the dimensions of clinical indicators are inherently low. Whether the high-dimensional data and low-dimensional data can be effectively integrated will have a great impact on the final results. Finding a feature fusion method that can successfully fuse these two different dimensions of information can be challenging. Consequently, we first fully leverage the advantages of each modality by training two separate models. Then a fusion model is used to learn from the two previous results and arrive at the final decision. This method overcomes the challenges of inconsistent dimensions between different modalities and the difficulty in effectively representing the fused features. Additionally, it can be extended to accommodate more modalities as needed.

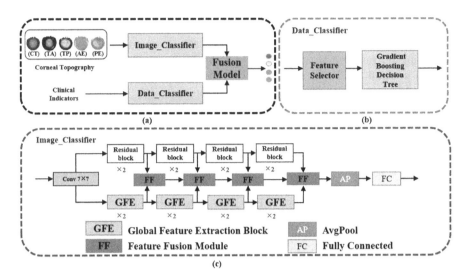

Fig. 1. (a) Diagram of the proposed KC grading framework, where Image_Classifier and Data_Classifier are used to process corneal topography and clinical indicators, respectively, and their structures are shown in (c) and (b). The fusion model is used to fuse the decisions of the two classifiers.

2.2   Image Classifier on Corneal Topography

The structure of the image classifier trained on corneal topography is shown in Fig. 1 (c), which is based on ResNet18 [6]. The unique residual learning of ResNet makes it widely used in image classification tasks. As it is widely recognized, the general convolution operation is limited to capturing local neighborhood information, thereby requiring a deeper network to capture long-range dependencies. However, this brings the problems of computational inefficiency, unstable gradients, and network degradation. For KC grading, it is important that the global information brought by long distance can obtain global features such as the overall shape of corneal topography. Therefore, on the basis of baseline network ResNet18, we add a branch to better acquire global features and design a feature fusion module to interact and fuse local features with global features.

Global Feature Extraction Block: Self-Attention [25] can calculate the relationship between any two pixels in an image directly, easily obtaining global features. Many previous studies utilized Self-Attention to obtain global features for improving image processing performance, and many of them chose Multi-Head Self-Attention (MHSA) [9,22], which allows network to focus on different aspects of information. However, MHSA may result in redundant information and has higher requirements on computational memory and power. To take advantage of Self-Attention and address the above problems, we propose a Global Feature Extraction (GFE) block (shown in Fig. 2), which is placed in parallel with the baseline. This module is similar to Residual block, where we replace the 3×3

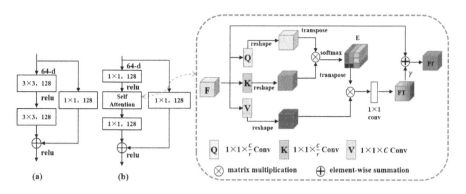

Fig. 2. (a) Residual block (b) Global Feature Extraction (GFE) block.

convolution with 1×1 convolution to maintain the same number of channels as the Residual block and increase non-linearity. Then add Self-Attention between the two to obtain global features with long range dependency. Self-Attention uses the output of a 1×1 convolution applied to the input feature map F as query (Q), key (K), and value (V). Once the similarity matrix E of Q and K is computed, the transpose of E is multiplied with V to obtain the spatial response matrix FT. Finally, Ff, the final spatial attention output, is obtained by element-wise summation of the F and weighted FT.

Feature Fusion Module: As shown in Fig. 3, the Feature Fusion (FF) module is utilized to combine global and local features, which are obtained by the GFE block and the Residual block, respectively. Starting from the second FF module, the output from the previous FF module are additionally fused, and after a 1×1 convolution, the channel and spatial attention maps are computed by two branches, respectively, where channel attention [8] uses global average-pooled features to exploit the inter-channel relationship. Spatial attention [26] is employed to identify the location on the map with the most aggregated information and to generate a spatial relationship map between features. Finally, the features are weighted for each channel and space using a scale operation.

2.3 Data Classifier on Clinical Indicators

Neural networks have been proven as robust and effective in processing unstructured data such as image and video [20]. However, for one-dimensional tabular data, tree-based machine learning model is more popular among researchers, and it can provide interpretability compared to neural networks. We use the Gradient Boosting Decision Tree (GBDT) [4] as the basic data classifier and utilize Analysis of variance (ANOVA), a statistical method for assessing the significance of differences, to remove redundant features.

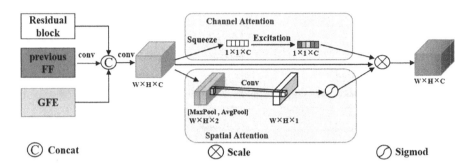

Fig. 3. The illustration of Feature Fusion (FF) module.

2.4   Fusion Strategy for Final Grading

In this paper, we use blending idea to fuse the graded results obtained by the two basic classifiers. We first divide all data into Train_Set and Test_Set, and then split a portion of Train_Set for training a second layer classifier, i.e., the fusion model. We call the data used for the first and second layer training as Train_Set1 and Train_Set2, respectively. The specific training process is as follows: First, we train image classifier and data classifier with a set of corneal topography and clinical data in Train_Set1, then these two models are predicted on the data in Train_Set2, and the two predictions obtained are concatenated as input of the fusion model to train it. The fusion model uses Light Gradient Boosting Machine (LightGBM) [11]. In the testing process, the corneal topography and clinical data in Test_Set are first predicted separately using image classifier and data classifier, and then the two predictions are merged into the fusion model to obtain the final grading decision.

3   Experiments and Results

3.1   Dataset

The dataset was collected in the hospital, and was approved by the Review Committee of the Hospital, which conforms to the principles of the Helsinki Declaration. All subjects obtained informed consent. The dataset contains the examination report of 488 eyes, which was provided by Sirius machine photography (CSOInc, Florence, Italy). All data were divided into normal (236 cases), mild (138 cases), moderate (63 cases) and severe (51 cases) according to Amsler-Kruemeich classification standard [24] and professional doctor's diagnosis. We obtained five corneal topographic maps with original dimensions of 640×480 in the report: corneal thickness (CT), tangential anterior (TA), anterior elevation (AE), tangential posterior (TP) and posterior elevation (PE) maps (shown in Fig. 1 (a)) and 15 numeric parameters measured by Sirius (listed in Table 1).

Table 1. 15 clinical parameters used for stage prediction of KC. K, Sim-K and Cyl mean keratometry reading, simulate K and corneal cylinder, respectively.

	Clinical Parameters
Features	Corneal thickness; Average K (Sim-k); Average K (Anterior 3 mm)
	Average K (Posterior 3 mm); Cyl (Sim-k); Cyl (Anterior 3 mm)
	Cyl (Posterior 3 mm); Symmetry index back; Symmetry index front
	Anterior zone of 6 mm root non-spherical index per unit area (A6 Q)
	Posterior zone of 6 mm root non-spherical index per unit area (P6 Q)
	Anterior zone of 6 mm root mean square values per unit area (A6 RMS /A)
	Posterior zone of 6 mm root mean square values per unit area (P6 RMS /A);
	Baiocchi Calossi Versaci index front; Baiocchi Calossi Versaci index back

3.2   Implementation Details

The proposed method was performed on the public platform Pytorch and one NVIDIA RTX 3060 GPU of 12G memory. The Adam was used as the optimizer, initial learning rate was set to 0.0001, the batch size was set to 8, and the number of epochs was 100. We merged 5 topographic maps into a 15-channel image as input and resized it to 256×256 to facilitate training and prevent loss of detailed information. Use the weighted categorical cross-entropy loss function to calculate the loss value. In order to comprehensively evaluate the performance of the proposed method, a 5-fold cross-validation strategy was used in all experiments, and 20% of the divided training set was used to train the second level fusion model. To ensure fairness, all the competing networks were trained with the same configuration.

3.3   Evaluation Metrics

In order to thoroughly and unbiasedly evaluate the classification performance of different methods, we use four common metrics to quantitatively analyze the experimental results, including weighted recall (W_R), weighted precision (W_P), weighted F1 score (W_F1), and weighted Kappa (W_K).

3.4   Results and Discussion

Since our dataset contains different modalities, we investigate on data from each modality separately to fairly explore the superiority of the two classifiers. In addition, comparison experiments of the different fusion methods are conducted to investigate their effect on the final KC grading performance.

Experiments on Corneal Topography: The proposed image classifier is compared with other stat-of-the-art algorithms on corneal topography, including ResNet34 [6], EfficientNetB1 [23], MoblieViT [15] SE_ResNet18 [8], ResNext50

[27], InceptionV4 [10], LKG-Net [5] and BoTNet50 [22]. For convenience, we refer to the basic ResNet18 as baseline. Furthermore, in order to verify the effectiveness of the proposed GFE and FF modules, we conduct ablation experiments of two modules. The experimental results are listed in Table 2, and it can be seen that our method achieves the best performance on all four evaluation metrics. While compared to LKG-Net with comparable model FLOPs, our method introduces more computational costs, but also has a improvement. InceptionV4 and BoTNet50 have also achieved relatively good performance, probably due to the large convolution of InceptionV4, which can provide a large receptive field to help classification. Similarly, BoTNet50 uses MHSA to obtain global information, but both methods have higher FLOPs. EfficientNetB1, MobileViT and SE_ResNet18 are slightly lower than ours in terms of FLOPs, but the classification performance is much worse. It is noteworthy that ResNet34 and ResNext50 not only have higher FLOPs, but also have much lower performance than the proposed image classifier. For the ablation experiments, it can be seen that the global features provided by GFE contribute significantly to the KC grading performance, increasing 1.03%, 0.39%, 0.99%, and 1.22% for W_R, W_P, W_F1, and W_K, respectively. The FF module helps the classifier to better integrate the extracted local and global features, resulting in a further improvement of W_R by 1.22%.

Table 2. The results of comparison experiments and ablation studies on corneal topography (Mean ± Standard deviation).

Methods	W_R(%)	W_P(%)	W_F1(%)	W_K(%)	FLOPs(G)
ResNet34 [6]	89.562.75	89.652.99	88.943.06	93.721.11	5.41
EfficientB1 [23]	87.512.66	87.252.80	87.112.86	92.642.53	1.63
MobileViT [15]	87.313.23	88.253.02	86.813.43	91.113.42	1.81
SE_ResNet18 [8]	89.152.16	89.002.62	88.832.60	94.361.30	3.00
LKG-Net [5]	90.781.81	91.042.09	90.492.29	94.861.56	**1.18**
InceptionV4 [10]	90.371.01	91.380.41	90.380.97	95.070.71	8.39
ResNext50 [27]	89.763.08	90.632.41	88.804.58	94.301.94	6.19
BoTNet50 [22]	90.162.11	90.752.21	89.702.83	94.381.03	5.84
Baseline	89.351.03	90.321.06	89.150.91	93.481.52	3.20
Baseline+GFE	90.381.63	90.711.25	90.141.58	94.701.30	3.51
Baseline+GFE+FF (proposed)	**91.601.74**	**91.401.91**	**91.321.95**	**95.771.03**	3.65

Experiments on Clinical Indicators: In terms of clinical indicators, we compare our data classifier with some popular machine learning algorithms, including Random Forest (RF) [16], eXtreme Gradient Boosting (XGBoost) [2], Decision Tree (DT) [19], and Support Vector Machines (SVM) [17]. Also, we compare a neural network-based learning method, a 3-layer Multi Layer Perceptron (MLP) [18]. The experimental results listed in Table 3 demonstrate that the tree model GBDT [4] is more suitable for tabular data and achieves the best results on all metrics. The MLP achieves the worst results, which indicates that the neural network is easily overfitted on the tabular data and lacks interpretability. When ANOVA is utilized to filter redundant information for feature selection, the classification performance is further improved.

Table 3. The results of comparison experiments and ablation studies on clinical indicators (Mean Standard deviation).

Methods	W_R(%)	W_P(%)	W_F1(%)	W_K(%)
DT [19]	90.371.65	91.211.50	90.241.78	94.161.59
RF [16]	90.171.98	90.741.32	89.971.72	94.710.80
XGBoost [2]	91.191.88	91.681.26	91.041.72	95.171.01
SVM [17]	88.121.37	88.511.28	87.691.19	93.561.33
MLP [18]	84.631.50	85.482.63	83.961.90	92.430.93
GBDT [4]	92.222.36	92.442.29	92.182.31	96.151.12
GBDT+ANOVA (proposed)	**92.632.35**	**93.062.40**	**92.592.26**	**96.341.10**

Experiments on Fusion: Table 4 shows the effects of different multimodal fusion methods, and it can be seen that the LightGBM [11] based on blending fusion strategy used in this paper achieves the best results. Also, using both corneal topography and clinical indicators performs better than using one modality alone. RFNet [28] and HDLM [14] are multimodal classification methods based on deep learning, and their performance is relatively poor on our task. Other decision-level fusion methods such as Means, Maximum and Entropy weight are also worse than the trainable blending fusion strategy. Furthermore, we compare the performance of different models under the blending strategy. Among them, LightGBM has the best performance and LR is the second best. It can be seen that under the blending strategy, the models all achieve good results, which also proves the effectiveness of blending.

Table 4. Performance of different fusion methods (Mean Standard deviation).

Strategies		W_R(%)	W_P(%)	W_F1(%)	W_K(%)
RFNet [28]		87.103.84	87.264.46	86.834.13	93.043.11
HDLM [14]		88.941.48	88.461.89	88.411.89	93.741.99
Means		92.630.74	93.140.94	92.550.77	96.290.50
Maximum		89.141.00	89.441.15	88.831.10	94.030.85
Entropy weight		94.061.51	94.471.54	93.921.52	97.010.75
Blending	LR [7]	94.271.52	94.581.42	94.281.45	97.140.78
	SVM [17]	93.851.44	94.321.50	93.771.40	96.920.73
	LightGBM [11]	**94.472.11**	**94.592.08**	**94.432.10**	**97.28 1.02**

4   Conclusion

In this paper, we propose a method for grading the severity of KC by combining data from two modalities, corneal topography and clinical indicators. We build models based on the data characteristics of each modality and then train a fusion model to make the final decision. For corneal topography, a GFE module to obtain image's global features and a FF module to fuse local and global information are proposed based on the baseline. For clinical indicators being tabular data, we choose the tree model GBDT and the feature selection of ANOVA for KC classification. For the final fusion model, we use the trainable blending fusion strategy to get the final decision. Compared with other state-of-the-art methods, the classifiers proposed in this paper all achieve the optimal classification performance and can additionally improve the W_R by 1.84% when using the fusion strategy.

References

1. Al-Timemy, A.H., Ghaeb, N.H., Mosa, Z.M., Escudero, J.: Deep transfer learning for improved detection of keratoconus using corneal topographic maps. Cogn. Comput. **14**(5), 1627–1642 (2022)
2. Chen, T., Guestrin, C.: Xgboost: a scalable tree boosting system. In: Proceedings of the 22nd ACM SIGKDD International Conference on Knowledge Discovery and Data Mining, pp. 785–794 (2016)
3. Feng, R., et al.: Kernet: a novel deep learning approach for keratoconus and subclinical keratoconus detection based on raw data of the pentacam hr system. IEEE J. Biomed. Health Inform. **25**(10), 3898–3910 (2021)
4. Friedman, J.H.: Greedy function approximation: a gradient boosting machine. Annals of statistics, pp. 1189–1232 (2001)
5. Gao, S., et al.: Lkg-net: lightweight keratoconus grading network based on corneal topography. Biomed. Opt. Express **14**(2), 799–814 (2023)
6. He, K., Zhang, X., Ren, S., Sun, J.: Deep residual learning for image recognition. In: Proceedings of the IEEE Conference on Computer Vision and Pattern Recognition, pp. 770–778 (2016)
7. Hosmer Jr, D.W., Lemeshow, S., Sturdivant, R.X.: Applied logistic regression, vol. 398. John Wiley & Sons (2013)
8. Hu, J., Shen, L., Sun, G.: Squeeze-and-excitation networks. In: Proceedings of the IEEE Conference on Computer Vision and Pattern Recognition, pp. 7132–7141 (2018)
9. Huo, X., et al.: Hifuse: hierarchical multi-scale feature fusion network for medical image classification. arXiv preprint arXiv:2209.10218 (2022)
10. Ioffe, S., Szegedy, C.: Batch normalization: accelerating deep network training by reducing internal covariate shift. In: International Conference on Machine Learning, pp. 448–456. PMLR (2015)
11. Ke, G., et al.: Lightgbm: a highly efficient gradient boosting decision tree. In: Advances in Neural Information Processing Systems 30 (2017)
12. Kuo, B.I., et al.: Keratoconus screening based on deep learning approach of corneal topography. Translational Vision Sci. Technol. **9**(2), 53–53 (2020)

13. Lavric, A., et al.: Keratoconus severity detection from elevation, topography and pachymetry raw data using a machine learning approach. IEEE Access **9**, 84344–84355 (2021)
14. Liu, T., Huang, J., Liao, T., Pu, R., Liu, S., Peng, Y.: A hybrid deep learning model for predicting molecular subtypes of human breast cancer using multimodal data. IRBM **43**(1), 62–74 (2022)
15. Mehta, S., Rastegari, M.: Mobilevit: light-weight, general-purpose, and mobile-friendly vision transformer. arXiv preprint arXiv:2110.02178 (2021)
16. Mitchell, T.M., Mitchell, T.M.: Machine learning, vol. 1. McGraw-hill New York (1997)
17. Platt, J.: Sequential minimal optimization: a fast algorithm for training support vector machines (1998)
18. Rosenblatt, F.: The perceptron: a probabilistic model for information storage and organization in the brain. Psychol. Rev. **65**(6), 386 (1958)
19. Salzberg, S.L.: C4. 5: programs for machine learning by j. ross quinlan. Morgan Kaufmann Publishers, Inc., 1993 (1994)
20. Sarkar, T.: Xbnet: an extremely boosted neural network. Intelligent Syst. Appli. **15**, 200097 (2022)
21. Sorkin, N., Varssano, D.: Corneal collagen crosslinking: a systematic review. Ophthalmologica **232**(1), 10–27 (2014)
22. Srinivas, A., Lin, T.Y., Parmar, N., Shlens, J., Abbeel, P., Vaswani, A.: Bottleneck transformers for visual recognition. In: Proceedings of the IEEE/CVF Conference on Computer Vision and Pattern Recognition, pp. 16519–16529 (2021)
23. Tan, M., Le, Q.: Efficientnet: rethinking model scaling for convolutional neural networks. In: International Conference on Machine Learning, pp. 6105–6114. PMLR (2019)
24. Vanathi, M., Sidhu, N.: Classifications and patterns of keratoconus. In: Keratoconus: Diagnosis and Treatment, pp. 59–67. Springer (2022). https://doi.org/10.1007/978-981-19-3571-8_18
25. Vaswani, A., et al.: Attention is all you need. In: Advances in Neural Information Processing Systems 30 (2017)
26. Woo, S., Park, J., Lee, J.-Y., Kweon, I.S.: CBAM: convolutional block attention module. In: Ferrari, V., Hebert, M., Sminchisescu, C., Weiss, Y. (eds.) ECCV 2018. LNCS, vol. 11211, pp. 3–19. Springer, Cham (2018). https://doi.org/10.1007/978-3-030-01234-2_1
27. Xie, S., Girshick, R., Dollár, P., Tu, Z., He, K.: Aggregated residual transformations for deep neural networks. In: Proceedings of the IEEE Conference on Computer Vision and Pattern Recognition, pp. 1492–1500 (2017)
28. Yan, R., et al.: Richer fusion network for breast cancer classification based on multimodal data. BMC Med. Inform. Decis. Mak. **21**(1), 1–15 (2021)

Automated Optic Disc Finder and Segmentation Using Deep Learning for Blood Flow Studies in the Eye

Noriyoshi Takahashi[1,2], Jui-Kai Wang[1,2,3]($\boxtimes$), Edward F. Linton[1,2],
Noor-Us-Sabah Ahmad[2], Julie K. Nellis[1,2], Mona K. Garvin[1,3],
and Randy H. Kardon[1,2]

[1] The Iowa City VA Center for the Prevention and Treatment of Visual Loss,
Iowa City VA Health Care System, Iowa City, IA, USA
{noriyoshi-takahashi,jui-kai-wang,mona-garvin,randy-kardon}@uiowa.edu
[2] Department of Ophthalmology and Visual Sciences,
The University of Iowa, Iowa City, IA, USA
[3] Department of Electrical and Computer Engineering,
The University of Iowa, Iowa City, IA, USA

Abstract. In-vivo imaging with laser speckle flowgraphy (LSFG) enables optical measurement of an index of blood flow in the retina. LSFG can help observe blood flow changes in various diseases, including optic nerve problems such as glaucoma, ischemic optic neuropathy, and others. However, identification of the optic disc in LSFG images is particularly challenging because of limited contour information in the rendered blood flow maps. In this study, we adopted a state-of-the-art U-Net approach (nnU-Net) to automatically identify the optic disc region based on input two-channel LSFG composite blood flow maps and infrared light intensity images. Since the optic disc contour is not always obvious in LSFG, a trained neuro-ophthalmologist (Expert 1) traced the optic discs in color fundus photographs from the same eye; these masks were then registered into the LSFG domain. One hundred subjects (training/test dataset ratio: 70/30) were used in this study. The nnU-Net was trained to identify the optic disc just based on the LSFG composite and light intensity images. After training, we compared the difference between nnU-Net's output and Expert 1 with the difference between Expert 1 and a second clinician (Expert 2) in the test dataset. Both the Dice coefficient and the intersection over union (IoU) index showed the nnU-Net's predictions were significantly closer to Expect 1's tracing than Export 2's (*p*-values < 0.001). In summary, having a robust optic disc segmentation in LSFG can reduce tedious manual tracing and will also be a foundation for future developments of automated region-based feature extraction in LSFG.

Keywords: Laser Speckle Flowgraphy (LSFG) · Optic Disc Segmentation · nnU-Net

© The Author(s), under exclusive license to Springer Nature Switzerland AG 2023
B. Antony et al. (Eds.): OMIA 2023, LNCS 14096, pp. 112–121, 2023.
https://doi.org/10.1007/978-3-031-44013-7_12

1   Introduction

In-vivo imaging with laser speckle flowgraphy (LSFG) enables optical measurement of an index of blood flow in living tissues in humans and animals. To image the retina and optic nerve within the eye, the device illuminates the fundus with a diode laser [2,16]. The random interference pattern of the laser spot (termed speckle pattern) is blurred by moving red blood cells. This blur is analyzed at each pixel in the image, and quantified with an index called the mean blur rate (MBR) that is linearly correlated with blood flow [9,17]. The average MBR at each pixel location over the entire sequence of images (device default setting: 120 frames in 4 s; LSFG-NAVI, Softcare Co., Ltd., Japan) is plotted to generate the composite image (or blood flow map), allowing visualization of overall perfusion (Fig. 1c and 1d). LSFG has been used to investigate blood flow in the optic nerve in a variety of blinding conditions, including optic nerve problems like glaucoma [1,3], ischemic optic neuropathy [11], optic neuritis [4], central retinal vein occlusion [12], and others. Delineation of the optic disc is a necessary step for quantification of optic nerve blood flow that currently must be tediously performed by hand [8]. A robust, automated segmentation approach to identify and demarcate the optic disc is needed to improve and streamline quantitative analysis of optic nerve head perfusion using LSFG. However, the frequent lack of a visible contour (Fig. 1b, 1c, and 1d) makes consistent delineation of the optic disc in such images very challenging.

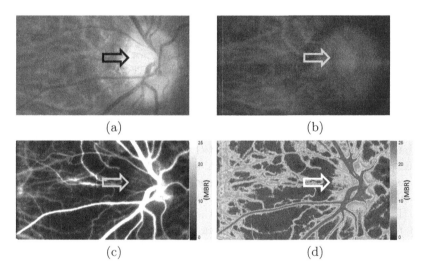

Fig. 1. An example of showing the optic disc in (a) a color fundus photograph, (b) the corresponding LSFG infrared light intensity image, (c) the corresponding LSFG composite image displaying the MBR values in a gray scale, and (d) in the default color scale used by the device. In (c) and (d), the lower blood flow (the lower MBR value) shows in a darker/blue color; the higher blood flow (the higher MBR value) shows in a brighter/red color. The temporal border of the optic disc is pointed by an arrow in all images. (Color figure online)

U-Net-based deep learning approaches have been widely applied in medical imaging [13,15]. Multiple studies have focused on the identification of the optic disc in color fundus photographs [7,10] but have not yet been implemented in LSFG. To fill this research gap, we adopt a state-of-the-art U-Net approach (nnU-Net [5]) to automatically identify the optic disc region based on an input comprised of two channels: the LSFG composite and infrared light intensity images (two-channel input). nnU-Net is an out-of-box tool that provides excellent segmentation results from an individual dataset without manually fine-tuning the data augmentation and the learning rate. However, nnU-Net is a supervised learning scheme, so the segmentation accuracy highly depends on the quality of the label provided. Because delineation of the optic nerve head from the LSFG images alone is challenging even for experts, we transferred ONH tracings from fundus photography of the same eye by a trained neuro-ophthalmologist (Expert 1) onto the LSFG input images after manual image registration. For validation, we had a second clinician (Expert 2) independently trace the optic disc using the same composite and infrared light intensity image pairs (same as the nnU-Net's input) in the test set. Details of the approaches are described in the following methods section; qualitative and quantitative evaluations are presented in the results section. Figure 2 shows the overall workflow, including data preparation (Sect. 2.1), nnU-Net model training (Sect. 2.2), and model evaluations (Sect. 2.3).

2   Methods

2.1   Data Preparation

The infrared light intensity and composite blood flow maps are two common images computed based on the LSFG raw data by averaging the light intensity reflection and the blood flow (in MBR) over the entire 120 LSFG time frames, respectively. However, it is challenging to directly identify the optic disc in the LSFG images because the contour of the disc is not always obvious [14] (Fig. 1). In this study, in order to obtain robust reference of the optic disc in LSFG, we first had a trained neuro-ophthalmologist (Expert 1) trace the optic disc in color fundus photographs of the same eye, which usually show a more distinct optic disc, using an iPad tablet and Apple Pencil (Apple, Inc.). Next, a customized manual registration tool was used to convert all the generated optic disc masks from the color fundus image domain to the LSFG image domain (Fig. 2a).

A total of 100 pairs of LSFG images and the corresponding color fundus photographs (100 different subjects from the University of Iowa Hospitals and Clinics) were used. These 100 subjects were randomly divided into a training (70 subjects) and a test dataset (30 subjects). Expert 1 marked the optic disc for all the 100 subjects in the color fundus photographs as the main optic disc reference. Note: All the eyes in this study were right eyes.

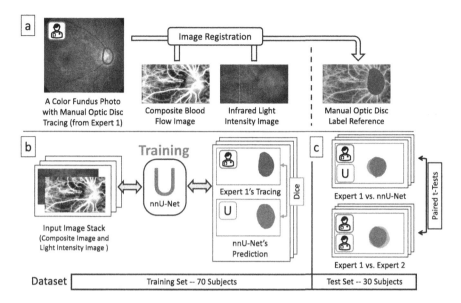

Fig. 2. Overview of the study design. (a) Data preparation: Expert 1 traced the optic disc in the color fundus photograph, and then the traced optic disc contours were registered into the LSFG image domain as the references. (b) The training process of nnU-Net: The nnU-Net's input was the stacked composite and infrared light intensity image pair (i.e., a two-channel input); the truth labels were the registered Expert 1's tracing. (c) Model validation: Paired t-tests were used to compare the differences between Export 1's tracing vs. the nnU-Net prediciton and Expert 1's vs. Expert 2's tracings. The goal is to demonstrate the nnU-Net's predicted optic disc region is closer to Expert 1's tracing than Expert 2's is.

2.2   Model Training

nnU-Net (no-new-UNet v2.1 [5]) is one of the state-of-the-art U-Net variations. It is an open-source tool and is specifically optimized to provide an automated framework (including pre-processing, post-processing, fine tuning parameters, etc.) for the design of segmentation methods reaching human experts' performance level.

In our design (shown in Fig. 2b), we used a two-channel input with light intensity (Channel 0) and composite (Channel 1) images as our nnU-Net input. For the infrared light intensity maps, we set the nnU-Net to normalize the images according to the z-score. For the composite images, we manually normalized the images after histogram equalization to enhance regions with low flow. Both the light intensity and composite images were resized to 750×420 pixels in 8 bits. For the loss function, nnU-Net compared the Dice coefficients between the nnU-Net's predictions and the registered optic disc masks (a binary map of optic disc value of 1 and background value of 0) obtained from Expert 1. A total of 1000 epochs and 5-fold cross-validation were performed by nnU-Net during the training. Only the images from the 70 subjects in the training dataset were used to train the model. The overall training time was approximately 110 h running in Ubuntu 18.04.4 LTS with Intel(R) Core(TM) i7-6800K CPU, GeForce GTX 1080 Ti GPU, and CUDA v10.2.

2.3 Model Evaluations

After training, the trained nnU-Net processed the 30 unseen LSFG composite and light intensity image pairs in the test set, generating 30 individual optic disc masks. To provide a fair comparison with nnU-Net's prediction, a second clinician (Expert 2) independently traced the optic disc in the same 30 test LSFG image pairs, which were aligned and saved as two layers on the iPad. When Expert 2 delineated the disc contour, each of the individual images could be observed and the display switched freely.

For quantification, the Dice coefficient and the intersection over union (IoU) index were used to test how closely the nnU-Net's predictions matched a trained neuro-ophthalmologist's original labeling (Expert 1). We used the same approach to compare Expert 2's ONH tracings to Expert 1's labeling (Fig. 2c). The goal of this comparison is to determine whether the trained nnU-Net can achieve or exceed human-level accuracy. The definitions, for regions A and B, of the Dice coefficient and the IoU index are listed below.

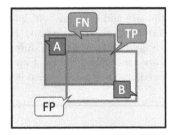

$$Dice = \frac{2\,|A \cap B|}{|A| + |B|} = \frac{2TP}{2TP + FP + FN}$$

$$IoU = \frac{|A \cap B|}{|A \cup B|} = \frac{TP}{TP + FP + FN}$$

Fig. 3. An illustration of the Dice coefficient and IoU index. (TP: True Positive, FP: False Positive, FN: False Negative)

It is worth noting that the Dice coefficient and IoU index are not completely independent to each other; the IoU index tends to penalize a single instance of inaccurate classification more than the Dice coefficient. Generally speaking, the Dice coefficient tends to reward the overlaid region (TP) difference between the prediction and reference, but the IoU index measures the worse-case scenarios (in other words, treating TP, FP, and FN equally). For regions A and B, both Dice coefficient and IoU index have a possible range from 0 (completely disjointed) to 1 (completely overlapped).

3 Results

After training was complete, the mean Dice coefficient comparing the nnU-Net output to Expert 1 labeling for the 70 subjects in the training dataset was 0.91.

Table 1. Comparisons between Expert 1's tracing vs. nnU-Net's prediction and Expert 1's vs. Expert 2's tracings.

	Dice	IoU
Expert 1 vs. nnU-Net	0.92 ± 0.04	0.86 ± 0.06
Expert 1 vs. Expert 2	0.89 ± 0.06	0.81 ± 0.09

For the independent 30 LSFG images in the test dataset, the mean (and standard deviation) Dice coefficient was 0.92 ± 0.04 between the nnU-Net and Expert 1's tracing and 0.89 ± 0.06 between Expert 2's and Expert 1's tracings, respectively. The mean IoU index was 0.86 ± 0.06 between the nnU-Net and Expert 1's tracing and 0.81 ± 0.09 between Expert 2's and Expert 1's tracings (Table 1). Figure 4 is a scatter plot showing the distributions of the 30 data points. Paired t tests showed that the nnU-Net predictions were significantly closer to Expert 1's tracing compared to Expert 2's tracing according to both Dice coefficients and IoU index in the independent test dataset (p-value < 0.001). In order to test the orientation robustness of nnU-Net, we horizontally and vertically flipped the 30 test images and re-ran the experiments, respectively. For both orientation experiments, the outcomes of the Dice coefficient and IoU index were not significantly different. All the segmentation results of the 30 test eyes are shown in Fig. 5.

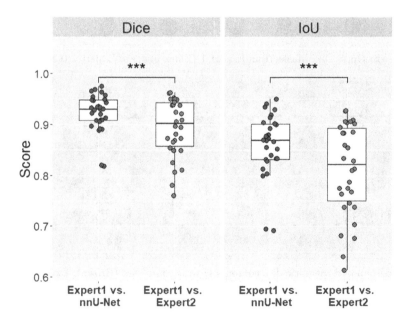

Fig. 4. Scatter plots of Dice coefficient and IoU index comparisons. [$\star\star\star$ represents significant difference (p-value < 0.001)]

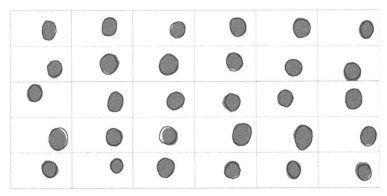

(a) Optic Disc Masks from Expert 1 (Black line) vs. nnU-Net (Brown)

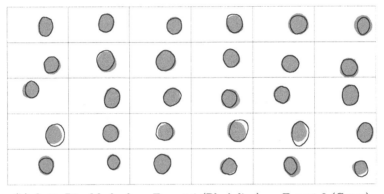

(b) Optic Disc Masks from Expert 1 (Black line) vs. Expert 2 (Green)

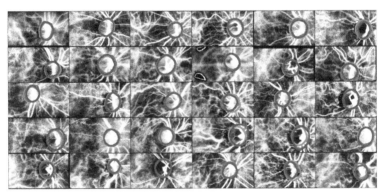

(c) Superimposed the optic disc contours from the nnU-Net (Brown), Expert 1 (Blue) and Expert 2 (Green) in the corresponding composite blood flow image.

Fig. 5. Qualitative results of the 30 subjects in the test dataset. (Color figure online)

4 Discussion and Conclusion

In this study, we successfully demonstrate that the nnU-Net has an outstanding ability to find and demarcate the optic nerve head from LSFG images alone, achieving a human expert's level, after training using high-quality fundus photography-derived labels. This is an important contribution, especially considering that the current standard approach for analyzing the blood flow in the disc from such images requires manual delineation. Given the need for automated approaches in LSFG images, an automated approach such as ours is expected to have a major impact in the field. The nnU-Net is an excellent tool for this task as it takes care of the optimization of the segmentation pipeline design (including pre- and post-processing, data augmentation, fine tuning learning rate, internal cross-validation, etc.), allowing investigators to focus on clinical issues, such as preparing good quality labels and trying novel image modalities (e.g., LSFG). Using fundus photographs to help generate a higher-quality reference standard is also an important observation/contribution, similar to a previous study regarding challenging cases of vessel segmentation in optical coherence tomography due to optic disc swelling [6]. The proposed method can also be applied to other image modalities where the disc border is critical, such as the *en-face* images derived from optical coherence tomography (OCT).

In Fig. 5a, we show that the nnU-Net's predictions overlap Expert 1's tracings quite well. This was true for a variety of optic disc morphologies. The worst of the nnU-Net's predictions (Dice coefficient: 0.82 and IoU index: 0.69) was for a case of optic disc edema with indistinct nerve margins (Fig. 6). Expert 2 had more trouble with larger nerves and sometimes overestimated the disc area when using the LSFG images alone.

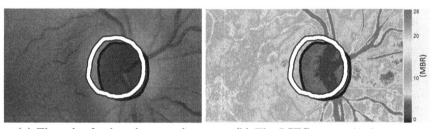

(a) The color fundus photograph   (b) The LSFG composite image

Fig. 6. A comparison between the nnU-Net prediction and Expert 1's tracing in a difficult case with a swollen optic disc. The optic disc is highlighted in white representing Expert 1's tracing and in black representing nnU-Net's prediction, respectively. (Color figure online)

A few limitations exist in this study. First, the process of manual registration is required to convert Expert 1's tracing from the color fundus photograph domain to the LSFG image domain. It will be worth developing an automated method to accelerate this step to allow for more streamlined labeling from fundus photography if we wish to train the approach on additional data in the future (as the registration is only required for training). Second, we randomly selected 100 subjects from the University of Iowa Hospitals and Clinics' LSFG database with no specific disease criteria. Future work will include automated identification of the vessel and artery trees in the LSFG images and identifying meaningful features regarding blood flow at the segmented vessel trees in different diseases or disorders.

Acknowledgements. This study was supported, in part, by the Department of Veteran Affairs (VA) Rehabilitation Research and Development (RR&D) I50RX003002, RR&D I01RX003797, and National Institutes of Health (NIH) R01EY031544.

References

1. Anraku, A., et al.: Ocular and systemic factors affecting laser speckle flowgraphy measurements in the optic nerve head. Trans. Vision Sci. Technol. **10**(1), 13: 1–12 (2021)
2. Fujii, H.: Visualisation of retinal blood flow by laser speckle flow-graphy. Med. Biol. Eng. Comput. **32**(3), 302–304 (1994)
3. Gardiner, S.K., Cull, G., Fortune, B.: Retinal vessel pulsatile characteristics associated with vascular stiffness can predict the rate of functional progression in glaucoma suspects. Investigative Ophthalmol. Visual Sci. **64**(7), 30: 1–11 (2023)
4. Hashimoto, R., Oyamada, M., Maeno, T.: Analysis of optic nerve head circulation using laser speckle flowgraphy in a case of pediatric optic neuritis. EC Ophthalmol. **9**, 572–581 (2018)
5. Isensee, F., Jaeger, P.F., Kohl, S.A.A., Petersen, J., Maier-Hein, K.H.: nnU-Net: a self-configuring method for deep learning-based biomedical image segmentation. Nat. Methods **18**(2), 203–211 (2021)
6. Islam, M.S., Wang, J.K., Johnson, S.S., Thurtell, M.J., Kardon, R.H., Garvin, M.K.: A deep-learning approach for automated OCT en-face retinal vessel segmentation in cases of optic disc swelling using multiple en-face images as input. Trans. Vis. Sci. Technol. **9**(2), 17: 1–15 (2020)
7. Jin, B., Liu, P., Wang, P., Shi, L., Zhao, J.: Optic disc segmentation using attention-based U-Net and the improved cross-entropy convolutional neural network. Entropy **22**(8), 844: 1–13 (2020)
8. Kiyota, N., Kunikata, H., Shiga, Y., Omodaka, K., Nakazawa, T.: Ocular microcirculation measurement with laser speckle flowgraphy and optical coherence tomography angiography in glaucoma. Acta Ophthalmol. **96**(4), e485–e492 (2018)
9. Konishi, N., Tokimoto, Y., Kohra, K., Fujii, H.: New laser speckle flowgraphy system using CCD camera. Opt. Rev. **9**(4), 163–169 (2002)
10. Liu, B., Pan, D., Song, H.: Joint optic disc and cup segmentation based on densely connected depthwise separable convolution deep network. BMC Med. Imaging **21**(1), 14: 1–12 (2021)
11. Maekubo, T., Chuman, H., Nao-i, N.: Laser speckle flowgraphy for differentiating between nonarteritic ischemic optic neuropathy and anterior optic neuritis. Jpn. J. Ophthalmol. **57**(4), 385–390 (2013)

12. Matsumoto, M., et al.: Retinal vascular resistance significantly correlates with visual acuity after 1 year of anti-VEGF therapy in central retinal vein occlusion. Trans. Vis. Sci. Technol. **10**(11), 19: 1–10 (2021)
13. Ronneberger, O., Fischer, P., Brox, T.: U-Net: convolutional networks for biomedical image segmentation. In: Medical Image Computing and Computer-Assisted Intervention - MICCAI 2015, pp. 234–241 (2015)
14. Sampietro, T., et al.: Acute increase in ocular microcirculation blood flow upon cholesterol removal. The eyes are the window of the heart. Am. J. Med. **136**(1), 108–114 (2023)
15. Siddique, N., Paheding, S., Elkin, C.P., Devabhaktuni, V.: U-Net and its variants for medical image segmentation: a review of theory and applications. IEEE Access **9**, 82031–82057 (2021)
16. Sugiyama, T.: Basic technology and clinical applications of the updated model of laser speckle flowgraphy to ocular diseases. Photonics **1**(3), 220–234 (2014)
17. Takahashi, H., et al.: Comparison of CCD-equipped laser speckle flowgraphy with hydrogen gas clearance method in the measurement of optic nerve head microcirculation in rabbits. Exp. Eye Res. **108**, 10–15 (2013)

Multi-relational Graph Convolutional Neural Networks for Carotid Artery Stenosis Diagnosis via Fundus Images

Junlong Qu[1], Hai Xie[1], Yingpeng Xie[1], Huiling Hu[2], Jiaqiang Li[1], Yunlong Sun[1], Guoming Zhang[2(✉)], and Baiying Lei[1(✉)]

[1] School of Biomedical Engineering, Health Science Center, National-Regional Key Technology Engineering Laboratory for Medical Ultrasound, Guangdong Key Laboratory for Biomedical Measurements and Ultrasound Imaging, Shenzhen University, Shenzhen, China
leiby@szu.edu.cn
[2] Shenzhen Eye Hospital, Jinan University, Shenzhen Eye Institute, Shenzhen, Guangdong, China
zhangguoming@sz-eyes.com

Abstract. The accumulation of carotid plaque leads to carotid artery stenosis, which in turn increases the risk of cerebrovascular disease. Non-invasive diagnosis of carotid stenosis using fundus images offers a promising approach. However, the challenge lies in extracting relevant features from these images, as convolutional neural networks(CNNs) or Transformers, which focus solely on individual images, fail to consider the interdependencies between them, leading to limited diagnostic accuracy. To address this issue, we propose a novel and effective network by combining CNNs and multi-relational graph convolutional neural networks(M-GCNs). Firstly, we feed the input images into four distinct branches, which consist of CNNs or Transformers, with each branch associated with a particular relation. This process generates unique feature vectors for each branch. Secondly, we construct a multi-graph for the four kinds of clinical data, such as gender, age, sex and pid, to obtain four adjacency matrices. Finally, the feature vectors and the corresponding four adjacency matrices are input into the graph convolutional network layer respectively to obtain the prediction features, and then the prediction results are obtained through the fully connected layer. Experiments are carried out on a private dataset and the results demonstrate that the accuracy of the proposed algorithm is **10%–20%** higher than that of the comparison model. Our code is available at https://github.com/momoyrz/Carotid-stenosis.

Keywords: Carotid artery stenosis · Fundus image classification · Multi-relational Graph Convolutional Neural Network

B. Antony et al. (Eds.): OMIA 2023, LNCS 14096, pp. 122–131, 2023.
https://doi.org/10.1007/978-3-031-44013-7_13

1   Introduction

Carotid artery stenosis refers to the narrowing or constriction of the carotid arteries, which are the major blood vessels located on either side of the neck that supply oxygenated blood to the brain [5,26]. Stenosis occurs when there is a buildup of plaque, consisting of cholesterol, fat, calcium, and other substances, along the inner walls of the carotid arteries [14,21]. This can lead to reduced blood flow to the brain, potentially resulting in serious complications such as stroke or transient ischemic attack. Retinal vessels and cerebral vessels belong to the branches of carotid artery, which can reflect the changes of cerebral vascular microcirculation [1]. As the only microvessels that can be observed in vivo under non-invasive conditions [3], retinal vessels provide the possibility of non-invasive vascular examination in vivo. In view of this, fundus images are used for the diagnosis of carotid stenosis. However, specialized ophthalmologists are unable to extract information related to carotid artery stenosis from fundus images. Therefore, it is crucial to utilize artificial intelligence(AI) techniques for computer-aided diagnosis. AI technology has revolutionized the field of medical diagnosis, particularly in the analysis of fundus images for detecting various ocular diseases [8]. Fundus images provide a detailed view of the retina, enabling the identification of abnormalities associated with conditions such as diabetic retinopathy, age-related macular degeneration, and glaucoma. AI algorithms trained on large datasets of fundus images, combined with deep learning techniques, have demonstrated remarkable accuracy and efficiency in diagnosing these diseases [15]. However, to the best of our knowledge, no investigators have used fundus images to make a diagnosis of carotid stenosis.

Learning the low-dimensional representation of images is a crucial objective in computer vision, and convolutional neural network (CNN) architectures, as a prominent deep learning technique, have made significant advancements in this area for image classification [13]. Additionally, the Transformer models has further enriched the field by enhancing the ability to capture long-range dependencies and enabling efficient attention-based mechanisms for image understanding [24]. Nonetheless, CNN and Transformer methods focus solely on individual images, disregarding the interdependencies between them [23]. Multi-relational Graph Convolutional Networks (M-GCNs) can simulate the association between patients and achieve excellent performance in node classification tasks with superior correlation capture ability [22,27]. The effectiveness of M-GCNs is evident in handling low-dimensional feature vectors in nodes. However, their applicability to high-dimensional data, such as images, is limited. In contrast, CNNs or Transformers excel at mapping high-dimensional images to low-dimensional feature vectors. Hence, we propose a novel and effective network by combining CNNs or Transformers and M-GCNs, enabling the learning of high-dimensional and unstructured features for accurate diagnosis of carotid stenosis. The main contributions are as follows: 1)According to the available literature, our study represents a pioneering effort in the integration of M-GCNs and CNNs or Transformers for the purpose of fundus image classification. 2)Extensive experiments

124   J. Qu et al.

have been conducted to substantiate the efficacy of our proposed method, aiming to enhance the diagnostic accuracy of carotid artery stenosis detection in fundus images.

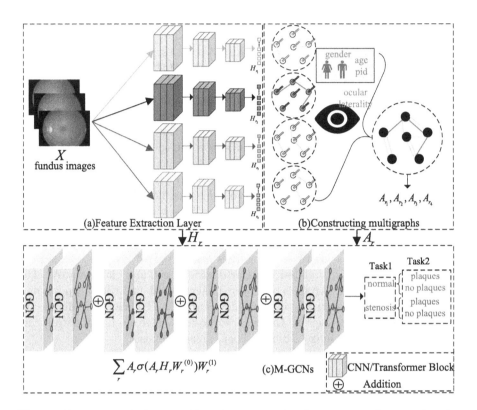

Fig. 1. Illustration of the overall architecture. We first extract features by feature extraction layer and construct a multi-graph by diverse clinical data. At last, the extracted features and multi-graphs are fed to M-GCNs for artery stenosis diagnosis.

2   Methodology

In this study, a new framework is devised for carotid stenosis detection. As shown in Fig. 1, the proposed method contains three modules: (1)Feature extraction layer, (2) Constructing multi-graphs, (3)M-GCNs. To be specific, the input image is fed into four distinct branches, each is specifically associated with a particular relation. Each branch yields a unique feature vector corresponding to its respective relation. Furthermore, considering the existence of four relationships within the image, a multi-graph is constructed, and four adjacency matrices are derived to represent these relationships. Finally, feature extraction is performed to obtain feature vectors, while the adjacency matrix, along with the extracted features, is utilized in the GCN layer. This integration facilitates the propagation of information and enhances the modeling capability by considering both learned features and the structural relationships present in the constructed multiple figure.

2.1 Feature Extraction Layer

Initially, the input images $X \in \mathbb{R}^{N \times C \times N \times W}$ undergo feature extraction via separate branches, where each branch corresponds to a distinct pretrained CNN or Transformer architecture. In each branch r_i, the last fully connected layer and classifier layer are excluded, while the remaining feature layers are retained to extract the feature maps. Subsequently, a global pooling layer is applied to the feature maps to generate feature vectors. The forward propagation process is shown in:

$$H_{r_i} = f_{r_i}(X), \tag{1}$$

where f_{r_i} is the feature extraction function, and H_{r_i} is the feature vector of the image with respect to the relation r_i. The inclusion of a feature extraction process for each relation results in a significant escalation in the total number of parameters within the model, thereby leading to the development of a large-scale model. Consequently, improving the performance of the model demands substantial computational resources and storage capacity, which poses challenges during the training process. To address this challenge, as shown in Fig. 2(b), we introduce a parameter sharing strategy in our proposed framework. Specifically, we adopt a unified CNN/Transformer architecture across all branches, ensuring that all branches except for the last fully connected layer of the feature extraction layer share the same structure [9,20]. This parameter sharing approach enables efficient utilization of model parameters by reducing redundancy and optimizing computational resources. By leveraging this strategy, we strike a balance between model complexity and computational efficiency, effectively alleviating

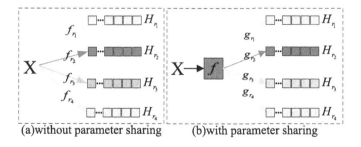

(a)without parameter sharing   (b)with parameter sharing

Fig. 2. Forward propagation process of feature extraction layer.(a) Without parameter sharing. (b) With parameter sharing.

the computational and storage burden associated with a large number of relations. Therefore, Eq. 1 can be further refined as:

$$H_{r_i} = g_{r_i}(f(X)), \tag{2}$$

where g_{r_i} is the fully connected layer and f is shared by all relations.

2.2   Constructing Multi-graphs

In the realm of precision medicine, there has been a growing recognition of the crucial role played by individualization, as well as demographic factors such as age and gender, in shaping patient-specific disease progression and outcomes [12]. In fundus image datasets, the existence of clinical data introduces diverse relationships among images [7,18]. To represent the relationships, we utilize a binary adjacency matrix A_r for each relation r. In this matrix, each element $A(i,j)$ corresponds to row i and column j, indicating a value of 1 if there exists a connection or association between image i and image j. Conversely, a value of 0 denotes the absence of such a relationship. The equation is expressed as:

$$A_r[i][j] = \begin{cases} 1, & the\, propertyr\, of\, image\, i\, and\, image\, j\, is\, equal \\ 0, & otherwise \end{cases}. \tag{3}$$

2.3   M-GCNs

GCN leverages both node features and graph structure to derive meaningful representations for nodes in a graph. GCNs employ a propagation rule based on spectral graph convolutions, specifically designed for undirected graphs, to learn node representations [2,6]. This propagation rule enables GCNs to effectively capture both feature information and relational dependencies present in the graph [11]:

$$H^{(l+1)} = \sigma(\widetilde{D}^{-\frac{1}{2}}\widetilde{A}\widetilde{D}^{-\frac{1}{2}}H^{(l)}W^{(l)}), \tag{4}$$

where $\widetilde{A} = A + I_n$ refers to the adjacency matrix of the undirected graph $\mathcal{G}$, augmented with self-connections, where $I_N \in \mathbb{R}^{N \times N}$ is an identity matrix of dimension N and A is the adjacency matrix of an undirected graph $\mathcal{G}$. $\widetilde{D}_{ii} = \sum_j \widetilde{A}_{ij}$ and $W^{(l)}$ is the trainable matrix in the lth layer, $\sigma()$ is the activation function, such as the ReLU. $H^{(l)} \in \mathbb{R}^{N \times D}$ is the node representation in the lth layer. One drawback of the traditional GCN (Eq. 4) is its limited capability to handle multiple relationship types or complex relational patterns [16]. By considering only a single relationship, the model may overlook important connections and dependencies within the graph data, leading to suboptimal performance in scenarios where multiple relationships exist. Therefore, in this study, we enhance the GCN model by extending it to accommodate multiple relationships [13]:

$$H_r^{(l+1)} = \phi\left(\sum_{r \in R} A_r H_r^{(l)} W_r^{(l)}\right). \tag{5}$$

This extension allows for a more comprehensive exploration of the interplay between different relations in the graph, leading to an enhanced modeling capability and improved performance in capturing the intricate relationships present in complex graph structures.

Table 1. Classification results compared with baseline models. The bold text means our method preforms best in all methods. The numerical values accompanying the upper arrows represent the extent of improvement achieved by our method in comparison to the baseline models.

Task	Method	ACC	AUC	Pre	Sen	F1	Spec	Kappa
Task1	CrossViT	59.47	56.57	58.64	57.58	57.07	57.58	15.6
	C-GCN	75.18	80.75	75.45	74.76	74.84	74.76	49.85
		(15.71)	(24.18)	(16.81)	(17.18)	(17.77)	(17.18)	(34.25)
	Swin-T	58.95	56.95	59.3	59.38	58.92	59.38	18.42
	S-GCN	73.04	78.14	75.69	75.14	75.27	76.09	51.22
		(14.09)	(21.19)	(16.39)	(15.76)	(16.35)	(16.71)	(32.8)
	ResNet34	60.88	60.67	60.31	58.88	58.33	58.88	18.33
	Res-GCN	79.56	84.12	**80.93**	78.89	79.02	78.89	58.49
		(18.68)	(23.45)	(20.62)	(20.01)	(20.69)	(20.01)	(40.16)
	EfficientNet	55.96	54.9	54.21	52.6	49.13	52.6	5.51
	E-GCN	**79.93**	**88.92**	80.68	**79.41**	**79.55**	**79.41**	**59.35**
		(23.97)	(34.02)	(26.47)	(26.81)	(30.42)	(26.81)	(53.84)
Task2	CrossViT	42.81	61.21	18.2	35	22.35	78	4.2
	C-GCN	54.74	73.86	48.23	45.17	45.46	83.33	32.97
		(11.93)	(12.65)	(30.03)	(10.17)	(23.11)	(5.33)	(28.77)
	Swin-T	43.33	62.7	33.3	28.61	24.01	77.18	8.64
	S-GCN	56.2	71.26	50.99	45.26	45.78	82.16	34.23
		(12.87)	(8.56)	(17.69)	(16.65)	(21.77)	(4.98)	(25.59)
	ResNet34	45.09	61.72	38.54	35.48	35.3	79.09	16.55
	Res-GCN	**63.37**	74.4	50.66	43.75	43.33	**85.31**	40.66
		(18.28)	(12.68)	(12.12)	(8.27)	(8.03)	(6.22)	(24.11)
	EfficientNet	41.75	58.61	32.09	27.51	23	76.46	5.79
	E-GCN	60.22	**80.13**	**56.98**	**52.27**	**53.61**	85.29	**41.4**
		(18.47)	(21.52)	(24.89)	(24.76)	(30.61)	(8.83)	(35.61)

3 Experiments and Results

3.1 Dataset

The study utilized data collected from the local health examination center, covering the period from January 2021 to January 2023. A total of 3033 fundus

photos, accompanied by carotid artery color Doppler ultrasound data, were analyzed. The examination population was divided into four groups based on carotid
ultrasound findings: group 1 (no stenosis or plaque), group 2 (plaque without
stenosis), group 3 (no plaque), and group 4 (both stenosis and plaque). Two
classification tasks were performed: the 2-class task, which focused on carotid
stenosis presence or absence in fundus images, and the 4-class task, which considered plaque presence or absence.

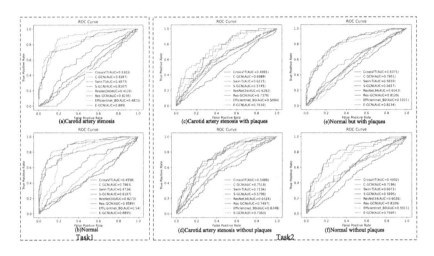

Fig. 3. ROC curves of different methods in different categories in two tasks.

3.2 Results

In this study, we use ResNet34 [10], EfficientNet-B0 [25], SwinTransformer-Tiny
[17], CrossViT-Tiny [4] as baseline models for the classification tasks within
our dataset. These baseline models were utilized as the feature extraction layer,
referred to as f, in our proposed framework. We conducted pairwise comparisons
among the eight models, considering both task 1 and task 2. The experimental
results and encompassing performance metrics are presented in Table 1. Table 1
demonstrates the significant improvement achieved by the proposed method in
nearly all classification metrics, ranging from 10% to 30%. These findings serve
as compelling evidence validating the efficacy and effectiveness of the approach
employed in this study. Furthermore, Fig. 3 presents the Receiver Operating
Characteristic (ROC) curves for both tasks. The ROC curves depict the performance of various classification methods, and notably, our proposed classification
method exhibits superior performance across both tasks. The higher position-
ing of our method's ROC curve indicates its superior discriminative power and
ability to accurately distinguish between different classes. In addition, we also
use t-SNE [19] to visualize the features learned by different models in the last
feature extraction layer, and the results of task 1 are shown in Fig. 4. The effectiveness of the method proposed in this study can be further demonstrated from
the t-SNE visualization results.

To assess the impact of each relationship on the final classification outcomes, a series of ablation experiments were conducted in this study. The findings of these ablation experiments are summarized in Table 2. The results indicate that all relationships lead to improved classification performance. Note that the best classification results are obtained when all four relationships are simultaneously employed. When considering individual relationships, the pid relationship exhibits notably superior performance compared to the other three relationships. The reason is that the pid relationship potentially captures relevant information pertaining to a patient's age, gender, and ocular laterality. Additionally, as depicted in Table 2, it is evident that the gender and ocular laterality relationships have the least influence on the classification results, as observed from the ablation experiments.

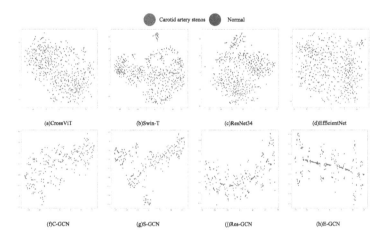

Fig. 4. t-SNE visualization results of task1 under different methods.

Table 2. The influence of individual relationships on the final outcomes is analyzed for both classification tasks. The highest value in each column is highlighted in bold, representing the maximum performance achieved.

	Relation	ACC	AUC	Pre	Sen	F1	Spec	Kappa
Task1	ocular laterality	57.66	63.12	57.42	57.35	57.34	57.35	14.75
	gender	58.76	57.43	59.64	57.36	55.42	57.36	15.09
	age	58.03	61.26	57.76	57.56	57.48	57.56	15.23
	pid	**74.82**	**87.11**	**75.92**	**74.11**	**74.12**	**74.11**	**48.83**
Task2	ocular laterality	40.15	62	33.99	30.56	29.55	77.07	8.56
	gender	41.24	64.52	35.69	33.07	33.02	77.86	11.81
	age	44.53	62.99	40.64	35.8	36.15	78.96	16.36
	pid	**52.92**	**74.98**	**47.46**	**43**	**43.51**	**82.35**	**29.56**

4   Conclusion

In this paper, we addresses a realistic and underexplored scenario in the field of fundus image analysis, where the distinctive features of fundus images are limited. In order to bridge this research gap, we present a novel framework based on M-GCNs that specifically targets classification in such challenging scenarios. Our proposed method effectively captures the intricate relationships between fundus images and utilizes this information to enhance the classification process. Significantly, our framework surpasses the performance of state-of-the-art models and even outperforms the clinical accuracy of expert doctors. By addressing the limitations of existing approaches, our research contributes to advancing the field of fundus image analysis and offers valuable insights for improved classification methodologies in similar contexts.

Acknowledgements. This work is supported in part by the National Natural Science Foundation of China(No.U22A2024, 62106153, 82271103), Guangdong Basic and Applied Basic Research Foundation(No.2020A1515110605, 2022A15150 12326) and Natural Science Foundation of Shenzhen(No.JCYJ20220818095809021).

References

1. Belotti, F., et al.: Ophthalmic artery originating from the anterior cerebral artery: anatomo-radiological study, histological analysis, and literature review. Neurosurg. Rev. **39**(3), 483–493 (2016)
2. Bruna, J., Zaremba, W., Szlam, A., LeCun, Y.: Spectral networks and locally connected networks on graphs (2014)
3. Chaikijurajai, T., Ehlers, J.P., Tang, W.H.W.: Retinal microvasculature: a potential window into heart failure prevention. JACC Heart Fail. **10**(11), 785–791 (2022)
4. Chen, C.F.R., Fan, Q., Panda, R.: Crossvit: cross-attention multi-scale vision transformer for image classification. In: Proceedings of the IEEE/CVF International Conference on Computer Vision, pp. 357–366 (2021)
5. Debrey, S.M., et al.: Diagnostic accuracy of magnetic resonance angiography for internal carotid artery disease: a systematic review and meta-analysis. Stroke **39**(8), 2237–2248 (2008)
6. Defferrard, M., Bresson, X., Vandergheynst, P.: Convolutional neural networks on graphs with fast localized spectral filtering (2017)
7. Fu, H., Cheng, J., Xu, Y., Wong, D.W.K., Liu, J., Cao, X.: Joint optic disc and cup segmentation based on multi-label deep network and polar transformation. IEEE Trans. Medical Imaging **37**(7), 1597–1605 (2018). https://doi.org/10.1109/TMI.2018.2791488
8. Gulshan, V., et al.: Development and validation of a deep learning algorithm for detection of diabetic retinopathy in retinal fundus photographs. JAMA **316**(22), 2402–2410 (2016)
9. Hamilton, W., Ying, Z., Leskovec, J.: Inductive representation learning on large graphs. Adv. Neural Inf. Process. Syst. **30**, 1–11 (2017)
10. He, K., Zhang, X., Ren, S., Sun, J.: Deep residual learning for image recognition. In: 2016 IEEE Conference on Computer Vision and Pattern Recognition (CVPR), pp. 770–778. IEEE, Las Vegas (2016)

11. Jiang, B., Zhang, Z., Lin, D., Tang, J., Luo, B.: Semi-supervised learning with graph learning-convolutional networks. In: 2019 IEEE/CVF Conference on Computer Vision and Pattern Recognition (CVPR), pp. 11305–11312 (2019)

12. Kohane, I.S.: Ten things we have to do to achieve precision medicine. Science **349**(6243), 37–38 (2015). https://doi.org/10.1126/science.aab1328

13. Krizhevsky, A., Sutskever, I., Hinton, G.E.: ImageNet classification with deep convolutional neural networks. Commun. ACM **60**(6), 84–90 (2017)

14. Lee, J.I., et al.: Stroke in patients with occlusion of the internal carotid artery: options for treatment. Expert Rev. Neurotherapeut. **14**(10), 1153–1167 (2014)

15. Li, F., et al.: Deep learning-based automated detection for diabetic retinopathy and diabetic macular oedema in retinal fundus photographs. Eye **36**(7), 1433–1441 (2022)

16. Li, X., Ng, M.K., Xu, G., Yip, A.: Multi-relational graph convolutional networks: Generalization guarantees and experiments. Neural Netw. **161**, 343–358 (2023). https://www.sciencedirect.com/science/article/abs/pii/S0893608023000576

17. Liu, Z., et al.: Swin transformer: hierarchical vision transformer using shifted windows. In: 2021 IEEE/CVF International Conference on Computer Vision (ICCV), pp. 9992–10002. IEEE, Montreal (2021)

18. Lu, W., Tong, Y., Yu, Y., Xing, Y., Chen, C., Shen, Y.: Deep learning-based automated classification of multi-categorical abnormalities from optical coherence tomography images. Transl. Vision Sci. Technol. **7**(6), 41–41 (2018)

19. van der Maaten, L., Hinton, G.: Visualizing data using t-sne. J. Mach. Learn. Res. **9**(86), 2579–2605 (2008). https://www.jmlr.org/papers/v9/vandermaaten08a.html

20. Mao, C., Yao, L., Luo, Y.: ImageGCN: multi-relational image graph convolutional networks for disease identification with chest x-rays. IEEE Trans. Med. Imaging **41**(8), 1990–2003 (2022)

21. Momjian-Mayor, I., Baron, J.C.: The pathophysiology of watershed infarction in internal carotid artery disease: review of cerebral perfusion studies. Stroke **36**(3), 567–577 (2005)

22. Schlichtkrull, M., Kipf, T.N., Bloem, P., van den Berg, R., Titov, I., Welling, M.: Modeling relational data with graph convolutional networks. In: Gangemi, A., et al. (eds.) ESWC 2018. LNCS, vol. 10843, pp. 593–607. Springer, Cham (2018). https://doi.org/10.1007/978-3-319-93417-4_38

23. Shaban, M., Awan, R., Fraz, M.M., Azam, A., Snead, D., Rajpoot, N.M.: Context-aware convolutional neural network for grading of colorectal cancer histology images (2019)

24. Shamshad, F., et al.: Transformers in medical imaging: a survey. Med. Image Anal. **88**, 102802 (2023)

25. Tan, M., Le, Q.: Efficientnet: rethinking model scaling for convolutional neural networks. In: International Conference on Machine Learning, pp. 6105–6114. PMLR (2019)

26. Wiebers, D.O., et al.: Pathogenesis, natural history, and treatment of unruptured intracranial aneurysms. In: Mayo Clinic Proceedings, vol. 79, pp. 1572–1583. Elsevier (2004)

27. Zitnik, M., Agrawal, M., Leskovec, J.: Modeling polypharmacy side effects with graph convolutional networks. Bioinformatics **34**(13), i457–i466 (2018)

Pretrained Deep 2.5D Models for Efficient Predictive Modeling from Retinal OCT: A PINNACLE Study Report

Taha Emre[1], Marzieh Oghbaie[2], Arunava Chakravarty[1], Antoine Rivail[2], Sophie Riedl[1], Julia Mai[1], Hendrik P.N. Scholl[6,7], Sobha Sivaprasad[3], Daniel Rueckert[4,5], Andrew Lotery[8], Ursula Schmidt-Erfurth[1], and Hrvoje Bogunović[2(✉)]

[1] Department of Ophthalmology and Optometry, Medical University of Vienna, Vienna, Austria
[2] Christian Doppler Lab for Artificial Intelligence in Retina, Department of Ophthalmology and Optometry, Medical University of Vienna, Vienna, Austria
{taha.emre,marzieh.oghbaie,hrvoje.bogunovic}@meduniwien.ac.at
[3] NIHR Moorfields Biomedical Research Centre, Moorfields Eye Hospital NHS Foundation Trust, London, UK
[4] BioMedIA, Imperial College London, London, UK
[5] Institute for AI and Informatics in Medicine, Klinikum rechts der Isar, Technical University Munich, Munich, Germany
[6] Institute of Molecular and Clinical Ophthalmology Basel, Basel, Switzerland
[7] Department of Ophthalmology, University of Basel, Basel, Switzerland
[8] Clinical and Experimental Sciences, Faculty of Medicine, University of Southampton, Southampton, UK

Abstract. In the field of medical imaging, 3D deep learning models play a crucial role in building powerful predictive models of disease progression. However, the size of these models presents significant challenges, both in terms of computational resources and data requirements. Moreover, achieving high-quality pretraining of 3D models proves to be even more challenging. To address these issues, hybrid 2.5D approaches provide an effective solution for utilizing 3D volumetric data efficiently using 2D models. Combining 2D and 3D techniques offers a promising avenue for optimizing performance while minimizing memory requirements. In this paper, we explore 2.5D architectures based on a combination of convolutional neural networks (CNNs), long short-term memory (LSTM), and Transformers. In addition, leveraging the benefits of recent non-contrastive pretraining approaches in 2D, we enhanced the performance and data efficiency of 2.5D techniques even further. We demonstrate the effectiveness of architectures and associated pretraining on a task of predicting progression to wet age-related macular degeneration (AMD) within a six-month period on two large longitudinal OCT datasets.

T. Emre and M. Oghbaie—These authors contributed equally to this work.

1   Introduction

3D imaging modalities are routinely employed in clinics for diagnosis, treatment planning and tracking disease progression. Thus, automated deep learning (DL) based methods for the classification of 3D image volumes can play an important role in reducing the time and effort of medical experts. However, the training and design of 3D classification models are challenging as they are computationally expensive, consume large amount of GPU memory during training and require large training datasets to prevent over-fitting. These issues are further exacerbated by the more recent Vision Transformer (ViT) architectures which have been shown to require significantly larger amounts of training data to outperform CNNs. Yet, in the medical domain, there is often a scarcity of labeled training data, especially in the case of 3D imaging modalities.

The gold-standard 3D imaging modality in ophthalmology is retinal Optical Coherence Tomography (OCT). It is of particular value in the management of patients with Age-Related Macular Degeneration (AMD), the leading cause of blindness in the elderly population. Although asymptomatic in the intermediate stage ($iAMD$), it may progress to a late stage known as $wet\text{-}AMD$, which is characterized by a significant vision loss. Thus, development of an effective personalized prognostic model of AMD using OCT would be of large clinical relevance. Given an input OCT scan of an eye in the $iAMD$ stage, we aim to develop efficient 3D prognostic models that can predict whether the eye will progress to the $wet\text{-}AMD$ stage within a clinically relevant time-window of 6 months, modeling the problem as a binary classification task. The lack of well-defined clinical biomarkers indicative of the future risk of progression, large inter-subject variability in the speed of AMD progression and large class imbalance between the progressors (minority class) and non-progressors (majority class) makes it a challenging machine learning task.

Given the above limitations, 2.5D architecture may be an effective approach for building prognostic models from volumetric OCT: it comprises a 2D network applied to each slice of the input volume followed by a second stage to aggregate the feature representations across the slices. Compared to 3D models, the 2D ones can be more effectively pretrained on large labeled natural image datasets such as ImageNet or on an unlabeled in-domain dataset of images of the same imaging modality using Self-Supervised Learning (SSL).

In this work, we analyze the impact of different DL architectures and pretraining schemes in the context of developing an effective prognostic classification model using OCT volumes of patients with AMD. We first address the problem of limited data availability with an effective in-domain SSL to pretrain 2D CNN weights. We then address the challenge of processing volumetric data by transferring the pretrained 2D CNN weights to a hybrid 2.5D deep learning framework. Our evaluation on two large longitudinal datasets underscores the advantages of such hybrid approach in 3D medical image analysis, and highlights the importance of in-domain pretraining in low data scenarios.

1.1 Related Work

Deep Neural Network Architectures for 3D Predictions. 3D CNNs employ large 3D isotropic convolutions, making them computationally expensive with a significantly increased number of trainable parameters. This makes them prone to over-fitting with limited training data. Moreover, pretrained models weights are more commonly available for 2D CNNs and they cannot be directly used to initialize the 3D networks for fine-tuning. To tackle these limitations, two main directions have been explored: inflating pretrained 2D CNNs into 3D networks or using Multiple Instance Learning (MIL) in a 2.5D setting. The first approach is based on the Inflated 3D Convnets [3] which were proposed as a new paradigm for an efficient video processing network using 2D pretrained weights. They achieved this by *inflating* 2D convolutional kernels along the time dimension with a scaling factor.

MIL is an efficient way of processing 3D volumes or videos [6]. The main idea is to process each 2D component (slice in a 3D volume or frame in a video) of the 3D data individually using a 2D CNN and then pool their output feature embeddings to obtain a single feature representation for the entire 3D data. Average Pooling is commonly employed to integrate the features from each 2D slice/frame in a linear and non-parametric manner. Alternatively, more complex architectures based on LSTMs have also been explored for pooling. Due to their directionality, vanilla LSTMs are better suited for processing videos by modeling the forward flow of time, and using the output from the last time-step as the feature for the entire video. However, a Bidirectional LSTM (BiLSTM) is required to capture the non-directional nature of 3D OCT volumes [12].

Recently, ViTs replaced CNN based models as state-of-the-art. One downside of ViTs is that they require large training datasets and extensive training duration, which are even amplified with 3D modalities. Indeed, the patch-based 3D/video processing ViTs [1,8,19] process videos through spatio-temporal attention, and 3D volumes with isotropic 3D images of voxels. On the other hand, it has been repeatedly demonstrated that ViTs benefit from the application of convolutional kernels in the earlier blocks [5,21]. Similar to the LSTM based approaches, hybrid ViTs have been successfully applied to video recognition tasks for memory efficiency and speed. In [16], the video frames are treated as patches and their embeddings are extracted using a ResNet18 which are forwarded to a transformer model. ViT hybrids focus on efficiency by first processing 2D instances (frames, cross-sectional volume slices), then obtaining a final score from the ViT which is used as a feature aggregator. In medical imaging, CNN + Transformer hybrids are already being used to address the MIL problems such as in whole-slide images [17] or histopathology images [14]. A 3D transformer ViViTs [1] were proposed for video analysis. They deploy different strategies to model the interactions between spatial and temporal dimensions at various levels of the model. One of the modes of ViViT denoted as Factorised Self-Attention (FSA), consists in factorizing the attention over the input dimensions. Each transformer block processes both spatial and temporal dimensions simultaneously instead of two separate encoders which makes the network adaptable for 3D volumes.

Self Supervised Pretraining. SSL pretraining aims to generate meaningful data representations without relying on manual labels. Utilizing pretrained network weights obtained through SSL reduces the requirement for labeled data while simultaneously boosting performance in downstream tasks. It is particularly useful when dealing with noisy and highly imbalanced class labels, as it helps prevent overfitting [2]. Contrastive learning [4] has emerged as one of the most successful SSL approaches. They aim to learn representations that are robust to expected real-world perturbations, while encoding distinctive structures that enable the discrimination of different instances. To achieve invariance against these perturbations, contrastive methods heavily rely on augmentations that create two transformed images, which the models try to bring together while pushing apart the representations of pairs from different instances.

Emre et al. [7] adapted contrastive augmentations for 2D B-scan characteristics. Additionally, they proposed to use two different scans of a patient from two different visit date as inputs to the contrastive pipeline. The extra temporal information was exploited through a time sensitive non-contrastive similarity loss, termed as *TINC* loss, to induce a difference in similarity between the pairs based on the time difference between them. In the end, they showed that the time sensitive image representations were more useful in longitudinal prediction tasks. In this study, we used *TINC* as the main pretraining method.

2   Methods: Predictive Model from Retinal OCT Volume

Predicting the progression to wet-AMD inherently involves a temporal aspect, as patients typically undergo multiple follow-up scans. However, the practicality of capturing temporal information is constrained by factors such as the availability of regularly scanned patients and computational costs. Therefore, we tackled the task as a binary risk classification problem from a given visit.

We explored two hybrid 2.5D architectures (Fig. 1), that utilize 2D CNN to generate B-scan embeddings, followed by either an LSTM or a Transformer network to produce volume-level predictions. The CNNs are based on ResNet50 and a B-scan representation is obtained by applying Global Average Pooling on the final feature map of the ResNet50 model, yielding a vector of size 2048. The CNNs were either pretrained in a non-contrastive manner, using *TINC* [7] on temporal OCT data, or *ImageNet* ResNet50 weights from the torchvision library [15] were used.

CNN + BiLSTM. Such networks have already been proposed for 3D OCTs [12]. Unlike standard LSTMs, BiLSTMs provide two outputs for each "time step" (in our case B-scan). Each output can be used for B-scan level prediction, if such labels are available as in [12]. However, wet-AMD progression prediction task is a MIL problem where the labels are available per OCT volume. The straightforward choice for aggregating the outputs would be average pooling but we hypothesised that OCT biomarkers indicative of wet-AMD progression are subtle and scarce. Thus, in order to make the predictions more robust, an

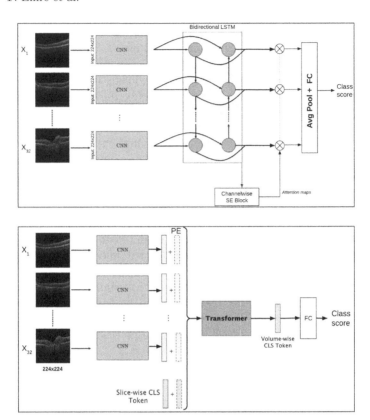

Fig. 1. Architecture of the two evaluated 2.5D approaches: (top) CNN + BiLSTM with attention, (bottom) CNN + Transformer

attention layer attached to the end of BiLSTM. The goal is to enforce B-scan level sparsity with attention such that subtle biomarkers do not blur out due to the global pooling operations. Moreover, we believe the B-scans with the highest attention weights will serve as ideal candidates for clinical inspection to discover novel biomarkers and phenotypes associated with progression to wet-AMD.

The BiLSTM comprises 32 time-steps (the number of B-scans used from an OCT volume) and a hidden state representation of size 512. For the final attention layer, we used a Squeeze-and-Excitation layer [11] adapted for stacked representations (Fig. 1). We will refer to this model as CNN + BiLSTM without explicitly mentioning the attention layer.

CNN + Transformer. ViTs are known for requiring longer training and larger datasets [13]. Moreover, in-domain pretrained weights for medical images are not as commonly available as they are for natural images. Motivated by this, we developed a hybrid CNN + Transformer model that leverages pretrained weights for the 2D CNN backbone. We attached a small Transformer on top of the 2D B-scan representations to obtain the final prediction. In this approach, each representation is treated as a patch embedding, representing one of the B-scans. Similar to BiLSTM, Transformers can capture the relation between the B-scans. However, unlike BiLSTM, Transformers do not require a pooling operation before the prediction head because they learn a single classification token that encapsulates the necessary information for making the prediction (Fig. 1). Additionally, self-attention inherently provides attention scores over the B-scans.

The Transformer network consists of 4 blocks, each with 2 self-attention heads. To handle the large dimension of the patch embedding (2048), the MLP output size in the transformer blocks is reduced to 1024, unlike in standard ViTs that scale up the dimensions in the MLP with respect to the patch embedding dimension. To prevent over-fitting on the small downstream dataset, we inserted Drop Path layers (Stochastic Depth [20]).

3D ViViT. We selected FSA ViViT that follows slow-fusion approach as opposed to hybrid models (late-fusion), where each Transformer block models both spatial and temporal interactions simultaneously. For ViViT, the model is first pretrained for binary OCT volume classification on the public DukeAMD dataset [9] that includes 269 intermediate age-related macular degeneration (iAMD) and 115 normal patients acquired with Bioptigen OCT device.

I3D. When using 2D weights for 3D convolutional kernels, we followed the paradigm of [3], and inflated a pretrained ResNet50 to process OCT volumes.

3   Experiments

The scans for the downstream predictive modeling task were manually labeled by ophthalmologists using a clinically relevant time interval of six months. All **scans** that convert to *wet*-AMD within the next 6 months have a positive label, while all **scans** that do not convert within the interval have a negative label.

Datasets: The models are trained and evaluated on the fellow-eye dataset from the HARBOR clinical trial[1] It is a longitudinal 3D OCT dataset where each patient is imaged monthly for a duration of 24 months with a Cirrus OCT scanner. Each OCT scan consists of 128, 2D cross-sectional B-scan slices covering a field of view of 6×6 mm^2. We split the dataset into pretraining and downstream (progression prediction) sets. The pretraining dataset comprises 540 patients and 12,506 scans and also includes images of the late stages of AMD. Among 463 patients, 113 are observed to progress to wet-AMD, yielding only 547 scans with a positive label out of a total of 10,108 scans. The extreme class imbalance makes the progression prediction a very challenging task.

A second longitudinal dataset, PINNACLE [18], is used only for the downstream task of progression prediction. Unlike HARBOR, the PINNACLE dataset was acquired with a TOPCON scanner. This resulted in a domain shift due to the

---

[1] NCT00891735. https://clinicaltrials.gov/ct2/show/NCT00891735.

difference in the acquisition settings and noise characteristics between the OCT scanner types. With the same labeling criteria, PINNACLE provided 127 converter **patients** out of 334 (536 positive scans out of 2813). Since the pretraining is only performed on unlabelled scans from the HARBOR dataset, experiments on the PINNACLE set are used to evaluate the performance of the pretraining method when the downstream dataset undergoes a domain shift.

In downstream tasks, both datasets were split in the following way: 20% of the patients were kept for hold-out test set, while the remaining scans in each dataset formed the training sets. A stratified 4-fold cross-validation at a patient-level was carried out on the training sets for hyper-parameter tuning. Treating each of the 4 folds as the validation set and the remaining data for training, resulted in an ensemble of 4 models. The mean and standard deviation of the performance of the 4 models on the hold-out test set is reported in Table 1.

Image Preprocessing. The curvature of the retina was flattened by shifting each A-scan (image column) in the volume such that the Bruch's membrane (extracted using the method in [10]) lies along a straight plane. Next, we extracted the central 32 B-scans, which were then resized to 224×224. During the progression prediction training, the input intensities were min-max scaled, followed by translation, small rotation, and horizontal flip as data augmentations. The same preprocessing was applied to both HARBOR and PINNACLE datasets. For the in-domain SSL-based pretraining, we followed the contrastive transformations outlined in [7].

Training Details. CNN+BiLSTM models were fine-tuned using an ADAM optimizer with a batch-size of 20, a learning rate of 0.0001, which is updated using cosine scheduler, and a weight decay of 10^{-6}. Similarly, in I3D experiments, we used ADAM with a batch-size of 64, a learning rate of 0.001, which is updated using cosine scheduler, and a weight decay of 10^{-6}. In CNN+Transformer, SGD optimizer with momentum was used, as it was found to perform better than ADAM, with a learning rate of 0.001 which is updated using cosine scheduler, no weight decay was used. We tested 2.5D models with frozen and end-to-end fine-tuning setup and picked the best. For ViViT, we used Adam optimizer with an initial learning rate of 10^{-5} which is updated by the cosine scheduler, no weight decay was used. For this experiment, the batch size is set to 8.

4   Results

The performances of four distinct architectures, I3D [3], ViViT with FSA [1], and the two proposed hybrid 2.5D models, i.e. CNN+BiLSTM and CNN+Transformer, are presented in Table 1. Each architecture was initialized either with ImageNet or TINC weights, with an exception of ViViT transformer,which was pretrained on DukeAMD dataset.

Firstly, comparing the two initialization strategies confirms the superiority of TINC pretraining in terms of AUROC score in all cases (Table 1). This finding highlights the advantage of in-domain pretraining with limited amount of

Table 1. Predictive performance of the evaluated models on the internal HARBOR and the external PINNACLE datasets.

Model	#Params	Pretraining	HARBOR		PINNACLE	
			AUROC	PRAUC	AUROC	PRAUC
I3D	46M	ImageNet	0.727 ± 0.012	0.134 ± 0.007	0.602 ± 0.036	0.157 ± 0.026
I3D	46M	*TINC*	0.750 ± 0.037	**0.162 ± 0.034**	0.644 ± 0.039	0.170 ± 0.023
CNN+BiLSTM	34M	ImageNet	0.742 ± 0.028	0.153 ± 0.012	0.622 ± 0.042	0.164 ± 0.028
CNN+BiLSTM	34M	*TINC*	**0.766 ± 0.012**	0.153 ± 0.003	0.646 ± 0.019	**0.190 ± 0.025**
CNN+Transf	108M	ImageNet	0.738 ± 0.032	0.152 ± 0.035	0.617 ± 0.055	0.156 ± 0.031
CNN+Transf	108M	*TINC*	**0.752 ± 0.022**	0.145 ± 0.023	**0.656 ± 0.027**	**0.179 ± 0.020**
ViViT$_{FSA}$	34M	DukeAMD	0.628 ± 0.064	0.098 ± 0.023	0.566 ± 0.054	0.121 ± 0.019

data over pretrained weights coming from a natural image dataset. Although it is probable that both natural and medical images share low-level features, we should emphasize on the drastic effects of the underlying noise characteristics originating from differences in modalities, standard views of the internal organs and tissues, and limited number of expected variances in medical images, on the model performance. Most of the cases, *TINC* improves PRAUC. On HARBOR dataset, CNN + Transformer with TINC is not better than ImageNet in terms of PRAUC score. This can be due to the fact that PRAUC is more sensitive to differences in probabilities, while AUROC is more concerned with the correct ranking of predictions, which is more relevant for progression prediction. The PINNACLE dataset, characterized by a strong domain shift caused by the intrinsic properties of the scanner, showed that TINC pretraining consistently outperformed ImageNet pretraining, despite a significant drop in AUROC range compared to the HARBOR dataset (Table 1).

When we compared the architectures, it is clear that 2.5D approaches outperform both of the 3D models. The CNN + BiLSTM model has significantly fewer trainable parameters than the CNN + Transformer model (34M vs 108M) with a similar number of FLOPs (130G and 133G, respectively). Despite its smaller size, CNN + BiLSTM outperformed CNN + Transformer in Table 1 for AUROC and PRAUC. In external data experiments on PINNACLE, it achieved comparable results for AUROC while outperforming CNN + Transformer for PRAUC in Table 1. This suggests that BiLSTM methods still have merit in the era of Transformers, especially under conditions such as limited and imbalanced 3D data. This can be attributed to the more data requirement of ViTs which affects CNN + Transformer model as well. It is important to highlight that both hybrid models outperformed the I3D model due to their explicit modeling of the relationship between individual B-scans and their better utilization of high-level representations. Similar to I3D, experiments regarding FSA ViViT also confirm that the simultaneous processing of both dimensions in the input volume did not provide extra benefit over the corresponding counterparts with the same number of parameters (~34M), indicating the advantage of less complicated models (CNN + BiLSTM/Transformer) for this specific task.

5   Conclusion

In this work, we performed a systematic evaluation of hybrid 2.5D models which utilize already available pretrained 2D backbones. Our results demonstrate that 2.5D approaches not only exhibit efficient memory and label usage, but also outperform larger 3D models when suitably pretrained. The addition of an attention layer to CNN + BiLSTM provides attention scores which in turn can facilitate model explainability. Thus, we conclude that deep learning models consisting of 2D CNNs in combination with LSTM continue to offer merits in predictive medical imaging tasks with limited data, outperforming both 2.5D and 3D ViTs. Furthermore, the in-domain pretraining approach *TINC* consistently outperformed the approaches with ImageNet-pretrained weights, highlighting the importance of domain information for predictive tasks. These findings provide valuable insights for further development of accurate and efficient predictive models of AMD progression in retinal OCT.

Acknowledgements. This work was supported in part by Wellcome Trust Collaborative Award (PINNACLE) Ref. 210572/Z/18/Z, Christian Doppler Research Association, and FWF (Austrian Science Fund; grant no. FG 9-N).

References

1. Arnab, A., Dehghani, M., Heigold, G., Sun, C., Lučić, M., Schmid, C.: ViViT: a video vision transformer. In: Proceedings of the IEEE/CVF International Conference on Computer Vision, pp. 6836–6846 (2021)
2. Balestriero, R., et al.: A cookbook of self-supervised learning. arXiv preprint arXiv:2304.12210 (2023)
3. Carreira, J., Zisserman, A.: Quo vadis, action recognition? a new model and the kinetics dataset. In: proceedings of the IEEE Conference on Computer Vision and Pattern Recognition, pp. 6299–6308 (2017)
4. Chen, T., Kornblith, S., Norouzi, M., Hinton, G.: A simple framework for contrastive learning of visual representations. In: International Conference on Machine Learning, pp. 1597–1607. PMLR (2020)
5. Chen, Z., Xie, L., Niu, J., Liu, X., Wei, L., Tian, Q.: Visformer: the vision-friendly transformer. In: Proceedings of the IEEE/CVF International Conference on Computer Vision, pp. 589–598 (2021)
6. Das, V., Prabhakararao, E., Dandapat, S., Bora, P.K.: B-scan attentive cnn for the classification of retinal optical coherence tomography volumes. IEEE Signal Process. Lett. **27**, 1025–1029 (2020)
7. Emre, T., Chakravarty, A., Rivail, A., Riedl, S., Schmidt-Erfurth, U., Bogunović, H.: TINC: temporally informed non-contrastive learning for disease progression modeling in retinal OCT volumes. In: Medical Image Computing and Computer Assisted Intervention-MICCAI 2022: 25th International Conference, Singapore, 18–22 September 2022, Proceedings, Part II, pp. 625–634. Springer, Heidelberg (2022). https://doi.org/10.1007/978-3-031-16434-7_60
8. Fan, H., et al.: Multiscale vision transformers. In: Proceedings of the IEEE/CVF International Conference on Computer Vision, pp. 6824–6835 (2021)

9. Farsiu, S., Chiu, S., O'Connell, R., Folgar, F.: Quantitative classification of Eyes with and without intermediate age-related macular degeneration using optical coherence tomography. Ophthalmology **121**(1), 162–172 (2014). www.sciencedirect.com/science/article/pii/S016164201300612X

10. Fazekas, B., Lachinov, D., Aresta, G., Mai, J., Schmidt-Erfurth, U., Bogunovic, H.: Segmentation of bruch's membrane in retinal oct with amd using anatomical priors and uncertainty quantification. IEEE J. Biomed. Health Inf. **27**(1), 41–52 (2023). https://doi.org/10.1109/JBHI.2022.3217962

11. Hu, J., Shen, L., Sun, G.: Squeeze-and-excitation networks. In: Proceedings of the IEEE Conference on Computer Vision and Pattern Recognition, pp. 7132–7141 (2018)

12. Kurmann, T., Márquez-Neila, P., Yu, S., Munk, M., Wolf, S., Sznitman, R.: Fused detection of retinal biomarkers in OCT volumes. In: Shen, D., et al. (eds.) MICCAI 2019. LNCS, vol. 11764, pp. 255–263. Springer, Cham (2019). https://doi.org/10.1007/978-3-030-32239-7_29

13. Lee, S.H., Lee, S., Song, B.C.: Vision transformer for small-size datasets. arXiv preprint arXiv:2112.13492 (2021)

14. Li, H., et al.: DT-MIL: deformable transformer for multi-instance learning on histopathological image. In: de Bruijne, M., et al. (eds.) MICCAI 2021. LNCS, vol. 12908, pp. 206–216. Springer, Cham (2021). https://doi.org/10.1007/978-3-030-87237-3_20

15. Maintainers, T.: Contributors: torchvision: pytorch's computer vision library (2016). www.github.com/pytorch/vision

16. Neimark, D., Bar, O., Zohar, M., Asselmann, D.: Video transformer network. In: Proceedings of the IEEE/CVF International Conference on Computer Vision (ICCV) Workshops, pp. 3163–3172 (2021)

17. Shao, Z., et al.: Transmil: transformer based correlated multiple instance learning for whole slide image classification. Adv. Neural Inf. Process. Syst. **34**, 2136–2147 (2021)

18. Sutton, J., et al.: Developing and validating a multivariable prediction model which predicts progression of intermediate to late age-related macular degeneration-the pinnacle trial protocol. In: Eye, pp. 1–9 (2022)

19. Tang, Y., et al.: Self-supervised pre-training of swin transformers for 3d medical image analysis. In: Proceedings of the IEEE/CVF Conference on Computer Vision and Pattern Recognition, pp. 20730–20740 (2022)

20. Touvron, H., Cord, M., Douze, M., Massa, F., Sablayrolles, A., Jégou, H.: Training data-efficient image transformers & distillation through attention. In: International Conference on Machine Learning, pp. 10347–10357. PMLR (2021)

21. Xiao, T., Singh, M., Mintun, E., Darrell, T., Dollár, P., Girshick, R.: Early convolutions help transformers see better. Adv. Neural Inf. Process. Syst. **34**, 30392–30400 (2021)

A Structure-Consistency GAN for Unpaired AS-OCT Image Inpainting

Guanhua Bai[1], Sanqian Li[2], He Zhang[1], Risa Higashita[1,2,3], Jiang Liu[1,2],
Jie Li[1(✉)], and Meng Zhang[1(✉)]

[1] Changchun University, Changchun, China
{lij69,zhangm72}@ccu.edu.cn
[2] Research Institute of Trustworthy Autonomous Systems and Department of
Computer Science and Engineering, Southern University of Science and Technology,
Shenzhen, China
[3] Tomey Corporation, Nagoya, Japan

Abstract. Anterior segment optical coherence tomography (AS-OCT)
is a crucial imaging modality in ophthalmology, providing valuable
insights into corneal pathologies. However, during AS-OCT imaging,
intense signals in highly reflective regions can easily lead to saturation
effects, resulting in pronounced stripes across the cornea. It compromises
the image visual quality and impacts automated ophthalmic analysis. To
address this issue, we propose an unsupervised Structure-Consistency
Generative Adversarial Network (SC-GAN) that captures the underlying semantic structural knowledge in both the spatial domain and frequency space within the generative model. This strategy aims to mitigate the influence of bright stripes and restore corneal structural details
in AS-OCT images. Specifically, SC-GAN introduces a stripe perceptual
loss to extract visual representations by utilizing the perceptual similarity between striped and stripe-free images. Moreover, Fourier feature
mapping is adopted to learn high-frequency information, thereby achieving crucial structure consistency. The experimental results demonstrate
that the proposed SC-GAN can removes stripes while preserving crucial
corneal structures, surpassing the competing algorithms. Furthermore,
we validate the benefits of SC-GAN in the corneal segmentation task.

Keywords: AS-OCT · Inpainting · GAN · structural consistency

1 Introduction

Anterior segment optical coherence tomography (AS-OCT) is a non-invasive
imaging technique widely employed in ophthalmology for diagnosing anterior
segment lesions, including glaucoma, cataract, and corneal diseases [1]. However, central artifacts inevitably occur due to back-reflections from the corneal
apex [2]. These artifacts saturate the spectrometer line camera and appear as

---

G. Bai and S. Li—Equal contribution.

stripes (Fig. 1.b) in AS-OCT image. The stripes significantly degrades the image quality and hampers subsequent clinical analysis, including accurate estimation of corneal thickness and curvature, thereby ultimately hindering the diagnosis of corneal diseases. Therefore, AS-OCT image inpainting plays a crucial role in improving image quality and facilitating clinical automated analysis.

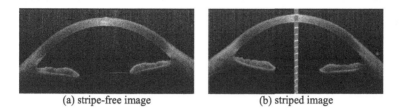

(a) stripe-free image   (b) striped image

Fig. 1. The visual comparison of the stripe-free and striped AS-OCT images.

Many traditional techniques have been developed to remove stripes in OCT images. The hardware-based method is representative research direction. For example, Li et al. [3] proposed a two-channel detector system to mitigate the occurrence of stripes. Besides, various post-processing algorithms have been proposed to remove stripes in OCT images. Huang et al. [4] utilized saturation detection and correction techniques to eliminate stripes, while Byers et al. [5] employed wavelet-FFT filtering methods to attenuate stripe artifacts. Although these methods offer ease of implementation, they tend to produce the artifact and neglect the structural knowledge inherent in the underlying images.

Recently, deep learning techniques have demonstrated the superiority in image restoration due to its powerful learning ability [6]. For instance, Cheong et al. [7] designed conditional Generative Adversarial Network (cGAN) [8] with weighted-mixture loss to effectively remove the stripes on the manually masked images. Ouyang et al. [9] used cGAN to remove stripes above the shallowest epithelium and achieved better corneal epithelium segmentation. Tang et al. [10] utilized a multi-scale sparse representation-based inpainting framework to remove the stripes on the cornea in AS-OCT images. Although these approaches can improve image quality and benefit subsequent clinical analysis, it is challenging for collecting paired clinical data. To relieve this requirement, many approaches including the CycleGAN [11], UNIT [12], CUT [13], and U-GAT-IT [14] have been proposed to achieve the unsupervised learning. Most of them attempt to learn representations in one domain and transfer its knowledge to another domain. For instance, Ma et al. [15] introduced a bi-directional GAN framework for enhancing the quality of medical images. Additionally, Mathew et al. [16] designed a directional discriminator to address the removal of specular highlights in medical images. This unpaired strategy facilitate the acquisition of domain-specific knowledge and provide avenues for overcoming data limitations.

Despite the notable advancements achieved in previous studies, deploying image inpainting methods to effectively remove stripes in AS-OCT images remains a challenging task: The stripes in AS-OCT images significantly corrupts

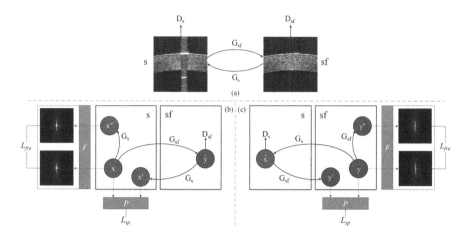

Fig. 2. (a) is the overall process of SC-GAN. It includes (b) forward cycle-consistency and (c) backward cycle-consistency. SC-GAN comprises two generators (G_s, G_{sf}), two discriminators (D_s, D_{sf}), the perceptual feature extractor P, and the Fourier transform module F. The input to (b) is $x \in s$, and the input to (c) is $y \in sf$. The proposed stripe perceptual loss and frequency loss are represented as L_{sp} and L_{fre}, respectively.

the structural context, which is crucial for accurate clinical corneal analysis. Additionally, existing unsupervised learning approaches often fail to adequately capture the underlying structural information, resulting in the loss of vital details [15]. Hence, it is of utmost importance to develop unsupervised methods that can effectively remove stripes while preserving the structural integrity.

Motivated by the idea of CycleGAN, which leverages cycle-consistency loss to achieve image translation between two domain, we propose a novel unsupervised inpainting approach, called Structure-Consistency Generative Adversarial Network (SC-GAN), to exploit the perceptual similarity properties between striped and stripe-free images for learning structural priori and facilitating stripe removal. Moreover, we achieve the structural consistency in both the spatial domain and frequency space to preserve the corneal structures in AS-OCT images. The contributions of this work can be summarized as follows:

- We treats AS-OCT image inpainting as a translation from striped to stripe-free images without paired images. We introduce the stripe perceptual loss to facilitate the extraction of essential features from regions affected by stripes.
- Furthermore, we explore the underlying representation learning by incorporating the Fast Fourier Transform (FFT), enabling the model to ensure a corneal structural consistency in both the spatial and frequency domains.
- The experimental results demonstrate the superiority of the SC-GAN in removing stripes from AS-OCT images while preserving the corneal structures, surpassing the competing methods. Additionally, the SC-GAN exhibits advantages in the corneal segmentation task, thus demonstrating its potential to subsequent clinical analysis.

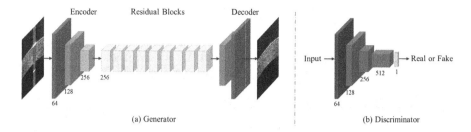

(a) Generator   (b) Discriminator

Fig. 3. The structure of generators G_{sf} (G_s) and discriminators D_{sf} (D_s). The generators adopt an encoder-decoder architecture with nine residual blocks, and the discriminators utilize PatchGAN [17] with five convolutional layers.

2 Proposed Method

In this work, we treat the AS-OCT image inpainting as a translation task from striped images to stripe-free data. Then we propose a novel unpaired learning framework, SC-GAN, for stripe removal. As shown in Fig. 2, SC-GAN also introduces two loss terms: stripe perceptual and frequency consistency loss.

2.1 Network Architecture

The proposed SC-GAN architecture is based on CycleGAN [11], it consists of two generators (G_{sf}, G_s) and two discriminators (D_{sf}, D_s). The G_{sf} generates stripe-free images, while the G_s generates striped images. The D_{sf} is trained to differentiate between real samples from stripe-free domain and generated images from the striped domain, or vice versa in D_s.

The generators G_{sf} and G_s employ an encoder-decoder architecture with residual blocks inspired by ResNet [18], as depicted in Fig. 3(a). The encoder consists of three convolutional layers and an InstanceNorm layer. The decoder comprises two transposed convolutional layers normalized by InstanceNorm, and one convolutional layer. The encoder and decoder are connected through the utilization of nine residual blocks, each residual block comprises two layers: a 3×3 Convolution-InstanceNorm-ReLU layer and a 3×3 Convolution-InstanceNorm layer. Furthermore, the residual blocks with a shortcut connection that connects the input and output of the block, facilitating the propagation of gradient information through the network.

Both the discriminator D_{sf} and D_s employ the PatchGAN architecture [17] for classifying an image as real or fake based on image patches. As shown in Fig. 3(b), The receptive field of PatchGAN to 70×70, it consists of five 4×4 convolutional layers, the first four layers incorporate LeakyReLU activation, while batch normalization is applied to the middle three layers.

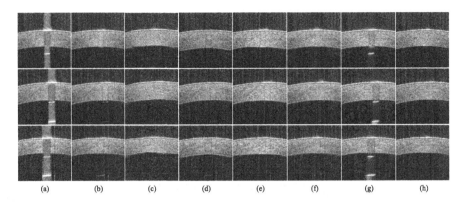

    (a)   (b)   (c)   (d)   (e)   (f)   (g)   (h)

Fig. 4. The visual comparison: (a) striped images, (b) CycleGAN, (c) UNIT, (d) AGGAN, (e) CUT, (f) U-GAT-IT, (g) XDCycleGAN, (h) SC-GAN.

2.2   Objective Function

As a bi-directional GAN framework, SC-GAN has the same objective functions: adversarial loss, cycle-consistency loss and identity mapping loss. Notably, the original cycle-consistency loss is replaced by the stripe perceptual loss to enhance the feature extraction. Additionally, SC-GAN introduces a novel term, frequency consistency constraint, to preserve subtle structural details for AS-OCT image inpainting.

Stripe Perceptual Loss. The stripe perceptual loss, denoted as L_{sp}, serves as the fundamental objective function within the SC-GAN framework. L_{sp} leverages both local and global features extracted from VGG [19] to guide the generator to reconstruct the backward mapping from the generated image to the real image. By exploiting the perceptual similarity between real samples and the generated images, L_{sp} enforces structural consistency in the generated images:

$$L_{sp}(G_{sf}, G_s) = E_{x \in s}[\|P(x') - P(x)\|_2] + E_{y \in sf}[\|P(y') - P(y)\|_2] \qquad (1)$$

where each $x \in s$ is denoted as $x \to \tilde{y} = G_{sf}(x) \to x' = G_s(\tilde{y}) \approx x$. This also holds for the each $y \in sf$: $y \to \tilde{x} = G_s(y) \to y' = G_{sf}(\tilde{x}) \approx y$. P denotes the perceptual feature extractor. This operator reduces the difference between x and x' (y and y') and improves the generative performance of G_s and G_{sf}.

Frequency Consistency Loss. Capturing corneal boundaries is crucial for clinical analysis, and solely focusing on image features in the spatial domain may not exploit tiny details. To further explore the tiny structure, we adopt the frequency consistency loss to learn high-frequency information in the Fourier domain [20]. We leverage the Fast Fourier Transform (FFT) to extract features in the frequency domain. This constraint enhances the network's sensitivity to

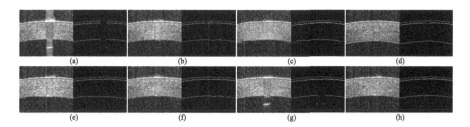

Fig. 5. The segmentation results: (a) striped images, (b) CycleGAN, (c) UNIT, (d) AGGAN, (e) CUT, (f) U-GAT-IT, (g) XDCycleGAN, (h) SC-GAN.

the frequency domain characteristics of the cornea, thereby ensuring improved structural consistency:

$$L_{fre}(G_s, G_{sf}) = E_{x \in s}[\|F(x") - F(x)\|_1] + E_{y \in sf}[\|F(y") - F(y)\|_1] \quad (2)$$

where $x" = G_s(x) \approx x$ and $y" = G_{sf}(y) \approx y$. F denotes the FFT operator, it means that transforming the image from spatial distribution to frequency domain by FFT, as shown in Fig. 2. The frequency consistency constraint further constrains x and $x"$ (y and $y"$) in the frequency domain. This has a vital role in preserving the corneal structure.

Basic Function. The same adversarial loss and identity loss is defined as the basic objective function of SC-GAN. In SC-GAN, the adversarial loss is applied to both the generator/discriminator pairs (G_s/D_{sf}, G_{sf}/D_s):

$$\begin{aligned} L_{adv}(G_s, G_{sf}, D_s, D_{sf}) = & E_{x \in s}[\log D_s(x)] + E_{x \in s}[\log (1 - D_{sf}(G_{sf}(x)))] \\ & + E_{y \in sf}[\log D_{sf}(y)] + E_{y \in sf}[\log (1 - D_s(G_s(y)))] \end{aligned} \quad (3)$$

To further enforce the generators to preserve the original characteristics from real domain, the identity mapping loss is employed to ensures that the generated image closely resembles the input image:

$$L_{idt}(G_s, G_{sf}) = E_{y \in sf}[\|G_{sf}(y) - y\|_1] + E_{x \in s}[\|G_s(x) - x\|_1] \quad (4)$$

Thus the overall objective function of the proposed SC-GAN for AS-OCT image inpainting is defined as:

$$L = L_{adv} + \lambda_1 L_{idt} + \lambda_2 L_{sp} + \lambda_3 L_{fre} \quad (5)$$

where λ_1, λ_2 and λ_3 are the weight coefficients of identity loss, stripe perceptual loss, and frequency consistency loss, respectively. Experimentally set as: $\lambda_1 = 5, \lambda_2 = 10, \lambda_3 = 5$.

3   Experiments

To evaluate the performance of the proposed SC-GAN in AS-OCT image inpainting, we conduct the comparative experiment and ablation study in evaluations, including inpainting evaluation and subsequent corneal segmentation.

Table 1. The inpainting performance of inpainted images using different approaches.

Method	Inpainting			Segmentation	
	CNR	XCOR	EPI	IoU	F1-Score
Striped Images	–	1.00	1.00	0.681	0.776
CycleGAN [11]	**6.36**	0.95	0.90	0.493	0.528
UNIT [12]	6.24	0.69	0.93	0.489	0.517
AGGAN [21]	4.99	0.57	0.91	0.597	0.681
CUT [13]	5.51	0.77	0.93	0.494	0.527
U-GAT-IT [14]	6.28	0.90	0.72	0.490	0.519
StillGAN [15]	5.41	0.98	0.69	0.490	0.516
XDCycleGAN [16]	2.09	0.95	0.79	0.487	0.513
SC-GAN w/o L_{sp}	4.88	**0.99**	0.92	0.491	0.517
SC-GAN w/o L_{fre}	6.17	**0.99**	0.94	0.492	0.519
SC-GAN	5.45	**0.99**	**1.00**	**0.690**	**0.783**

Dataset Preparation. The AS-OCT dataset consists of the 450 striped and 450 unpaired stripe-free images, collected from the CASIA1 ophthalmology device (Tomey Inc., Japan). 410 striped and 410 stripe-free images are randomly selected for training, and the rest are for testing. Ophthalmologists annotated the three corneal boundaries on images: the epithelium, Bowman's Layer, and endothelium.

Implementation Settings. The SC-GAN was implemented with the PyTorch library, and all experiments were conducted on a NVIDIA GPU (GeForce RTX 3090, 24GB). All training images were resized to the size of 256×256. The network training process employed the Adam optimizer [22], with an initial learning rate set to 0.0002. A batch size of 1 was utilized during the training process. These experienced setting ensured efficient training and optimization of the SC-GAN model. All competing approaches are conducted with the default setting.

Evaluation on AS-OCT Image Inpainting. The inpainting performance of the proposed SC-GAN was evaluated using non-parametric indices, including the contrast noise ratio (CNR) [23], cross-correlation function (XCOR) [24], and edge preservation index (EPI) [25]. Comparative analysis was conducted against several state-of-the-art methods, including CycleGAN [11], UNIT [12], AGGAN [21], CUT [13], U-GAT-IT [14], StillGAN [15], and XDCycleGAN [16]. The higher CNR and the closer XCOR and EPI to 1 indicate better image quality. The quantitative results are shown Table 1, it can be observed that our SC-GAN achieve superior performance in terms of XCOR and EPI, demonstrating its ability to remove stripes while preserving corneal structures. Although CycleGAN exhibits the best CNR, it fails to preserve corneal structure; and the UNIT, AGGAN, and U-GAT-IT can remove stripes but severely lose corneal structural information; while the SC-GAN achieve the best performance with the best visual quality and structure consistency, as shown in Fig. 4.

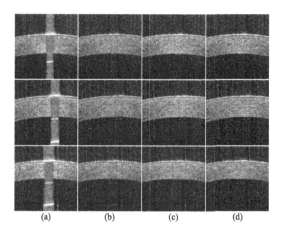

Fig. 6. The ablation study: (a) striped images, (b) SC-GAN w/o L_{sp}, (c) SC-GAN w/o L_{fre}, (d) SC-GAN.

Evaluation on Segmentation. To validate the clinical benefits of the SC-GAN, we conducted experiments on a corneal segmentation task. Specifically, a U-Net segmentation model [26] was trained using the labelled AS-OCT stripe-free images. As depicted in Fig. 5, the visual segmentation results demonstrate that the SC-GAN achieves the best performance. It successfully removes stripes while preserving the corneal structure owing to the utilization of perceptual similarity and the frequency consistency constraint. Moreover, quantitative evaluation results in Table 1 reveal that SC-GAN outperforms other methods, exhibiting the highest Intersection over Union (IoU) and F1-Score scores. The superior segmentation results obtained by SC-GAN, both visually and quantitatively, confirm its efficacy in enhancing corneal segmentation.

Ablation Studies. We evaluate the effectiveness of the stripe perceptual loss and frequency consistency constraint. In SC-GAN w/o L_{sp}, we removed stripe perceptual loss and replaced it with cycle-consistency loss. In SC-GAN w/o L_{fre}, we removed frequency consistency loss. The experimental results are shown in Fig. 6 and Table 1. We can observe that the stripe removal ability of SC-GAN becomes weaker with the removal of stripe perceptual loss. And SC-GAN is unable to further restore the corneal structure with the removal of frequency consistency loss, although it performs better in CNR. SC-GAN leads in XCOR and EPI scores. Therefore, the proposed SC-GAN achieve the best performance both thanks the perceptual similarity and the frequency consistency constraint.

4   Conclusion

Due to the limitation of the existing AS-OCT technique, the stripes often affect the corneal and hinder the subsequent clinical analysis. In this paper, we propose an unsupervised structural-consistency GAN (SC-GAN) for restoring the corneal structures in AS-OCT images. The proposed SC-GAN achieve the AS-OCT image inpainting by image translation and preserving the subtle but vital morphological details by incorporating perceptual similarity properties and learning the structural knowledge between the spatial and frequency domain. The experimental results demonstrate the SC-GAN can remove stripes and preserve the corneal structural details simultaneously. The further corneal segmentation task validates the SC-GAN benefits for the subsequent clinical analysis.

References

1. Holden, B., Mertz, G., McNally, J.: Corneal swelling response to contact lenses worn under extended wear conditions. Invest. Ophthalmol. Visual Sci. **24**(2), 218–226 (1983)
2. LaRocca, F., Chiu, S.J., McNabb, R.P., Kuo, A.N., Izatt, J.A., Farsiu, S.: Robust automatic segmentation of corneal layer boundaries in sdoct images using graph theory and dynamic programming. Biomed. Opt. Express **2**(6), 1524–1538 (2011)
3. Li, X., Liang, S., Zhang, J.: Correction of saturation effects in endoscopic swept-source optical coherence tomography based on dual-channel detection. J. Biomed. Opt. **23**(3), 030502–030502 (2018)
4. Huang, Y., Kang, J.U.: Real-time reference a-line subtraction and saturation artifact removal using graphics processing unit for high-frame-rate fourier-domain optical coherence tomography video imaging. Opt. Eng. **51**(7), 073203–073203 (2012)
5. Byers, R., Matcher, S.: Attenuation of stripe artifacts in optical coherence tomography images through wavelet-fft filtering. Biomed. Opt. Express **10**(8), 4179–4189 (2019)
6. Li, S., Qin, B., Xiao, J., Liu, Q., Wang, Y., Liang, D.: Multi-channel and multi-model-based autoencoding prior for grayscale image restoration. IEEE Trans. Image Process. **29**, 142–156 (2019)
7. Cheong, H., et al.: Deshadowgan: a deep learning approach to remove shadows from optical coherence tomography images. Transl. Vision Sci. Technol. **9**(2), 23–23 (2020)
8. Mirza, M., Osindero, S.: Conditional generative adversarial nets. arXiv preprint arXiv:1411.1784 (2014)

9. Ouyang, J., Mathai, T.S., Lathrop, K., Galeotti, J.: Accurate tissue interface segmentation via adversarial pre-segmentation of anterior segment oct images. Biomed. Opt. Express **10**(10), 5291–5324 (2019)

10. Tang, Y., et al.: Multi-scale sparse representation-based shadow inpainting for retinal oct images. In: Medical Imaging 2022: Image Processing, vol. 12032, pp. 9–17. SPIE (2022)

11. Zhu, J.Y., Park, T., Isola, P., Efros, A.A.: Unpaired image-to-image translation using cycle-consistent adversarial networks. In: IEEE International Conference on Computer Vision, pp. 2242–2251 (2017)

12. Liu, M.Y., Breuel, T., Kautz, J.: Unsupervised image-to-image translation networks. Adv. Neural Inf. Process. Syst. **30** (2017)

13. Park, T., Efros, A.A., Zhang, R., Zhu, J.-Y.: Contrastive learning for unpaired image-to-image translation. In: Vedaldi, A., Bischof, H., Brox, T., Frahm, J.-M. (eds.) ECCV 2020. LNCS, vol. 12354, pp. 319–345. Springer, Cham (2020). https://doi.org/10.1007/978-3-030-58545-7_19

14. Kim, J., Kim, M., Kang, H., Lee, K.H.: U-gat-it: unsupervised generative attentional networks with adaptive layer-instance normalization for image-to-image translation. In: International Conference on Learning Representations (2020)

15. Ma, Y., et al.: Structure and illumination constrained gan for medical image enhancement. IEEE Trans. Med. Imaging **40**(12), 3955–3967 (2021)

16. Mathew, S., Nadeem, S., Kumari, S., Kaufman, A.: Augmenting colonoscopy using extended and directional cyclegan for lossy image translation. In: IEEE Conference on Computer Vision and Pattern Recognition, pp. 4696–4705 (2020)

17. Isola, P., Zhu, J.Y., Zhou, T., Efros, A.A.: Image-to-image translation with conditional adversarial networks. In: IEEE Conference on Computer Vision and Pattern Recognition, pp. 1125–1134 (2017)

18. He, K., Zhang, X., Ren, S., Sun, J.: Deep residual learning for image recognition. In: IEEE Conference on Computer Vision and Pattern Recognition, pp. 770–778 (2016)

19. Zhang, R., Isola, P., Efros, A.A., Shechtman, E., Wang, O.: The unreasonable effectiveness of deep features as a perceptual metric. In: IEEE Conference on Computer Vision and Pattern Recognition, pp. 586–595 (2018)

20. Qiao, C., et al.: Evaluation and development of deep neural networks for image super-resolution in optical microscopy. Nat. Methods **18**(2), 194–202 (2021)

21. Tang, H., Xu, D., Sebe, N., Yan, Y.: Attention-guided generative adversarial networks for unsupervised image-to-image translation. In: International Joint Conference on Neural Networks, pp. 1–8. IEEE (2019)

22. Kingma, D.P., Ba, J.: Adam: a method for stochastic optimization. In: International Conference on Learning Representations (2015)

23. Patterson, M., Foster, F.: The improvement and quantitative assessment of b-mode images produced by an annular array/cone hybrid. Ultrason. Imaging **5**(3), 195–213 (1983)

24. Fisher, R.: On the "probable error" of a coefficient of correlation. Metron **1**, 3–32 (1920)

25. Sattar, F., Floreby, L., Salomonsson, G., Lovstrom, B.: Image enhancement based on a nonlinear multiscale method. IEEE Trans. Image Process. **6**(6), 888–895 (1997)

26. Ronneberger, O., Fischer, P., Brox, T.: U-Net: convolutional networks for biomedical image segmentation. In: Navab, N., Hornegger, J., Wells, W.M., Frangi, A.F. (eds.) MICCAI 2015. LNCS, vol. 9351, pp. 234–241. Springer, Cham (2015). https://doi.org/10.1007/978-3-319-24574-4_28

STAGE Challenge: Structural-Functional Transition in Glaucoma Assessment Challenge in MICCAI 2023

Huihui Fang[1,2], Fei Li[3], Hanyi Yu[1,2], Dongyang Zhao[4], Xiang Li[4], Zhuoling Li[5], Huazhu Fu[6], Xiulan Zhang[3(✉)], and Yanwu Xu[1,2(✉)]

[1] School of Future Technology, South China University of Technology, Guangzhou, China
xuyanwu@scut.edu.cn
[2] Pazhou Lab, Guangzhou, China
[3] State Key Laboratory of Ophthalmology, Zhongshan Ophthalmic Center, Sun Yat-sen University, Guangdong Provincial Key Laboratory of Ophthalmology and Visual Science, Guangzhou, China
zhangxl2@mail.sysu.edu.cn
[4] Shenzhen Institute for Advanced Study, University of Electronic Science and Technology of China, Shenzhen, China
[5] Central South University, Changsha, China
[6] Institute of High Performance Computing, Agency for Science, Technology and Research, Singapore, Singapore

Abstract. Glaucoma leads to irreversible vision impairment due to optic nerve damage, and there is currently no cure available. The visual field (VF) test is a reference standard examination to assess visual function and determine glaucomatous optic nerve damage. However, the VF test is time-consuming, requires patient cooperation, and may have poor repeatability. Optical Coherence Tomography (OCT) is widely used for eye structure examination. OCT images provide objective cross-sectional information of the fundus structure, aiding glaucoma diagnosis. Moreover, monocular OCT imaging is significantly faster than monocular visual field test. Therefore, we aim to use structural OCT images for predicting VF test indicators. We have organized the STAGE challenge, in conjunction with the International Conference on Medical Image Computing and Computer Assisted Intervention (MICCAI) 2023. The challenge involves three tasks: 1) predicting mean deviation (MD) values; 2) forecasting sensitivity maps; and 3) estimating pattern deviation probability maps. Participants will access to a dataset of 400 volume OCT data samples with corresponding MD values, sensitivity maps, and pattern deviation probability map labels from VF test reports. The STAGE Challenge is accessible at https://aistudio.baidu.com/aistudio/competition/detail/968.

Keywords: Glaucoma · Structural imaging · Functional test · OCT · Visual field test

© The Author(s), under exclusive license to Springer Nature Switzerland AG 2023
B. Antony et al. (Eds.): OMIA 2023, LNCS 14096, pp. 152–160, 2023.
https://doi.org/10.1007/978-3-031-44013-7_16

1 Introduction

Glaucoma is a chronic eye disease that gradually damages the optic nerve. As glaucoma progresses, the damage to the optic nerve becomes irreversible, leading to a gradual loss of vision. Glaucoma has a significant impact on visual function and is one of the primary causes of irreversible vision loss. The clinical standard for glaucoma diagnosis is to decide whether there is glaucomatous optic nerve damage [7]. A visual field (VF) test is a reference standard examination to assess visual function damage. It is a subjective examination that requires the subject to remain calm and focused and to cooperate with the physician. The monocular VF test takes approximately 15 min. In addition to the functional tests, Optical Coherence Tomography (OCT) is the most commonly used imaging modality for fundus structural examination, which provides objective cross-sectional information of the structures in the fundus, facilitating the physician's observation of structural thickness changes, and is an important basis in the diagnosis of glaucoma [16]. There is now much evidence to support the role of OCT imaging in the detection of glaucoma [1,4,8,18]. Furthermore, there is a moderate to good correlation between retinal layer thickness and central VF sensitivities or other markers of optic nerve function [13]. Moreover, a monocular volume OCT scan takes only about 3 s. Therefore, we aim to investigate the transition from structural information to functional information in glaucoma assessment. It is to seek the mapping relationship between the fundus structure and visual function, which is important for understanding the underlying causes of visual defects.

We hold a STAGE Challenge in conjunction with MICCAI 2023, aiming to use objective and easy-to-acquire structural OCT images to predict key indicators in VF test reports. The key indicators focused on in this challenge are the mean deviation (MD) value, sensitivity map, and pattern deviation probability map. MD value [2] reflects the decrease in mean visual sensitivity caused by the death of ganglion cells in glaucoma, and it is around 0 dB in normal individuals. The sensitivity map [3], also known as the threshold map, is the raw data obtained during visual field tests, i.e., the photosensitivity observable at each test point. The automatic visual field analyzer uses a threshold cursor intensity to express photosensitivity in dB, with 0 dB being the strongest photosensitivity and 100 dB being the weakest photosensitivity. There are 52 test points in the 24-2 visual field test, and each point in the sensitivity map has a corresponding photosensitivity value, which represents the weakest photosensitivity to which this test point can respond. In the visual field report, the pattern deviation probability map [3] reflects the statistical significance of the remaining local sensitivity reduction after excluding the generalized sensitivity reduction from the overall sensitivity reduction. That is, the probability that the patient has a visual field defect in a certain area after removing interference factors such as anterior segments (e.g., cataracts, small pupils), which can highlight a meaningful local visual deficit. There are also 52 test points in the 24-2 visual field test, and each point belongs to one of the five categories of visual loss in the pattern deviation probability map. These 5 categories of cases are normal visual field, probability of normal visual field less than 5%, less than 2%, less than 1%, and less than

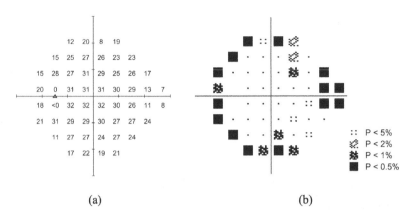

Fig. 1. Schematic diagram of (a) sensitivity map and (b) pattern deviation probability map in the 24-2 VF test report.

0.5%. Among them, the probability of a normal visual field is less than 0.5% is the most serious case of visual field loss. In clinical diagnosis, the MD value, sensitivity map, and pattern deviation probability map are the key parameters in both the H-P-A [14] and Mills visual [12] grading methods. Therefore, in the STAGE challenge, we treat the prediction of these key indicators as the task to predict functional information based on the structural images (Fig. 1).

Hence, three tasks are proposed in this challenge: 1) mean deviation (MD) value prediction; 2) sensitivity map prediction; 3) pattern deviation probability map prediction. For the STAGE Challenge, Zhongshan Ophthalmic Center, Sun Yat-sen University has contributed 400 volume OCT data samples with corresponding MD values, sensitivity maps, and pattern deviation probability map labels. This paper mainly introduces the released dataset, provides baselines for the three tasks, and also describes the evaluation rules in detail.

2   Dataset

The STAGE challenge provides 400 volume OCT data and corresponding MD value, sensitivity map, and pattern deviation probability map labels of the VF test report. The raw 3D OCT volumes are collected by Topcon DRI OCT Triton, and each volume is stored in 256 images. And personal information except age and sex is removed.

The labels for the indicator prediction task are derived from the report of the VF test in clinical practice. All the VFs are automated white-on-white perimetry SITA 24-2 standard/fast VFs acquired by Humphrey Field Analyzers (Carl Zeiss Meditec, Dublin, CA). VF test results are considered reliable if the VF with fixation losses of less than 2/13, false-positive rate less than 15%, and false-negative rate less than 25% [9]. The MD values in the VF reports are the ground truth of task 1. The sensitivity maps are the ground truth of task 2. The label of each sample contains 52 values (value of 0–100) corresponding to 52 positions in the sensitivity map. Similarly, the pattern deviation probability maps in the VF report are the ground truth of task 3. Each label also contains 52 values corresponding to 52 positions in the pattern deviation probability map. Unlike task 2, these 52 values are taken to be 0–4, representing the degree of visual field deficit at that location falling into one of the five categories. Similar to GAMMA [17] and GOALS [6] challenges, the samples released in the STAGE challenge are randomly selected from the glaucoma study cohort (200) and the high myopia study cohort (200) at the Zhongshan Ophthalmic Center, Sun Yat-sen University.

Of the 400 released samples, 200 macular OCT data and corresponding labels will be released to the teams for model training in the preliminary round. 100 macular OCT data will also be released in the preliminary round. The remaining 100 macular OCT data will be released in the final round for the evaluation of the model. To have a balanced distribution of samples across the data subsets, the 400 samples will be assigned to ensure a consistent distribution of age groups, gender, and disease conditions. Among them, the distribution of non-glaucoma samples, early glaucoma samples, intermediate glaucoma samples, and advanced glaucoma samples will be at 50%, 25%, 15%, and 10% in each subset.

3 Baseline

We have established baselines for each of the three tasks. For task 1, a group of OCT images is fed into the baseline network (ResNet34), and output the single channel predictive value and glaucoma grading results at the same time. Scale them to [0,1] through the sigmoid Activation function. During the training process, use the glaucoma auxiliary information in the dataset to scale the data to get the predictive value. During the prediction process, use the glaucoma grading results to scale the data to get the predictive value.

For task 2, the data consists of two modalities: a set of stacked slices (sampled from the 3D OCT along the slicing direction) and glaucoma grading information. These two modalities are separately input into the EfficientNet and the Embedding layer. EfficientNet is responsible for extracting image features, while the Embedding layer maps the category information into a continuous and dense vector feature space. The features obtained from both modalities are then concatenated and fed into the Linear regression head for further predicting 52 values (Fig. 2).

The baseline pipeline of task 3 is as follows: using ResNet to encode OCT features and concatenate them with learnable data_info embeddings. Subsequently, the concatenation is fed into Multi-Layer Perception for ordinal regression [17].

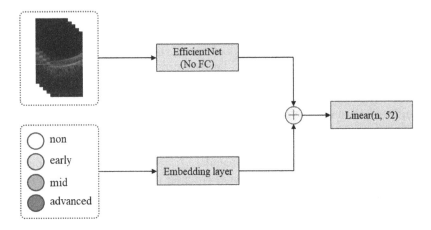

Fig. 2. A baseline framework for sensitivity map prediction(task 2).

4 Evaluation

For the value regression task in tasks 1 and 2, the Symmetric Mean Absolute Percentage Error (SMAPE) measure is used. Compared to the Mean Absolute Error (MAE) commonly used for regression tasks, SMAPE is more reflective of the degree of error and is bound, with the lower bound of 0% implying a perfect fit, and the upper bound of 200% [5,11], which is friendlier for the score calculation in the challenge. SMAPE is progressively gaining momentum in biomedical applications due to its interesting properties [10,15]. In the STAGE Challenge, SMAPE is used to calculate the difference between the predicted value and the target value. If both the target and predicted values are 0, then SMAPE for this case will be recorded as 0. In task 1, we evaluate the performance using SMAPE for all the test samples (Eq. 1). In Task 2, we first calculate the SMAPE for each of the 52 positions in every sample and then take the average of SMAPE values across all test samples as the final evaluation metric (Eq. 2).

$$SMAPE = \frac{100\%}{n} \sum_{i=1}^{n} \frac{|\hat{y}_i - y_i|}{(|\hat{y}_i| + |y_i|)/2} \tag{1}$$

where, n represents the number of test samples, $\hat{y}_i$ and y_i represent the predicted and true values of the ith sample, respectively.

$$SMAPE_{average} = \frac{1}{n} \sum_{j=1}^{n} (\frac{100\%}{52} \sum_{i=1}^{52} \frac{|\hat{y_{j,i}} - y_{j,i}|}{(|\hat{y_{j,i}}| + |y_{j,i}|)/2}) \tag{2}$$

where, n represents the number of test samples, $\hat{y_{j,i}}$ and $y_{y,i}$ represent the predicted value and the true value for the ith test point of the jth sample, respectively.

In addition, R^2 is used as an evaluation index to measure the degree of numerical fit of the model. Similar to using SMAPE as the evaluation metric, when using R^2 as the evaluation metric, Task 1 considers the R^2 value for all samples (Eq. 3), while Task 2 calculates the mean R^2 value after considering the R^2 values for each of the 52 test points in every sample (Eq. 4).

$$R^2 = 1 - \frac{\sum_{i=1}^{n}(\hat{y}_i - y_i)^2}{\sum_{i=1}^{n}(y_i - \bar{y})^2} \tag{3}$$

where $\bar{y}$ represents the mean of all the true values in the samples.

$$R^2_{average} = \frac{1}{n}\sum_{j=1}^{n}(1 - \frac{\sum_{i=1}^{52}(\hat{y_{j,i}} - y_{j,i})^2}{\sum_{i=1}^{52}(y_{j,i} - \bar{y_j})^2}) \tag{4}$$

where $\bar{y}_j$ represents the mean of all the true values in jth sample. The scores for tasks 1 and 2 are calculated by SMAPE and R_2, as shown in Eqs. 5 and 6.

$$Score_1 = 0.5 \times (\frac{1}{SMAPE + 0.1}) + 0.5 \times (R^2 \times 10) \tag{5}$$

$$Score_2 = 0.5 \times (\frac{1}{SMAPE_{average} + 0.1}) + 0.5 \times (R^2_{average} \times 10) \tag{6}$$

The $micro - F_1$ (Eq. 7–10) and $macro - F_1$ (Eq. 11–15) are used to evaluate the five-category classification results of the 52 points in the pattern deviation probability map.

$$micro - F_{1average} = \frac{1}{n}\sum_{j=1}^{n} micro - F_{1j} \tag{7}$$

$$= \frac{1}{n}\sum_{j=1}^{n}(\frac{2 \times Recall_{m_j} \times Precision_{m_j}}{Recall_{m_j} + Precision_{m_j}}) \tag{8}$$

where $micro - F_{1average}$ represents the average of $(micro - F_{1j})$ for the n test samples. $Recall_{m_j}$ and $Precision_{m_j}$ refer to the multiclass recall and precision, respectively, for the jth test sample.

$$Recall_{m_j} = \frac{\sum_{c=1}^{5} TP_{jc}}{\sum_{c=1}^{5} TP_{jc} + \sum_{c=1}^{5} FN_{jc}} \tag{9}$$

$$Precision_{m_j} = \frac{\sum_{c=1}^{5} TP_{jc}}{\sum_{c=1}^{5} TP_{jc} + \sum_{c=1}^{5} FP_{jc}} \tag{10}$$

where TP_{jc}, FN_{jc} and FP_{jc} represent the number of true positives, false negatives, and false positives, respectively, for class c in the jth test sample across the 52 test points.

$$macro - F1_{average} = \frac{1}{n} \sum_{j=1}^{n} macro - F1_j \tag{11}$$

$$= \frac{1}{n} \sum_{j=1}^{n} (\frac{1}{c} \sum_{c=1}^{5} F1_{jc}) \tag{12}$$

$$= \frac{1}{n} \sum_{j=1}^{n} (\frac{1}{c} \sum_{c=1}^{5} \frac{2 \times Recall_{jc} \times Precision_{jc}}{Recall_{jc} + Precision_{jc}}) \tag{13}$$

where $macro - F1_{average}$ represents the average of the $macro - F1$ scores, calculated individually for each of the nth test samples. $macro - F1_j$ is the $macro - F1$ score for the jth sample, which is computed based on the $F1_{jc}$ scores for each class c involved in the calculation.

$$Recall_{jc} = \frac{TP_{jc}}{TP_{jc} + FN_{jc}} \tag{14}$$

$$Precision_{jc} = \frac{TP_{jc}}{TP_{jc} + FP_{jc}} \tag{15}$$

The score for task 3 is calculated as follow:

$$Score_3 = 0.5 \times (micro - F1_{average} \times 10) + 0.5 \times (macro - F1_{average} \times 10) \tag{16}$$

The total score of the three sub-tasks is:

$$Score = 0.3 \times Score_1 + 0.3 \times Score_2 + 0.4 \times Score_3 \tag{17}$$

In the final ranking, we consider both the preliminary and final performances. Because the teams can adjust their models after seeing the performance on the preliminary dataset through the leaderboard, we set the preliminary weight at 0.3. Compared with the predicted results in the preliminary round, those in the final round can reflect the real generalizability of the models due that the final dataset is unknown to the teams. Hence, we set the final weight at 0.7.

$$Score_{total} = 0.3 \times Score_{preliminary} + 0.7 \times Score_{final} \tag{18}$$

5   Conclusion

This paper presents an overview of the STAGE Challenge held at the MICCAI 2023. The challenge focuses on utilizing more objective and easily obtainable eye structural information to predict visual field functionality, aiming to find a way to replace the subjective and time-consuming visual field test in clinical practice. The challenge comprises three sub-tasks, namely predicting mean deviation values, sensitivity maps, and pattern deviation probability maps. With the collaboration of Zhongshan Ophthalmic Center at Sun Yat-sen University, the challenge provides a dataset of 400 samples, including age, gender, glaucoma status, and the three main indicators to be predicted in the visual field reports. Detailed descriptions of the dataset and evaluation criteria are presented in the paper. Participants can access them via https://aistudio.baidu.com/aistudio/competition/detail/968. The provided dataset and evaluation platform offers a valuable resource for researchers to explore and validate their algorithms, ultimately contributing to the improvement of glaucoma diagnosis in clinical practice. We hope this challenge will inspire more innovative solutions in the development of cutting-edge technologies for glaucoma assessment.

References

1. Asrani, S., Rosdahl, J.A., Allingham, R.R.: Novel software strategy for glaucoma diagnosis: asymmetry analysis of retinal thickness. Arch. Ophthalmol. **129**(9), 1205–1211 (2011)
2. Banegas, S.A., et al.: Evaluation of the retinal nerve fiber layer thickness, the mean deviation, and the visual field index in progressive glaucoma. J. Glaucoma **25**(3), e229–e235 (2016)
3. Bengtsson, B., Heijl, A.: A visual field index for calculation of glaucoma rate of progression. Am. J. Ophthalmol. **145**(2), 343–353 (2008)
4. Chen, M.J., Chang, Y.F., Kuo, Y.S., Hsu, C.C., Ko, Y.C., Liu, C.J.L.: Macular ganglion cell-inner plexiform vs retinal nerve fiber layer measurement to detect early glaucoma with superior or inferior hemifield defects. J. Chin. Med. Assoc. **82**(4), 335–339 (2019)
5. Chicco, D., Warrens, M.J., Jurman, G.: The coefficient of determination r-squared is more informative than smape, mae, mape, mse and rmse in regression analysis evaluation. PeerJ Comput. Sci. **7**, e623 (2021)
6. Fang, H., Li, F., Fu, H., Wu, J., Zhang, X., Xu, Y.: Dataset and evaluation algorithm design for goals challenge. In: International Workshop on Ophthalmic Medical Image Analysis, pp. 135–142. Springer, Heidelberg (2022). https://doi.org/10.1007/978-3-031-16525-2_14
7. Garway-Heath, D.F., Poinoosawmy, D., Fitzke, F.W., Hitchings, R.A.: Mapping the visual field to the optic disc in normal tension glaucoma eyes. Ophthalmology **107**(10), 1809–1815 (2000)
8. Kim, K.E., Park, K.H.: Macular imaging by optical coherence tomography in the diagnosis and management of glaucoma. Brit. J. Ophthalmol. **102**(6), 718–724 (2018)
9. Li, F., et al.: Development and clinical deployment of a smartphone-based visual field deep learning system for glaucoma detection. NPJ Dig. Med. **3**(1), 123 (2020)
10. Lucano, E., et al.: Assessing the electromagnetic fields generated by a radiofrequency mri body coil at 64 mhz: defeaturing versus accuracy. IEEE Trans. Biomed. Eng. **63**(8), 1591–1601 (2015)
11. Makridakis, S.: Accuracy measures: theoretical and practical concerns. Int. J. Forecast. **9**(4), 527–529 (1993)
12. Mills, R.P., et al.: Categorizing the stage of glaucoma from pre-diagnosis to end-stage disease. Am. J. Ophthalmol. **141**(1), 24–30 (2006)

13. Mohammadzadeh, V., et al.: Macular imaging with optical coherence tomography in glaucoma. Surv. Ophthalmol. **65**(6), 597–638 (2020)
14. Perkins, T.W.: Clinical decisions in glaucoma. Arch. Ophthalmol. **112**(12), 1518–1519 (1994)
15. Purkayastha, S., et al.: A comparison of five epidemiological models for transmission of sars-cov-2 in India. BMC Infect. Dis. **21**(1), 1–23 (2021)
16. Schuman, J.S., et al.: Optical coherence tomography: a new tool for glaucoma diagnosis. Curr. Opin. Ophthalmol. **6**(2), 89–95 (1995)
17. Wu, J., et al.: Gamma challenge: glaucoma grading from multi-modality images. arXiv preprint arXiv:2202.06511 (2022)
18. Wu, Z., Weng, D.S., Thenappan, A., Ritch, R., Hood, D.C.: Evaluation of a region-of-interest approach for detecting progressive glaucomatous macular damage on optical coherence tomography. Transl. Vision Sci. Technol. **7**(2), 14 (2018)

Author Index

B. Antony et al. (Eds.): OMIA 2023, LNCS 14096, pp. 161–162, 2023.
https://doi.org/10.1007/978-3-031-44013-7

Printed in the United States
by Baker & Taylor Publisher Services